SO-BRS-739

WITHDRAWN

Date

May 28 '51

PAUL W. PORTERFIELD

WITHDRAWN

# MARK TWAIN
## SON OF MISSOURI

# MARK TWAIN
## SON OF MISSOURI

BY

MINNIE M. BRASHEAR

CHAPEL HILL
THE UNIVERSITY OF NORTH CAROLINA PRESS
1934

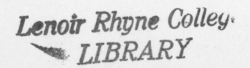
Lenoir Rhyne Colley
LIBRARY

Copyright, 1934, by
The University of North Carolina Press

PRINTED IN THE UNITED STATES OF AMERICA BY
THE SEEMAN PRESS, DURHAM, NORTH CAROLINA

817.4
B75m

To
the Memory of
MY FATHER

". . . Whatsoever a man is, is due to his *make,* and to the *influences* brought to bear upon it by his heredities, his habitat, his associations. He is moved, directed, COMMANDED, by *exterior* influences—*solely.* He *originates* nothing, not even a thought."—The Old Man, in *What Is Man? and Other Essays.*

# PREFACE

No ONE in his own lifetime was so fully aware of the contradictory undercurrent of opinion that paralleled the great wave of popularity attending his career as was Mark Twain himself, and to no one would the contradictions in the interpretations appearing since his death have been so real and so impossible to solve; for in the end the humorist "eluded himself."

An essay on Mark Twain, appearing in 1908, anticipated at least three of the fuller and more searching criticisms that have come out since his death. In his book, *The New American Type*, H. D. Sedgwick pointed out a resemblance between Mark Twain and Cervantes, such as might have suggested O. H. Moore's study. His representation of the western writer as "the voice, the type, the effigy" of a nation might have furnished the theme for Stuart P. Sherman's essay in the *Cambridge History of American Literature*. And his phrase "everybody's neighbor" might have supplied the theme for one of Van Wyck Brooks's chapters. It was the publication of the twenty-five volume edition of Mark Twain's complete works in 1910 that facilitated the fuller appraisal.

In 1913 John Macy published *The Spirit of American Literature* with an important chapter on Mark Twain, in which, after examination of the whole record, he concluded that Mark Twain's portrait of mankind is "the greatest canvas that any American has painted."

Fred Lewis Pattee, in his *A History of American Literature Since 1870*, published in 1915, reviewed the

chronological unfolding of Mark Twain's genius. A large
part of Mark Twain's strength, he believed, came from the
fact that he spent the first thirty years of his life in a part
of the country "unshadowed by Europe." "He was the
first voice of the new West and of the new era." Pattee
follows the suggestion of Howells that Mark Twain was
"at heart romantic," and he was one of the first to make it
clear that the Missourian rose to fame on the shoulders
of a large group of other American humorists born between "the magic years," 1833-1843. He also credits
Mark Twain with having been the first to make American
literature national. After *Life on the Mississippi* and
*Huckleberry Finn* it was no longer the voice of a narrow
strip of Atlantic seaboard, but of a nation beginning to be
conscious of its immense growth.

Perhaps the two interpretations of Mark Twain that
have come nearest to satisfying Americans are those of
William Dean Howells of the earlier period and Stuart P.
Sherman of more recent years. The first of the two essays
by the latter, published in the book *On Contemporary Literature*, in 1917, is entitled "The Democracy of Mark
Twain." Most of it had appeared as reviews in *The Nation*, part of it as early as 1910. The second is the chapter
in the *Cambridge History of American Literature*. The
theme of both essays is contained in the words: "He
fulfilled the promise of American life. He proves the
virtues of the land and society in which he was born and
fostered." This, of course, might be a double-edged statement. "He does not give us much help in realizing our
best selves," Sherman believes—he would not inure us to
the cooler climate where the saving remnant dwells—"but

he is a rock of refuge when the ordinary self, the 'divine average,' is in danger." On three counts, Sherman finds, Mark Twain must be recognized as an influence because he was an innovator: for his "disillusioned treatment of history," for his "fearless exploitation of the natural man," and for "a certain strain of naturalistic pessimism."

All these studies were slight, however, compared with that of Van Wyck Brooks, which was the sensational book of 1920. *The Ordeal of Mark Twain* has been useful and stimulating, chiefly because a writing so definitely negative, aiming, as it does, to prick a popular bubble, is a challenge. As Mark Twain himself said, if a personality is not vigorous enough to stand "that much friction," the point of the criticism probably stands proved. Van Wyck Brooks, applying the methods and principles of the new psychology, as he understood it, to Mark Twain's case, elaborated the theory that the humorist was the victim of an environment that crushed out the artist in him. The censorship of his mother and his wife—the most effective weapon of that environment—had such authority with him that his larger self could not gain expression, and this failure to live up to his real possibilities was, in Brooks's opinion, the cause of the philosophical bitterness expressed in Mark Twain's later writings. In a different environment and with a different training his vigorous and poetic genius might have made of him a Voltaire, a Rabelais, a Swift, or even a Cervantes.

The book has caused a reëxamination of everything pertaining to Mark Twain. The writings, letters, and other autobiographical data have taken on new significance since 1920. Two types of study have received new incentive since this criticism appeared. One type is noncritical in its purpose. It adds something to the Mark Twain source-book by searching out writings which he himself did not choose to have preserved, but which are important for what they reveal about the growth of his mind and art. The Huntington Library in California has made an extensive collection of letters. The State Historical Society of Missouri has made accessible files of early Hannibal, Missouri, papers, upon part of which Sam Clemens worked. The *Iowa Journal of History and Politics* has published the investigation of Fred W. Lorch concerning Sam and Orion Clemens's experience in Muscatine and Keokuk, Iowa. An effort has been made to discover the letters which, during his pilot days, he contributed to New Orleans papers.

The second type of investigation seeks to discover, by careful observation, what are the significant literary elements in the writings of Mark Twain. One of the most painstaking is Henry Pochmann's unpublished study, "The Mind of Mark Twain," a tabulation of all the books and authors which it can be found the humorist read. This study may have had its inspiration from a paper by O. H. Moore entitled "Mark Twain and Don Quixote," appearing in the *Publications of the Modern Language Association* in 1922, in which the author attempted to refute the idea that Mark Twain's genius, like Topsy, just grew. The most original of American writers, this critic insists, "drew much of his inspiration for his most American books from European models; . . . he was in earnest when he declared in a heated controversy that 'there is not a single characteristic which can be safely labeled as American.' " O. H. Moore finds *Don Quixote* influence from *Innocents Abroad* through *Life on the Mississippi*, the Tom Sawyer books, *Huckleberry Finn,* and *A Connecticut Yankee,* and, incidentally, believes that the influence of Cervantes may have been responsible for the repression of Mark Twain's "romantic instinct."

A slighter study, with somewhat the same purpose, is Friedrich Schönemann's note, "Mark Twain and Wilbrandt," *Modern Language Notes,* June, 1919, in which he offers the theory that Wilbrandt's *Meister von Palmyra* may have furnished inspiration for the humorist's "two most important philosophic works," the essay "What is Man?" and the story "The Mysterious Stranger." With these studies may be classed, also, Herbert Edward Mierow's article, "Cicero and Mark Twain," *Classical Journal,* December, 1924, in which he contrasts the "Olympian serenity" of Cicero after the death of his daughter Tullia with Mark Twain's destructive pessimism expressed in "The Death of Jean" and "The Mysterious Stranger."

The most penetrating critical study of Mark Twain's mind and art, however, is Friedrich Schönemann's *Mark Twain als literarische Persönlichkeit,* which seeks to break down Van Wyck Brooks's thesis, with the view that Mark Twain was so thoroughgoing a literary man in mood and training, irregular as the latter may have been, that the theory that he failed to realize his larger possibilities as artist because he compromised with an unfavorable environment is untenable. He criticises Brooks for attempting, American fashion, to apply a sort of pseudo-Freudian method to the case of the American humorist, and charges the critic with the untruth of overemphasis. His own view is that Mark Twain had a great personality and was an artist of great distinction. He supports this view by

combing Mark Twain's works and the criticisms of them
for evidence that as a humorist, a literary personality, a
social philosopher, and a master of prose style he shows
kinship with many of the greatest English and American
writers; that, in fact, his models extend into world literature.

He analyses the western origin of Mark Twain's
humor. His is *"der frischeste und wildeste Humor von
der Welt,"* but it has an undercurrent that suggests constantly the tragedy of life on the borders of civilization.
*"Man entspannte sich im Lachen, und je grösser die
Spannung gewesen war, desto krampfhafter klang nach-
her das Gelächter."* Humor was a means by which the
young man maintained himself in a pioneer society, when
it turned against him because he was "different." Consequently, contrary to Van Wyck Brooks's view, he really
came into his own in the West—found himself not only
as a humorist but also as a prose stylist. The German
critic discusses also the corrective passion of his humor as
dramatized in *A Connecticut Yankee.* He compares Mark
Twain and Franklin and discovers a fineness of feeling in
the western writer which the Philadelphian lacked. In
him, finally, was a *"Dualismus von Verstand und
Gefühl."* He is the "Mysterious Stranger" and "the
friend of mankind." Schönemann cites Howells's theory
that "at heart Mark Twain was romantic" and Moore's
view that the repressed romantic *Zug* in the western
humorist was due to his early reading of Cervantes, and
finds in the mind and temperament of Mark Twain an
*exemplum* of the theory of romantic irony.

It is clear from all this that criticism since Van Wyck
Brooks's study appeared has been almost wholly an at-

tempt to answer the question, "How is Mark Twain to be accounted for?"

The present study attempts to answer this question in part, by pointing out formative elements in Mark Twain's immediate inheritance and environment—by turning the telescope back as steadily as possible upon the first twenty-five years of his life. It is necessary, however, in order to make any profitable analysis of what is found there, to view it in the light of Mark Twain's later career—his own conception of it and the judgment of his contemporaries upon it. The introductory chapter, therefore, traces the growth and flowering of the Mark Twain legend.

The book was begun in the faith that it is more profitable to know how an important American writer reacted to persons and objects in his environment than to theorize about how he ought to have reacted. Such conclusions as are suggested are offered, in every case, with full realization that all conclusions are merely tentative, and experimental, and human. An Einstein pries away the results of the most accurate-seeming observation and the most logical reasoning.

I have lived, temporarily, both in Hannibal, Missouri, and in Pike County. One of my great-grandfathers entered land in 1832 within twenty-five miles of Florida, in Monroe County. This book is an attempt to verify an impression, formed from personal observation, that commentaries on Mark Twain which have pointed to his Middle West up-bringing as unfortunate, even tragic in its suppressions, are not true accounts.

For suggestions about the form and method employed in the study I am indebted to Professor Norman Foerster, of the University of Iowa, Professor Howard Mumford

xiv PREFACE

Jones, of the University of Michigan, and Professor Gregory Paine, of the University of North Carolina, to Professors Henry M. Belden, James W. Rankin, and Robert L. Ramsay, of the University of Missouri, to Dr. Louise Dudley, of Stephens Junior College, and to Professor Frances Grinstead, of the School of Journalism of the University of Missouri; for aid in assembling materials, to the library staff of the University of North Carolina, especially to Mrs. Edna Lane, secretary to the librarian; to Mr. F. C. Shoemaker, Miss Sarah Guitar, Mr. Roy King, and Mr. Monas Squires of the State Historical Society of Missouri; for help with the materials themselves I owe a very special debt to Professor Friedrich Schönemann, whose study, *Mark Twain als Literarische Persönlichkeit*, I have found particularly illuminating, and to Professor Henry Pochmann, of the Mississippi Agricultural and Technical College, who very generously permitted me to make use of findings from his study "The Mind of Mark Twain," not published. I wish also to express appreciation to Harper and Brothers for permission to quote from *Mark Twain's Letters*, *Mark Twain's Autobiography*, *Mark Twain, a Biography*, by Albert Bigelow Paine, and certain of Mark Twain's works copyrighted by them.

MINNIE M. BRASHEAR

*Columbia, Missouri*
*January 1, 1933*

# TABLE OF CONTENTS

# LIST OF ILLUSTRATIONS

*(The illustrations, except two maps, face the pages indicated.)*

# MARK TWAIN
## SON OF MISSOURI

# I

## INTRODUCTION

## THE MARK TWAIN LEGEND

### §1

No AMERICAN writer has offered a more insistent challenge to critics than Mark Twain. The early popularity of his humorous lectures was much extended by the publication under his name of pirated collections of "funny sayings." The *Jumping Frog* book, first of his own publications, had wide vogue with a varied class of readers. So general, in fact, was the curiosity about the author come out of the West that from the time when, as he said, he "stumbled into literature," in 1867, until the posthumous appearance of *The Mysterious Stranger* in 1916, indeed until the present time, a many-sided question concerning the status of Samuel Langhorne Clemens has intrigued the world. "How many sheep has Mark Twain?" his Arab guide asked of Richard Watson Gilder on the pyramid of Gizeh.

A review of the criticism called forth by the publication of his writings shows that the question has come from two main angles. The earlier critics apparently felt themselves to be attempting an answer to the inquiry, "What title has this fun-maker to be considered a legitimate author?" Later, after the publication of the Albert Bigelow Paine biography in 1912, and of *The Mysterious*

[ 3 ]

*Stranger* in 1916, the question became a psychological rather than a purely literary one: "Given so arresting a mind and personality, how is it to be accounted for?"

It was the prompt recognition, in 1869, of *Innocents Abroad* as something unusual of its kind, by so conservative a magazine as *The Atlantic Monthly* that first caused discriminating readers to wonder. "Under his *nom de plume* of Mark Twain," Howells said, "Mr. Clemens is well known to the very large world of newspaper-readers; and this book ought to secure him something better than the uncertain standing of a popular favorite. It is no business of ours to fix his rank among the humorists California has given us, but we think he is, in an entirely different way from all the others, quite worthy of the company of the best."[1]

It is not surprising that readers of *Innocents Abroad*, for all their enjoyment of its sheer audacity, hesitated to admit literary merit in the book. The author himself up to that time had been, in his own eyes, a mere journalist;[2] and he looked upon book-making chiefly as a means to attain a competency so that he might marry. He was thirty-four years old, and he expected to spend the rest of his life as a newspaper man. He was satisfied with the acknowledgment he received from Oliver Wendell Holmes, to whom he had sent a copy of the book: "I always like to hear what one of my fellow-countrymen who is not a Hebrew scholar, or a reader of hieroglyphics, but a good-humored traveler with a pair of sharp, twinkling Yankee . . . eyes in his head, has to say about the things that

[1] *The Atlantic Monthly*, XXIV (Dec., 1869), 766.
[2] A. B. Paine, ed., *Mark Twain's Letters*, I, 162. Hereafter referred to as *Letters*.

learned travelers often make unintelligible, and sentimental ones ridiculous or absurd."[3]

In the letter of forgiveness, however, with which Holmes acknowledged Mark Twain's explanation of his having unconsciously adopted for *Innocents Abroad* the poet's dedication of his volume of verse, the New Englander wrote generously, "I rather think *The Innocents Abroad* will have many more readers than *Songs in Many Keys.* . . . You will be stolen from a great deal oftener than you will borrow from other people."[4]    Carl Van Doren speaks of "the sudden, the almost explosive fame which the book brought him";[5] but in spite of the unprecedented sales of *Innocents Abroad* there were adverse criticisms on both sides of the Atlantic.    The New York *Nation,* conceding, in an unsigned review, that none of it was "really poor, and much of it very good," found in it "all the prominent characteristics of our peculiar school of humorists—their audacity, their extravagance and exaggeration."    While the author had some merits of his own, he had also some literary vices: "he pads" and "he grimaces."[6]    This and *Blackwood's* criticism were warnings to the new author of what strides he had to make before he could attain to the kind of approval he desired:

. . . he sets a slur of commonness upon beauty and splendour. With the vanity of a crude civilisation he finds every custom ridiculous that does not conform with the standard of the United States. . . . Nor does he understand that there are certain institu-

[3] *Ibid.,* I, 166.

[4] A. B. Paine, *Mark Twain, A Biography,* II, 660.    (Hereafter referred to as A. B. P.)

[5] *The American Novel,* p. 162.    *Cf.* A. B. P., I, 426: "At the end of a year from its publication the *Innocents* had sold up to 67,000, and was continuing at the rate of several thousand monthly."

[6] IX (Sept. 2, 1869), 194.

tions, certain manifestations of genius, which should be sacred even for the jester. Newness is not the only virtue known to the world, and he who laughs at what is old . . . proves a lack of intelligence which no whimsicality can excuse.[7]

## §2

BETWEEN the publication of *Innocents Abroad* in 1869 and *Roughing It* in 1872, the author's mood toward himself and toward his work changed considerably. He had bought a share in the *Buffalo Express* in the late summer of 1869. In February, 1870, he married into a well-to-do New York family of considerable culture, and what he knew he lacked in taste, he thenceforth trusted his wife to coach him in. In August of the same year his father-in-law died. In September he began *Roughing It,* and in November his son was born. The success of *Innocents Abroad,* together with the possibility of an assured income, brought the hope that he might give up journalism and turn to authorship permanently—a career which had lured him from his Hannibal days. As early as 1868, after the return of the *Quaker City* excursion, he had written to Orion from Washington, *"then* [when I marry] I am done with literature . . . to please the general public. I shall write to please myself then." In the meantime, misgivings concerning the sort of reputation that had come to him from *Innocents Abroad,* together with domestic anxieties, threw him into a mood of discouragement. "The newspaper praises bestowed upon the 'Innocents Abroad,' " he wrote Howells afterward, "were large and generous, but somehow I hadn't *confidence* in the critical

---

[7] Anon., "Mark Twain's Message of Mirth," *Blackwood's Magazine,* CLXXXII (August, 1907), 279.

judgment of the parties who furnished them."[8] His dream of a regular writer's career was in danger of coming to nothing. Only the reassurance of Joe Goodman, friend of his Nevada days, fortified him to finish the new book. "You are doing a great book!" Goodman exclaimed after reading the manuscript.[9] He sold the *Buffalo Express* in the spring of 1871. In the fall he finished *Roughing It*, and moved his family to Hartford in order to be near his publisher. The book appeared in February, 1872. But again it was Howells's review that brought real recognition. His criticism was defensive of the author, if at the same time guarded:

The grotesque exaggeration and broad irony with which the life is described are conjecturably the truest colors that could have been used, for all existence there must have looked like an extravagant joke, the humor of which was only deepened by its netherside of tragedy . . . everything far-fetched or near at hand is interwoven, and yet the complex is a sort of "harmony of colors" which is not less than triumphant . . . the work of a human being, it is not unbrokenly nor infallibly funny; nor is it to be always praised for all the literary virtues; but it is singularly entertaining, and its humor is always amiable, manly, and generous.[10]

*Harper's Magazine, The North American Review,* and *The Nation* took no notice of the book, but in general, even if it did not receive the sensational reception of its predecessor, it was ranked with *Innocents Abroad.* This meant, of course, that it was looked upon as a funny book, of the journalistic sort, and Mark Twain had moved to Hartford with the ambition to attain to a higher level than that.

[8] *Letters,* I, 263.          [9] A. B. P., I, 436.
[10] *The Atlantic Monthly,* XXIX (June, 1872), 754-55.

Archibald Henderson quotes Mark Twain as having said to him, "The first great lesson of my life was the discovery that I had a reputation to live down. When I began to lecture, and in my early writings, my sole idea was to make comic capital out of everything I saw and heard," and he told the story of the rebuke he had received during his Nevada days from his friend Tom Fitch because he "sold" his audience in a cleverly flippant way.[11]   It was the ability to take a suggestion that kept the humorist constantly trying for something better.   Howells's concession to readers of *The Atlantic Monthly* that there was something to be desired in his work in the way of "literary virtues" was a spur that kept him in a state of unrest.   He was aware, when he went about, of "such drifting exclamations as, 'There he is!  There goes Mark Twain!' People came out on the street to see him pass. . . . In his note-book he wrote, 'Fame is a vapor, popularity an accident; the only earthly certainty oblivion.' "[12]   He had set it as his goal to correct the impression that he was merely a high class jester.

His third adventure into authorship was of an entirely different sort from the first two.   Although the incident that ended in his collaboration with Charles Dudley Warner in writing *The Gilded Age* appears quite casual, the same serious sort of realization that caused Joseph Conrad to seek the collaboration of Ford Madox Hueffer must have lain behind Mark Twain's agreement with the New England writer.   He "had the beginning of a story in his mind,"[13] but he had no experience to help him chart the way for a full-length story.   Charles Dudley Warner was

[11] *Mark Twain*, p. 99.
[12] A. B. P., I, 373.          [13] *Ibid.*, I, 477.

an experienced and successful literary man; the westerner was canny enough to realize the advantage of working with him, but in doing so he lost none of his independence. It was a miscarriage of the announcement of *The Gilded Age* which drew down upon the critics Clemens's sharpest sarcasm. The incident is related in the *Autobiography*. The editor of the *Daily Graphic* had agreed that, if he were given an advance copy of the novel, he would make no use of it until after *The Atlantic Monthly* notice had come out. But his ambition for the credit of his paper was evidently too strong for him; he published the notice ahead of any other periodical. "I could not really complain," Clemens said, "because he had only given me his word of honor as security. I ought to have required of him something substantial." The book was so much more in the manner of the conventional fiction of the day than anything Mark Twain had before attempted that the *Daily Graphic* said that Charles Dudley Warner must have been the real author, and that Mark Twain, counting upon Warner's popularity with American readers to sell the book, had sought to deceive the public by announcing their joint authorship. The story of his dishonesty was copied in newspapers as far west as the Chicago *Tribune*. "It is the will of God that we must have critics, and missionaries, and congressmen, and humorists," the author said, in concluding the reminiscence, "and we must bear the burden."[14] *The Gilded Age* was issued a day or two before Christmas, 1873. The *Daily Graphic* story had doubtless served as effective advertising, for in spite of the business depression which Mark Twain had feared would affect

[14] *Mark Twain's Autobiography*, II, 70-71.

the sales,[15] it ran into the third edition soon after the holidays, and by the end of February forty thousand copies had been sold. The dramatization of the story, and its production on the stage, did a good deal to extend Mark Twain's fame.

When the collection of early writings entitled *Sketches New and Old* was put out the year before *Tom Sawyer* appeared, Howells commented on the "growing seriousness of meaning in the apparently unmoralized drolling." After pointing out a like growth in Dickens and Thackeray, he instanced the sketch of the Negro woman, entitled "A True Story," as showing "a gift in the author for the simple, dramatic report of reality which we have seen equaled in no other American writer."[16] Mark Twain's acknowledgment of the review shows how anxious he and Mrs. Clemens were about his reputation:

Yours is the recognized critical Court of Last Resort in this country; from its decision there is no appeal; and so, to have gained this decree of yours before I am forty years old, I regard as a thing to be rightdown proud of. Mrs. Clemens says, "Tell him *I* am just as grateful to him as I can be." (It sounds as if she were grateful to you for heroically trampling the truth under foot in order to praise me—but in reality it means that she is grateful to you for being bold enough to utter a truth which she fully believes all competent people know, but which none has heretofore been brave enough to utter.) You see, the thing that gravels her is that I am so persistently glorified as a mere buffoon, as if that entirely covered my case—which she denies with venom.[17]

The author still had it clearly in mind, evidently, that he had a reputation to live down. Archibald Henderson's

---

[15] For an account of Mark Twain's part in writing *The Gilded Age* and of its publication, see his letter to Dr. John Brown of Feb. 28, 1874, in *Letters*, I, 214.

[16] *My Mark Twain*, pp. 120-24.     [17] *Letters*, I, 263.

account of the change in him, from the time he "settled down in a Connecticut town" is not just. He says that Mark Twain "foreswore the creeds and principles of his native section and underwent a new transformation." More true is his description of the humorist's attitude after travel in Europe. The experience, he says, "far from diminishing his racial consciousness, tended still further to accentuate the national characteristics."[18]   It was because Mark Twain knew how to be a western man in the East that men were so sure of his worth. The change that Archibald Henderson observes, however, came from his determination not to be a "mere buffoon." The two supports he could depend upon in his new rôle were William Dean Howells and his wife.[19]

## §3

THE PUBLICATION of *Tom Sawyer* brought commendation from those who knew him best and censure from more orthodox circles. Howells had wanted the story for *The Atlantic Monthly*, but because his household expenses were "something almost ghastly," Clemens felt that he must find the most profitable way to put it out. Because of Mrs. Clemens's doubt about parts of it, Howells had been asked to read the manuscript. He sat up until one o'clock finishing it and then declared that it was the best boy's story he had ever read. "Give me a hint when it's to be out," he wrote, "and I'll start the sheep to jumping in the right places." In his *Autobiography* Mark Twain acknowledged the debt he owed to Howells, as he had often done in letters. Man's inability to pronounce a

[18] *Op. cit.*, p. 157.          [19] *Cf. My Mark Twain*, p. 10.

fearless, independent judgment was a constant subject of Mark Twain's irony:

In the matter of slavish imitation, man is the monkey's superior all the time. The average man is destitute of independence of opinion. He is not interested in contriving an opinion of his own, by study and reflection, but is only anxious to find out what his neighbor's opinion is and slavishly adopt it. A generation ago, I found out that the latest review of a book was pretty sure to be just a reflection of the *earliest* review of it. That whatever the first reviewer found to praise or censure in the book would be repeated in the latest reviewer's report, with nothing fresh added. Therefore more than once I took the precaution of sending my book, in manuscript, to Mr. Howells, when he was editor of the *Atlantic Monthly*, so that he could prepare a review of it at leisure. I knew he would say the truth about the book—I also knew that he would find more merit than demerit in it, because I already knew that that was the condition of the book. I allowed no copy of that book to go out to the press until after Mr. Howells's notice of it had appeared. That book was always safe. There wasn't a man behind a pen in all America that had the courage to find anything in the book which Mr. Howells had not found—there wasn't a man behind a pen in America that had spirit enough to say a brave and original thing about the book on his own responsibility.

I believe that the trade of critic, in literature, music, and the drama, is the most degraded of all trades, and that it has no real value—certainly no large value.[20]

But scorn of critics is not the only thing apparent in this passage. It also shows how much the author's native shrewdness in insuring the right kind of publicity for his books had to do with their fortunes.

There is no accounting for all the complex elements that lie behind such congeniality of spirit as existed be-

[20] II, 68-69.

tween Mark Twain and William Dean Howells. Their western origin, of much the same kind, and their literary feeling for the importance of realistic detail, doubtless temperamental, insured mutual understanding. On the side of the magazine editor, the economic motive could scarcely have been absent. Mark Twain's writings brought in dividends at an amazing rate. Furthermore, the pride of discovery must have afforded considerable satisfaction to his vanity. Clemens, on the other side, had felt immense gratitude for the *Atlantic* review of *Innocents Abroad*. Henceforth he trusted the editor's judgment and cultivated his friendship. He would naturally have been attracted by Howells's sensitiveness and broad humanity, but it was one more proof that he had been born under a lucky star that Fate should have sent him such a literary sponsor.

The adverse opinions of *Tom Sawyer* came from very orthodox circles. The irreverence in the earlier books had drawn out frequent protests, but what many conscientious people considered the questionable parts of *Tom Sawyer* caused them to refuse to read it. Some years later, when a public library in Brooklyn ruled it and *Huckleberry Finn* out of the reading room for children, an indignant librarian wrote to Mark Twain privately about the matter. He replied:

Dear Sir,—I am greatly troubled by what you say. I wrote *Tom Sawyer* & *Huck Finn* for adults exclusively, & it always distresses me when I find that boys & girls have been allowed access to them. The mind that becomes soiled in youth can never again be washed clean. I know this by my own experience, & to this day I cherish an unappeasable bitterness against the unfaithful guardians of my young life, who not only permitted but compelled me to read an unexpurgated Bible through before I was 15 years old.  None can do that and ever draw a clean, sweet breath again this side of the grave. . . .

Sincerely yours,

S. L. Clemens.[21].

New York reporters got wind of the letter, "and *Huck* and *Tom* had a perfectly fresh crop of advertising."  One of the most enthusiastic readers of *Tom Sawyer* was Colonel Henry Watterson of the Louisville *Courier,* who classed its author with the greatest British novelists:

I have just laid down *Tom Sawyer,* and cannot resist the pressure. It is immense!  I read every word of it, didn't skip a line, and nearly disgraced myself several times in the presence of a sleeping-car full of honorable and pious people.  Once I had to get to one side and have a cry, and as for an internal compound of laughter and tears there was no end to it. . . . The "funeral" of the boys, the cave business, and the hunt for the hidden treasure are as dramatic as anything I know of in fiction, while the pathos—particularly everything relating to Huck and Aunt Polly—makes a cross between Dickens's skill and Thackeray's nature, which, resembling neither, is thoroughly impressive and original.[22]

§4

THE PUBLICATION of *The Prince and the Pauper* in 1881 drew forth two types of comment.  That which was favorable made much of the versatility of an author who could turn from broad western humor to archaic quaintness and antiquarian appeal.  Unfavorable critics advised the author to stick to his last.  *Scribner's Monthly* had heretofore taken no notice of the western writer,[23] but its editor,

---

[21] A. B. P., III, 1280-81.          [22] A. B. P., II, 586.

[23] This conservative policy seems to have been continued by the new *Scribner's.* The editor in July, 1890, speaks with asperity of "certain optimistic critics of new

J. G. Holland, after reading *Innocents Abroad*, had referred to the author as a "mere fun-maker of ephemeral popularity."[24]   Richard Watson Gilder, however, who was its editor when it became the *Century* in 1881 just before *The Prince and the Pauper* came out, reviewed the book.  He was doubtful about the author's new manner, but very positive as to his quality:

So far as it was the author's purpose to produce a work of art after the old models, and to prove that the humorous story-teller and ingenious homely philosopher, Mark Twain, can be a literary purist, a scholar, and an antiquary, we do not think his "new departure" is a conspicuous success.  It was not necessary for the author to prop his literary reputation with archaic English and a somewhat conventional manner.  His recent humorous writings abound in passages of great excellence as serious compositions, and his serious, nervous style is the natural expression of an acute mind, that in its most fanciful moods is seldom superficial in its view.  Indeed, it is because Mark Twain is a satirist, and in a measure a true philosopher, that his broadly humorous books and speeches have met with wide and permanent popular favor.[25]

How sane and well balanced Mark Twain's attitude toward criticism was at this time is seen in a letter written to Howells in January, 1882.  A friend thought that he had discovered a disposition in the New York *Tribune* to conduct a crusade against Mark Twain.  After careful investigation, the latter sifted the whole matter down to four counts, all of which he considered negligible.  "Adverse criticism which is not malicious," he said, "is a thing which none but fools irritate themselves about. . . . If I

writers."  Concerning Howells's recent defense of "his native contemporary writers," he says that the *Atlantic* editor takes them "at the pitch of their aspirations rather than their deeds."

[24] A. B. P., I, 382.

[25] *Century*, I, n.s. (March, 1882), 783-84.

can't stand that amount of friction, I certainly need reconstruction."[26]

## §5

THE TWO books following *The Prince and the Pauper* stand at the crest of his purely literary achievement. *Life on the Mississippi*, published in 1883, and *Huckleberry Finn*, in 1884, are to be considered together not only for their importance in the development of Mark Twain's genius, but also for their contemporary success. Both were forming themselves in the author's mind at the same time: the writing of both extended over a period of almost ten years, and both had the vigor to persist through the complexity of other interests.

In spite of the fact that *Harper's* was the first eastern magazine to publish any writing by Mark Twain,[27] no review of his books appeared in the magazine until *Life on the Mississippi* came out, and then it was not for its literary merit that the reviewer found it valuable, but, chiefly, for its historical and regional interest: "Aside from the humor with which the narration is enlivened, and the instances of personal adventure and heroism with which it is embellished, the volume is an invaluable souvenir of a phase of American life and manners that has passed away never to be revived."[28]  The reviewer of the English reprint, four years later, found Mark Twain's humor more decorous when it was turned upon American than upon European objects. The comparison is to the disparagement of *A Tramp Abroad:* " . . . His broad pleasantry is in better keeping with raftsmen, back-woods settlers,

[26] *Letters*, I, 413-16.
[27] "Forty-three Days in an Open Boat," *Harper's Magazine*, XXXIV (Dec., 1866), 104-13. (An error in the signature made it Mark Swain.)
[28] "Editor's Literary Record," *Harper's Magazine*, LXVII (Oct., 1883), 799.

and gold-diggers than with monks, mountains, kings, cathedrals and other sanctities of old-fashioned Europe. . . . a volume which does not contain a dull page."[29]

In general, *Life on the Mississippi* did more than anything published by Mark Twain up to that time to gain him recognition, both in America and in Europe, as something more than a humorist. "Why don't people understand that Mark Twain is not merely a great humorist?" Thomas Hardy said to William Dean Howells at a dinner.[30] The Emperor William of Germany and the porter of Mark Twain's lodging in Berlin both assured the author that *Life on the Mississippi* was their favorite American book.[31]

*Huckleberry Finn* was issued in December to take advantage of the Christmas trade. The "account of the famous Grangerford-Shepherdson feud," prefaced with the "argument" of the earlier part of the story, had appeared in the Christmas number of the *Century* under the heading "An Adventure of Huckleberry Finn."[32] The criticism called forth by its publication in America was very different from that which had formerly been bestowed upon Mark Twain. Instead of the vague, impressionistic appraisal which earlier works had received, there appeared comments on the methods by which the author secured his effects. T. S. Perry, reviewing for the *Century*, compared it with *Tom Sawyer* in this respect. The earlier story is "an apparently fortuitous collection of incidents"; *Huckle-*

[29] A review by Robert Brown, in the Literature section of *The Academy*, XXIV (July 28, 1883), 58.

[30] Howells, *Life in Letters*, I, 349.

[31] A. B. P., II, 746.

[32] *Century*, VII, n.s. (Dec., 1884), 546-67. Two other sections of the story were published by the same magazine: in January, 1885, "Jim's Investment and King Sollerman," and in February, "Royalty on the Mississippi."

*berry Finn* has "a more intelligible plot." The autobiographical form secures better unity through

. . . the reflection of the whole varied series of adventures in the mind of the young scapegrace of a hero. His undying fertility of invention, his courage, his manliness in every trial, are an incarnation of the better side of the ruffianism that is one result of the independence of Americans . . . an absence of morbidness in the . . . account of the feud between the Shepherdsons and the Grangerfords [is notable. The story is told] as it would appear to a semi-civilized boy of fourteen.[33]

After the favorable reception of *Life on the Mississippi* and *Huckleberry Finn,* Mark Twain and his sponsors must have felt that fame of a really lasting sort had finally come to him. A little earlier Edwin Whipple had said, "Mark Twain is regarded chiefly as a humorist, but the exercise of his real talents would rank him with the ablest of our authors in the past fifty years."[34] After the appearance of the Grangerford-Shepherdson chapter in the *Century,* E. C. Stedman wrote to the author, "To my mind it is not only the most finished and condensed thing you have done, but as dramatic and powerful an episode as I know in modern literature."[35] His real talents were at last apparent. Writing in 1920 on "The Literary Status of Mark Twain," H. H. Peckham compared him with Whittier, Holmes, Lowell, Whitman, Howells, and Harte in the eighties, and found that in the sales of his books, number of translations, favorable reviews, popularity of his lectures, and distinguished friends and patrons, Mark Twain superseded them all; that he was the most

[33] *Century,* VIII, n.s. (May, 1885), 171.
[34] A. B. P., I, 474.
[35] *Ibid.,* II, 793 n.

representative author in America in the eighties in the realm of pure literature.[36]

But Mark Twain had become an enthusiastic admirer of England—almost an Anglomaniac[37]—and he wanted English approval. Andrew Lang's enthusiastic appreciation of *Huckleberry Finn* carried a sting with it:

They [people of culture] call him a Barbarian. They won't hear of him, they hurry from the subject; they pass by on the other side of the way. . . . Let it be admitted that Mark Twain often sins against good taste . . . nothing can be more true and more humorous than the narrative of the outcast boy . . . no novel has better touches of natural description . . . the book remains a nearly flawless gem of romance and humor . . . but "cultured critics" are probably unaware of its singular value. . . .

Andrew Lang guessed that the story might be "the great American novel which has escaped the eyes of those who watched to see this new planet swim into their ken."[38]

## §6

IT WAS about this time that Clemens decided to give up the lecture-platform. George W. Cable tells of his surprise when, after an apparently successful and satisfactory evening's entertainment, Mark Twain said, on his way back to the hotel in the carriage, "Oh, Cable, . . . I am allowing myself to be a mere buffoon. It's ghastly. I can't endure it any longer."[39] The stories are numerous of his discomfiture when he discovered that he could not

---

[36] *South Atlantic Quarterly*, XIX (October, 1920), 332-40.
[37] *My Mark Twain*, p. 12.
[38] "The Art of S. L. Clemens," *Critic*, XIX, o.s. (July 25, 1891), 45.
[39] A. B. P., II, 786.

be taken seriously, and he resented the effect of his reputation upon the reception of his more serious writings.

In the late eighties, Mark Twain staked his whole
fortune upon the Paige type-setting machine. *A Connecticut Yankee* was written partly to make money to keep
the work on that enterprise going. It is possible that the
importance the machine had assumed in his mind stimulated his imagination, as much as did "old Sir Thomas's
enchanting book," to the grotesque, retroactive exercise of
projecting a Yankee mechanic into sixth-century England.
Always distrustful of his own taste, he depended upon
Howells and Stedman, when the book was published
(1889), to read the proofs, and, as he wrote, "waste-
basket" the parts that could not be admitted. Whether
Howells's "inner check" deserted him in his enthusiasm
for the satire upon monarchy and aristocracy that he
found in the story, or whether he was right in his judgment, only the future can prove. He pronounced it "a
mighty great book": "The book is glorious—simply noble; what masses of virgin truth never touched in print
before! . . . a greatly imagined and symmetrically developed tale."[40]   And Stedman considered it "titanic."

But W. T. Stead of the London *Review of Reviews*
was the only British reviewer who thought it important:

. . . to those who endeavor to understand what the mass of men
who speak English are thinking, as opposed to those who merely
care about what they think they ought to be thinking, this book
of Mark Twain's is one of the most significant of our time. . . .
The average English-speaking man . . . prefers Longfellow to
Browning, and as a humorist he enjoys Mark Twain more than
all the dainty wits whose delicately flavored quips and cranks de-

[40] *Letters*, II, 513.

light the boudoir and the drawing-room. This may be most deplorable from the point of view of the supercilious aesthetes, but the fact in all its brutality cannot be too frankly recognized.[41]

J. A. Noble, in the *Academy*, condemned the book as utterly unworthy of its author:

Though burlesque is the cheapest kind of humour which can be produced by men whose humorous faculty is of the slenderest sort, it has a field in which it may legitimately exploit itself; but the Arthurian legends, which, to us of the age of Tennyson have become saturated with spiritual beauty and suggestiveness, lie a long way outside the boundary of this "scanty plot."[42]

*A Connecticut Yankee*, in fact, brought to the surface all the English distrust of Mark Twain's irreverence. Even Andrew Lang, his friend, disapproved:

I have abstained from reading his work on an American at the Court of King Arthur, because here Mark Twain is not, and cannot be, at the proper point of view. He has not knowledge which would enable him to be a sound critic of the ideal of the Middle Ages. An Arthurian Knight in New York or in Washington would find as much to blame, and justly, as a Yankee at Camelot.[43]

Mark Twain's misgivings had not prepared him for the English criticism of *A Connecticut Yankee*. It caused him to attempt to rationalize his deep distrust of "those parties who miscall themselves critics."[44] Howells, he believed, had developed a "new art" of criticism: "man courteously reasoning with man . . . [instead of] a superior being lecturing a boy." He answered Andrew Lang

---

[41] *Review of Reviews* (London), I, 145-56.
[42] "New Novels," *Academy*, XXXVII (Feb. 22, 1890), 130.
[43] "The Art of S. L. Clemens," *loc. cit.*
[44] *Letters*, II, 513.

with his famous defense of a democratic aesthetic. It was a protest against the type of arrogant judgment that refuses recognition to James Whitcomb Riley because he is not Shakespeare and to Abbey's Knights of the Graal because they cannot be admitted to the Raphael stanza— "the ancient habit of judging all books by one standard." He pleaded for a democratic theory of criticism that would seek to discover the creative impulse in the less important contribution to art—and that would make its power to touch the masses the real test of its validity.[45]

He wished to win the English over to approval of his idea of art, which would mean approval of that kind of flower which the American experiment could put forth. Their most serious charge against him—it is the most serious wherever his work is considered—was that of irreverence. It had been one of his favorite tenets that, as he phrased it near the end of his life, "the word Irreverance will be regarded as the most meaningless, and foolish, and self-conceited, and insolent, and impudent, and dictatorial word in the language."[46] He set out to show what sort of reverence he was capable of, and his Joan of Arc book was the result. He had written *The Prince and the Pauper* to prove what he could do with a more conventional model, and the new book was to be "a companion piece" to that. He had wished to put *The Prince and the Pauper* out anonymously; now he said to his family: "I shall never be accepted seriously over my own signature. People always want to laugh over what I write and are disappointed if they don't find a joke in it. . . . It [the Joan of Arc book] means more

---

[45] *Ibid.*, II, 525.
[46] *What is Man? and Other Essays*, p. 369. (Unless otherwise stated references are to the Uniform Edition.)

to me than anything I have ever undertaken. I shall write it anonymously."[47] In spite of the high favor with which the author and his biographer always regarded *Joan*, reviewers were not enthusiastic about it; and there were many angles for the objections as there were writers. English critics, distrustful still of the author's irreverence, but always much interested in his personality and sturdy character, referred to him at this time as "a charming writer of whimsical historical romance";[48] in America Barrett Wendell said, "In this he showed himself an historical novelist of positive importance."[49] But W. P. Trent, finding that in it alone of all his writings, Mark Twain "challenged criticism as a historical novelist, properly speaking," asks the question, "Has he succeeded in writing a great book or even a thoroughly satisfactory historical novel?" And he has to answer, 'No. . . . He has failed . . . to fuse properly the historic and the purely imaginative or fictive elements of his narrative. . . . His admiration for [Joan of Arc] . . . has prevented him from making her really human and alive."[50]

## §7

THE PUBLICATION of *Joan of Arc* came at the crisis in Mark Twain's literary and public life—its book publication followed upon the heels of the collapse of the typesetting venture and the consequent failure of the Webster Publishing House. His friend, Henry Rogers, the financier, arranged a plan by which his creditors agreed to al-

[47] A. B. P., II, 959.            [48] *Spectator*, May 25, 1907.
[49] *History of Literature in America*, p. 423.
[50] "Mark Twain as an Historical Novelist," *Bookman*, III (May, 1896), 207-10.

low Mark Twain time to make a lecture tour around the world. With the proceeds he proposed to pay the debt in full.

From this trip he returned an international hero. Academic honors came to crown a venerable old age. But his lucky star had betrayed him. He had written to Henry Rogers of his failure in the business venture which he had set his heart upon: "There's one thing which makes it difficult for me to soberly realize that my ten year dream is actually dissolved; and that is, that it reverses my horoscope. The proverb says, 'Born lucky, *always* lucky,' and I am very superstitious. As a small boy I was notoriously lucky. . . ." And he reviewed instances to show that his luck had served him throughout his life.[51]

The Mark Twain legend, so far as it represented the sentiment about him attending his active career, had written itself. Its early loud echoes would gradually fade, but it would gather more trustworthy connotations, perhaps, in the lapse of time. It had been developed through thirty years of hard work—the inevitable persistence of genius, impatient of limitation, seeking the best expression its light could point to, and it had been attended by much vain inflation. His personal gifts laid him open to adulation. It was of Mark Twain as the "Belle of New York" that President Frank Lawrence, introducing him at a Lotus Club banquet held to welcome him back from Europe, said, "Whose name is there in literature that can be likened to his? Perhaps some of the distinguished gentlemen about this table can tell us, but I know of none. Himself his only parallel, it seems to me. He is all our own—a ripe and perfect product of the American soil."[52]

From an external view, life had brought him all that

---

[51] *Letters*, II, 621.     [52] A. B. P., II, 971.

he had hoped for; with his constant help, the Mark Twain legend had written itself large, but he had not been able to content his own spirit. Though his devotion to the masses had remained firm, the final irony of his position was that he was not satisfied with their judgment of his worth. He who had kept his finger so cannily upon the critical pulse had to realize the waverings that he had not been able to overcome. He is a great man of letters, insisted William Dean Howells; he has never been accepted by serious critics, declared opponents of this point of view—chiefly British. His significance is mainly historical and regional, a reviewer in *Harper's* asserted; his record is so casually written and diffuse that ultimately he will be viewed as a mere fun-maker, said the J. G. Holland type of critic. His real significance lies in his philosophical and moral teaching, said some; his philosophy is sophomoric, said others. He is remarkable for his "mastery of all the devices of rhetoric," wrote a distinguished teacher of English; "he cannot be considered a real artist," because his writings are too nearly formless and journalistic, said a later *Atlantic* critic. He is America's greatest humorist— one of the world's greatest humorists, said one; his humor is coarse and ephemeral, said another. He is like Dr. Johnson, a great literary figure destined to adorn the story of *belles lettres* rather as a great human being than as the author of any one book or character, in the view of some critics; but others believed that it was his colossal vanity that kept him so long in the public eye, and that in the final analysis it will be found that his fame has faded away.

One reason why the riddle has been difficult, why he has been a legendary character, is that, until O. H.

Moore's paper was published in 1922, it was believed that he was an original genius who was as free from any influence out of the past as a man could be. Fred Lewis Pattee, quoting Hawthorne's wish that he might see a part of America where the chilling "shadow of Europe had never fallen,"[53] declared that Mark Twain "spent his life in such unshadowed places. When he wrote he wrote without a thought of other writings. . . ."[54] But this statement was written before the Mark Twain *Letters* appeared in 1917. These show that there were shadows along the way, and that the young Sam Clemens occasionally sought refuge in their cool spaces. Even in the cabin of Jim Gillis on Jackass Hill was a "library which included the standard authors."[55] But Mark Twain himself encouraged the widespread belief that he was an "unliterary literary man." Both he and Howells counted on his reversion to the "virgin soil" in his writings, to win readers for them, and the public valued most his bold originality of matter and manner. Carl Van Doren suggested, in a slight way, that there was a provenience, but Henry Pochmann and Friedrich Schönemann have most nearly discovered its extent. Every close search through his works leads to the discovery that the diversity of his materials "can be accounted for only by a breadth of reading." V. R. West, writing on *Folk Lore in the Writings of Mark Twain,* says that that reading must have ranged from current robber and pirate tales, through Homer, Shakespeare, Macpherson's *Ossian,* the Bible, the *Arabian Nights,* and *Robin Hood,* to the most detailed

[53] *Cf.* W. D. Howells, *Life in Letters,* I, 275.
[54] *A History of American Literature Since 1870,* p. 45.
[55] A. B. P., I, 266.

period-histories available in his day.[56] And late in life, after his attention had been called to some of his unconscious borrowings, Mark Twain said what Oliver Wendell Holmes had taught him many years before, "all our phrasings are spiritualized shadows cast multitudinously from our readings."[57]

But another reason for the mystery attending Mark Twain's literary career, and closely related to the first, has lain in the common misconception concerning his early environment. Recently Bernard De Voto, in his *Mark Twain's America* (1932), with its large-scale, interpretative pictures of the whole American frontier, from the Mississippi to the Pacific, has done much to correct the impression conveyed by certain critics that the frontier was culturally barren, but even he seems to believe that it was unshadowed by Europe.[58] Stephen Leacock's *Mark Twain* (1933), a readable commentary on his life, does

[56] *University of Nebraska Studies in Language, Literature, and Criticism*, No. 10, p. 8.

[57] *Autobiography*, I, 241. Extensive studies being conducted by Dr. R. L. Ramsay of the University of Missouri are described in the following:

"A series of detailed investigations of Mark Twain's contribution to American speech, with lists of his Americanisms, nineteenth century words, archaisms, and other significant elements of his vocabulary, have been made with a view to use in the *Historical Dictionary of American English* now being edited by Professor William E. Craigie at the University of Chicago. Already completed and accessible in manuscript in the library of the University of Missouri are M.A. theses on 'The Vocabulary of *The Gilded Age*' by Alma Borth Martin (1929); 'The Vocabulary of *Huckleberry Finn*' by Frances Guthrie Emberson (1930); and 'The Vocabulary of *Tom Sawyer*' by Emma Orr Woods (1932); and others are in progress. All these preliminary studies for the M.A. degree on single books will be combined and supplemented in the Ph.D. dissertation by Frances Guthrie Emberson on 'The Vocabulary of Mark Twain till 1885' already announced. The thesis by Alma Borth Martin mentioned above was published in condensed form as 'A Vocabulary Study of Mark Twain's *Gilded Age* with an Introduction by R. L. Ramsay and a Foreword by Hamlin Garland,' by the Mark Twain Society in 1930. Copies obtainable from Mr. Cyril Clemens, President of the Mark Twain Society, Webster Groves, Missouri."—*American Literature*, IV (May, 1933), p. 214.

[58] P. 99.

not discuss this particular problem. In general, Mark Twain's case has been considered much like that of Lincoln: that he came out of discouraging frontier conditions, where there were few books and where no adequate standard of living had been developed. And out of this conception has developed the legend: Here was a man, possessed of such charm that, with his tongue and his pen, he could amuse the whole world, sprung unaccountably from the western wilderness. As a matter of fact, it is doubtful whether, anywhere in America, there could have been found in the forties and fifties a small section of country more favorable for his start in life than northeast Missouri.

# II

## THE PRE-HANNIBAL PERIOD

### §1

THE MISSOURI toward which the Clemens family turned their faces in 1835 had been a part of the United States less than half a century, but it was conscious of more than a hundred years' tradition of French and Spanish occupation, and from 1765 had had a considerable proportion of English-speaking people in its population. Its tradition was first of all of fur-trading and lead-mining activity, but commerce of various kinds had been developed with New Orleans for almost a hundred years—by means of river barge and keel boat until 1817, when the first steamboat made its way up the Mississippi as far as St. Louis. Frederick J. Turner says:

Down the Mississippi floated a multitude of craft: lumber rafts from the Allegheny, the old-time arks, with cattle, flour, and bacon, hay-boats, keel-boats, and skiffs, all mingled with the steamboats which plied the Western waters. Flatboatmen, raftsmen, and deck-hands constituted a turbulent and reckless population, living on the country through which they passed, fighting and drinking in a true "half-horse, half-alligator" style.[1]

Furthermore, St. Louis had been an outfitting station for expeditions adventuring into the Louisiana Territory to the west, of which it was the heart and center. There had fol-

[1] F. J. Turner, "Colonization of the West," *American Historical Review*, XI (Jan., 1906), 323.

lowed the expulsion of the Indians, the opening up of travel on the Missouri River and across the prairies—development from a loose territorial outpost into a rough border state, with agitation concerning slavery, upon which its economic future seemed to hinge. And, more recently, the movement to expel the Mormons had aroused the zeal of those citizens who would be provident for both the prosperity and the morality of the new commonwealth.

On the tide of immigration that followed the Missouri Compromise, several members of Jane Lampton Clemens's family had come into the state and found homes near the village of Florida, a little over a hundred miles north of St. Louis. John Quarles, Mrs. Clemens's brother-in-law, was prosperous in Florida. Back in Kentucky John Marshall Clemens, whose fortunes at that time had slumped, when the news came of the promise of the new land had decided to follow the family trail west. Thoroughgoing pioneers that they were, the family must have heard tales, as they sailed down the Ohio River, convincing them that they were not making an unwise move. On the boat may have been Germans who would be their traveling companions as far as St. Charles and who would repeat to them the glowing reports of the state of Missouri sent back to Germany by Gottfried Duden.[2] If they had read Cooper's *The Prairie* (1827), or Irving's *A Tour of the Prairies* (1835), and were doubtful, after their experience of reality in the interior of Kentucky, about the romantic pictures they found in them, perhaps they had been reassured by John Bradbury's *Travels in the Interior*

[2] William G. Bek, "The Followers of Duden," *Missouri Historical Review*, XIV, 29.

utch Re
No min-
g to the
icted by
he Pub
p of two
wo Meth-
ans. No
word can
the mem-
.
sionaries
r of any
luals are
iestion is,
re have
gaged in
only be-
ined.
e Union
s. The
political
b encour
iation of
ribe any
schools,
v set of
h denom-
t free to
hools as
ools con-
not even
r publi
very res
to induce
ls. Whe-
whether
not, they
isto ope-
that they
we invite
e places
rejudices
d they op-
of proper
d plans.
covered
signs in
ny to the
ubers for
terprize
ee, quil-
ng them
ex el us.
ourselves

pointed consisting of Chairman and Secretary, to take measures to increase the sum to at least $1000, which amount it was thought reasonable to hope might be obtained from the Baptists in this city, to aid this noble undertaking. We have no doubt but that many of our brethren in other places will forward this design according to their power, and we feel assured that as Christians, the cause has a large claim upon our prayers, liberality and labours.

W. T. BRANTLY, Chair'n
NOAH DAVIS, Secretary.

P. S. Circumstances beyond our control did not permit us to attend the above menti ned meeting; yet we most cordially unite in the sentiments and Resolutions adopted.

THOMAS J KITTS,
*Pastor of the 2d Baptist Church, Pa.*
JOHN L DAGG,
*Pastor of the 5th Bap. Church, Pa.*"

When such names are before the public, as vouchers for the purity of the American Sunday School Union, what candid man will doubt? And who can avoid the reflection, that the proceedings of the late meeting, were the offspring of ignorance, endeavoring to hide the light? To the foregoing testimony we now add the names of Jackson, Grundy, Webster, Hayne, Wickliffe, and other leading men, who, differing widely on political subjects, are united in proclaiming the excellence of the Sunday School system. Doubtless, when the Haden men, in hot pursuit of liberty, arrive at the "polls," they will be constrained to vote for themselves. Oh Liberty! driven from the Capitol, thou hast found a last retreat among thy *tried friends* in Fayette! U. S. T.

P. S. The writer has seen a short paragraph in the Western Monitor, refusing to publish his

## LOTS FOR SALE
### IN THE TOWN OF
# FLORIDA.

THE Proprietors will offer for sale at public auction, on the first day of June next, a quantity of LOTS, in the town of FLORIDA, on a credit of s x and twelve months; (purchasers giving bond with approved security.)

FLORIDA is situated on a ridge, half a mile from the junction, and immediately between, the North and South Forks of Salt River, Monroe county, Missouri, in the centre of an extensive and fertile region of country, which at present embraces several good settlements, and from the tide of emigration, will, in a very short time be densely populated. From the local situation of *Florida*, few places in the interior of Missouri possess equal advantages: Salt River is navigable for Keels, Batteaux, and Flat Boats, several months in the year, at the Forks; and arrangements have been made by the Leg sl ture, for the opening of said river to the junction, which will make *Florida* the principal place of deposit for all the surplus produce raised within thirty or forty miles of said place. There are at present two good Grist, and one Saw Mill, (now in operation,) on each side, and within half a mile of the Cite; and yet enough water power to put in operation an immense quantity of machinery.

*Florida* being situated about 30 miles from Hannibal Palmyra, and New-London, and no probability of any Village being established between it and those places, must cause an extensive business to concentrate at said place.

Persons wishing to purchase Town property, will do well to call and examine for themselves

WILLIAM KEENAN.
WILLIAM N. PENN.
H. A. HICKMAN.
J. T GRIGSBY.
ROBERT DONALDSON.
JOHN WITT.

*Monroe County, April 1. 1831.*

ADVERTISEMENT OF FLORIDA LOTS FROM THE COLUMBIA
*Missouri Intelligencer,* APRIL 16, 1831.

*of America.*[3]   And if they read a warning in William
Faux's *Memorable Days in America*,[4] they had assurance
of something different from the Lamptons; in Missouri
there was "enough for all, and to spare."[5]   If from travelers returning John Clemens heard of the rough life of
the "gray backs," as the scattered population of western
Missouri was called, he would make a stern resolve to
bring up his family to be of a different sort.   Orion
Clemens, a lad of ten, lounging among the passengers on
the lower deck of the river boat, may have heard the kind
of story that delighted the young Walter Raleigh when he
sought the haunts of travelers returned from America two
centuries and a half before.   There would have been on
the boat such people as were found by Timothy Flint, the
missionary, on the banks of the Mississippi:

Some had been hunters on the Missouri; some had explored the
Mississippi above the Falls of St. Anthony; others knew the region
of the Great Lakes and Canada; others had wandered far south,
on the Red River and on the lagoons near the Gulf of Mexico.
They had stories to tell of river and forest, of war and the hunt,
of Spanish and Frenchmen.   Sometimes we had details of their
dusky loves, that no feature of romance might be wanting.[6]

[3] "The vast tract of prairie extending through all these regions is an important
object of consideration . . . it will be one of the most beautiful countries in the
world."—Thwaites, *Early Western Travels*, V, 38.   *Cf.* Lyman Beecher, *A Plea
for the West:* The Mississippi Valley "is the largest territory, and the most
beneficent in soil, and mineral wealth, and commercial facilities, ever prepared for
the habitation of man, and qualified to sustain the densest population on the globe."
p. 35.

[4] "But to those of *decreasing* means, and *increasing* families, uprooted, with-
ering, and seeking a transplantation *somewhere*, full of hard, dirty-handed industry . . . I would say, 'Haste away; you have no other refuge from poverty.' "
—Thwaites, XI, 303.

[5] See *The Gilded Age*, chap. I, Beriah Sellers's letter.

[6] *Recollections of the Last Ten Years in the Valley of the Mississippi* (1826),
p. 94.   Quoted by W. H. Venable, *Beginnings of Literary Culture in the Ohio
Valley*, p. 339.   *Cf.* R. L. Rusk, *The Literature of the Middle Western Frontier*,
I, 126.

The Clemens family may well have had some such anxious moment on their journey as that of Washington Irving three years before:

Our voyage was prolonged by our repeatedly running aground in the Ohio from the lowness of the water. Twice we remained aground for the greater part of twenty-four hours. The last evening of our voyage we were nearly run down and sent to the bottom by a huge steamboat, the *Yellow Stone*, which came down the river under "high pressure" and a rapid current. Fortunately our pilot managed the helm so as to receive the blow obliquely, which tore away part of the wheel, and staved in all the upper works of one side of our boat. We made shift to limp through the remainder of the voyage.[7]

As they passed by Ste. Genevieve on their way up the Mississippi to St. Louis, they may have seen on the levee signs of a fête to celebrate the centennial of the founding of the town. Settled by the Acadians from Canada, the town was a "relic of the time when one could travel from the mouth of the Mississippi to Quebec and be on French territory and under French rule all the way."[8] Their boat may have taken on lead ore to be put off at a shot tower at Herculaneum, thirty miles below St. Louis.[9] From passengers embarking there they could learn that almost half the population of the town were Negroes, many of them brought up through New Orleans from Santo Domingo

[7] From a letter to Irving's sister, Mrs. Paris, written September 13, 1832. *Life and Letters of Washington Irving* (ed. P. M. Irving, 1882), I, 247.

[8] *Life on the Mississippi*, chap. XXIII. *See* Lucien Carr, *Missouri*, p. 24.

[9] Herculaneum is "environed by high bluffs, the tops of which are surrounded with shot towers, where vast quantities of shot are manufactured."—Robert Baird, *View of the Valley of the Mississippi* (1832), p. 227. *Cf. Missouri Historical Review*, XX, 214-16, "The first shot tower west of Pittsburgh was erected in 1809 at the top of this cliff. Shot made by dropping molten lead from it and bullets molded from lead smelted nearby were used by the American troops during the War of 1812."

by the first white men in the district, to work in the iron and lead mines;[10] and they may have talked with officials from the French school to which Henry Marie Bracken-ridge was sent from Pittsburg in 1793, as a boy of seven, to learn to speak French[11]—the same H. M. Brackenridge whose *Recollections of Persons and Places in the West* (1834), they may have read.

With their "barouche and four horses" the Clemens family probably left the river boat in St. Louis, near the confluence of the two rivers that unite to form the largest river in the world—of which their son, born seven months or so later, was to be the chief historian. In 1835 the city had about ten thousand inhabitants,[12] but its importance was greater than those figures would indicate to a casual reader. At a time when waterways were railroads, tel-egraph lines, and pony express routes, it was the key to most of the country that lay to the west, as well as to the immediate east.

St. Louis occupied a unique position, as the entrepôt of the important fur trade of the upper Mississippi and the vast water system of the Missouri, as well as the outfitting point for Missouri settlements. The French element was still important, but was gradually giving way to adventurous Americans. St. Louis's interests included the far-off region of the Columbia, and the ancient Spanish settlement about Santa Fé. It was the capital for the far West. . . .[13]

[10] "The feverish desire of wealth of the early French explorers led to the introduction of negro slavery into Missouri. The Sieur de Renault purchased hundreds of slaves in Santo Domingo to work his mines in the Ste. Genevieve district. In 1722 there were in the district nearly three hundred slaves to four hundred free men."—James Hall, *Romance of Western History* (1857), p. 321.

[11] Alexandre De Menil, *Literature of the Louisiana Territory* (1904), p. 125. H. M. Brackenridge was the son of H. H. Brackenridge, author of *Modern Chivalry* (1792).

[12] *Cf.* Samuel E. Moffett, "Mark Twain, a Biographical Sketch," *The $30,000 Bequest*, p. 330.

[13] Turner, "Colonization of the West," *loc. cit.*, p. 320.

Relatively, the importance of the city at the confluence of the Mississippi and the Missouri was far greater than it is today.

Viewed from the standpoint of transportation, the western country in that day can be likened in shape to a fan. The handle was that portion which extended from St. Louis to the mouth of the Kansas River. Thence the various routes to all parts of the country diverged along the arms of the fan, which were outspread from Santa Fé on the south to Fort Union on the north. Most of the business below the point of divergence was done by steamboat. Vessels in large numbers plied the river over this first four hundred miles, and the amount of freight and passenger traffic carried by them was very great.[14]

In St. Louis, John Clemens, because he was a lawyer and had had experience among men, probably talked with patriarchs who had seen the Louisiana Territory formally turned over to the United States in 1804; with William Clark, one of the leaders of the Lewis and Clark Expedition and second territorial governor;[15] with William Ashley, the fur-trader and Indian fighter who had discovered the Great Southern Pass in the Rocky Mountains; with persons who had had an active part in the debate over the Missouri Compromise in the State Constitutional Convention fifteen years before; or with Thomas Hart Benton, whose politics his sons were to attack in their paper fifteen years later. In St. Louis he may have purchased a copy of Angus Umphraville's *Missourian Lays, and Other Western Ditties*, published there in 1821.[16] "He

[14] H. M. Chittenden, *Early Steamboat Navigation on the Missouri River*, I, 174.

[15] William Clark died in St. Louis in 1838. Territorial governor of Missouri, 1813-20.

[16] M. M. Brashear, "Missouri Verse and Verse-Writers," *Missouri Historical Review*, XIX, 87.

bought a book now and then," Mr. Paine says, "and sub-
scribed for *Peter Parley's Magazine*."[17]   He may even
have purchased, among other books, to save his family
from the uncouthness of life in the new country, a copy of
*Don Quixote*, which was to have a formative influence
upon the mood and writings of one of his sons.   He would
have been following the example of at least one adventurer into the West if he had done so: H. M. Brackenridge wrote in his *Journal*, "I had also had the precaution
to provide myself with some well selected books; among
the rest, *Don Quixote*. . . ."[18]   And John Clemens may
have arranged for the *Missouri Republican*[19] to be sent to
him and John Quarles up in the country.

The family probably did not tarry long in St. Louis,
but took the road directly across to St. Charles twenty
miles away on the Missouri River; or they may have gone
by boat up the Mississippi around to St. Charles, into the
Missouri a few miles below the town.   They may have
heard French Canadian river-men singing the same boat
song that Manuel Lisa, the Cuban fur-trader, sang fourteen years before to hearten the men that took him and
H. M. Brackenridge up the Missouri River.[20]

If the family stopped in St. Charles to load their
barouche with what provisions it would carry up country,
they still must have been cheered concerning their destination.   Founded by French Canadians in 1804, St.
Charles by 1835 ranked second in the state, with a population of about fifteen hundred.[21]   From 1820 till 1826 it

[17] A. B. P., I, 14.
[18] H. M. Brackenridge, *Journal*, in Thwaites, VI, 54.
[19] R. L. Rusk, *op. cit.*, I, 140.
[20] Thwaites, VI, 57; V, 40.
[21] In 1840, five years later, St. Charles had 2,818 population, of which 419 were slaves.

had been the capital of the state. The General Assembly of Missouri early in the spring of that year had passed an act incorporating the St. Charles Library Company. Seven years later John Clemens would organize a like company in Hannibal. Through the streets of St. Charles, from its beginning, traders and adventurers had passed, to embark on the Missouri.[22] Since 1821 those people were more likely to travel by land by the Boonslick Road to Franklin, half way across the state, where they were outfitted before proceeding on the Santa Fé Trail.[23] Near St. Charles Timothy Flint, early chronicler of the West, had lived as missionary for six years, and near there Daniel Boone had finished out his life. The family may have met, in St. Charles, traders from New Mexico who told them of the well developed Spanish life there; and they would certainly have heard of the trip of the *Yellowstone* up the Missouri in 1832 to the mouth of the Yellowstone River. They would have had pointed out to them, on the streets of St. Charles, Mormons starting out with supplies to their settlement at Independence, and they may have heard threats against the state within a state which was being formed there. Among the travelers talked about in the town would be Washington Irving, and the story would already have taken on the halo of legend, that, going up the river horseback, with a party of explorers, as the local story has it, he had met Kit Carson and his squaw wife at the Arrow Rock Tavern just

[22] "As early as 1703 a party of twenty set out to go from Kaskaskia to New Mexico, by way of the Missouri River."—Lucien Carr, *Missouri*, p. 22.

[23] *Journals* of Captain Thomas Becknell, founder of the Santa Fé Trail, 1821, *Missouri Historical Review*, IV, 75, 309. "An hundred persons have been numbered in a day passing through St. Charles either to Boone's Lick or Salt River."—Flint's *Recollections*, p. 313.

above Franklin, where he had to ford the Missouri. Irving had written back to his sister:

Our journey has been a very interesting one, leading us across fine prairies and through noble forests, dotted here and there by farms and log houses, at which we found rough but wholesome and abundant fare, and very civil treatment. Many parts of these prairies of the Missouri are extremely beautiful, resembling cultivated countries embellished with parks and groves, rather than the savage rudeness of the wilderness. . . . The fertility of all this western country is truly astonishing. The soil is like that of a garden, and the luxuriance and beauty of the forest exceed anything I have ever seen. We have gradually been advancing, however, toward rougher and rougher life, and are now at a little straggling frontier village that has only been five years in existence. . . .[24]

More important still, the Clemenses would probably talk with some of those German immigrants who were transforming the banks of the Missouri at Washington, forty miles above St. Charles, into a pastoral refuge, and what they heard must have heartened them for the last lap of their journey.[25]

[24] *Life and Letters of Irving*, I, 248.

[25] F. Steines, a follower of Gottfried Duden, writes back to Germany the description of a farm which he bought in 1830, twenty or thirty miles up the Missouri from St. Charles: "I bought not only the farm, but also the crop, consisting of corn, wheat, oats, potatoes, cotton, pumpkins, also the stock—1 horse, 10 head of cattle, 11 sheep, about 50 hogs, chickens, and beehives, moreover, plows and other farm implements, harness, etc., [158 acres of land, with thirty acres under cultivation] all for $1000. . . . In half an hour I can walk to . . . the Missouri. Three miles east of us we have a highway, the Franklin road, which makes communication with St. Louis and other places easy. . . . The schools are very poorly taken care of, but somehow American life seems to compensate for many other omissions. I have traveled much in my neighborhood, but everywhere I was made to feel that I was among educated people."—Bek, "The Followers of Duden," *Missouri Historical Review*, XV, 534, 535, 538.

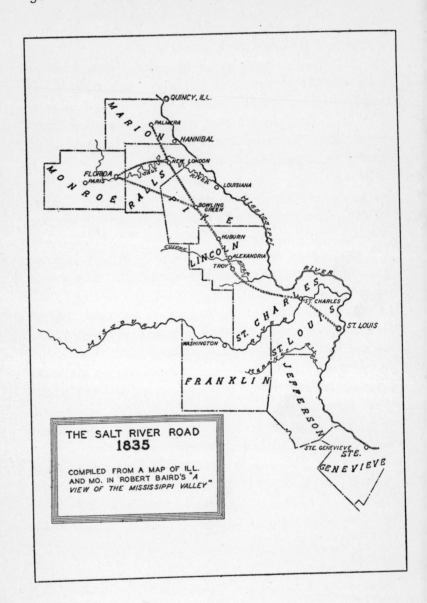

THE SALT RIVER ROAD
**1835**

COMPILED FROM A MAP OF ILL.
AND MO. IN ROBERT BAIRD'S "*A
VIEW OF THE MISSISSIPPI VALLEY*"

## §2

FROM ST. CHARLES John Clemens must have set out over the Salt River Road, which has been followed rather closely by the present U. S. Highway 61, from St. Louis to Hannibal: "The Salt River Road passed out from St. Charles to St. Peters, thence along the Mississippi bluffs to Burkles; thence by Wellsburgh, Flint Hill to Troy, thence by Alexandria, Auburn, Prairieville (now Eolia), Bowling Green, New London, to Palmyra."[26] As they proceeded on their slow journey through St. Charles County, John Clemens was no doubt interested to discover the large cleared areas under cultivation. The county had a population of about six thousand in 1835, over a thousand of whom were engaged in agriculture. One-fourth of the population were slaves.

When the travelers reached Troy, the county seat of Lincoln, next county above St. Charles, they would have turned due north into Pike County.

If the Clemens family had come to live on the banks of the Salt River sixteen years earlier, Mark Twain would have been born in Pike County,[27] the section of the state most famous in song and story. Even his fame cannot invest Marion County with an aura equal to that won for Pike by the Missouri Argonauts. It came to stand not only for all Missouri among forty-niners, but also for all the West. Like Pike County, Illinois, opposite to it on

[26] G. C. Broadhead, "Early Missouri Roads," *Missouri Historical Review*, VIII (Jan., 1914), 91.

[27] "As first erected, Pike County comprised an indefinite region north of Lincoln and Montgomery counties, bounded on the north by the Iowa line and on the west by the Pacific Ocean! Marion, Ralls, Monroe, and other counties were carved out of it. It was reduced to its present limits in 1818. It extends, in an angle, about ten miles north of the confluence of Salt river with the Mississippi."— Clayton Keith, *Centennial History of Pike County* (1876).

the east bank of the Mississippi—John Hay's county—it was named for Lieutenant Zebulon Pike, who, in 1805, was commissioned by the government to take a party in a keel-boat to explore the head waters of the Mississippi.[28] From the close of the War of 1812, in which Lieutenant Pike was killed, settlers had been coming into the Salt River country from the Carolinas, from Virginia, from Tennessee, and, in large numbers, from Kentucky. As the chief landing place in the region was at Louisiana, in the northeast corner of the county, that place was made the temporary county seat.[29] When the town which in 1824 became the permanent county seat was laid out in 1819, in the center of the county, loyal Kentuckians named it Bowling Green. The first newspaper published at the county seat was the *Salt River Journal*, established two years before John Clemens came through Bowling Green. By 1835 the county had a population of seven thousand with two thousand slaves.

As in southeast Missouri, the excitement connected with land speculation, since the time of large French and Spanish land grants, had imparted some importance to this section, from the first. With slaves to do their work, the southerners who came to Pike County had time for a vivid public life. Called on to furnish contingents of men to the various Indian wars, the county had acquired such

[28] In 1810 Lieutenant Pike published his *Journal* (1805-1806), in which he described northeast Missouri. On August 15, 1805, he saw, on the west, Salt River, which the Indians called the Auhaha, flowing into the Mississippi: "about one hundred or one hundred and twenty yards wide at its entrance . . . about one day's sail up this river there are salt springs, which have been worked for four years."

[29] Apparently Louisiana is near the site of a town called, on early maps of the county, Petersburg. As the oldest river town in the state north of St. Louis, it probably suggested the name Mark Twain chose for Tom Sawyer's town: "the poor little shabby village of St. Petersburg."—*The Adventures of Tom Sawyer*, p. 7.

local spirit that it often called itself the State of Pike. When, therefore, twenty years later, Colonel Abner Mc-Pike collected a band of two hundred gold-seekers to cross the plains, they were proud to call themselves Pike County Men. It was due to this band that, in distinction from Yankee emigrants to California from east of the Mississippi, those from west of its banks came to be known as Pikers or Pikes.

The fame of Pike County in literature comes from its having given its name to the dialect which became the vehicle for certain western humorous writings. How this happened is so lost in legend that the historical facts can probably not be come at. But Henry Childs Merwin in his *Life of Bret Harte* gives what he believes to be an authentic account. He quotes "an intelligent pioneer" as saying, "We recognize in California but two types of the republican character, the Yankee and the Missourian. The latter term was first used to represent the entire population of the West, but Pike county superseded, first, the name of the state, and soon that of the whole West." Henry Childs Merwin attributes the fame of a district not over sixty miles square to the Joe Bowers ballad. He believes that he has sources to prove that Joe Bowers was an ox-driver in General McPike's company, who, to relieve the tedium of travel across the plains, "soon made a reputation . . . as a humorist, as an 'original,' as a 'greenhorn,' and as a good fellow generally. Joe Bowers was poor, he was in love, he was making a fortune in order that he might lay it at the feet of his sweetheart, and the whole company became his confidants and sympathizers." In the company, according to this version of the story, was a young journalist by the name of Frank Swift—in some versions it is Frank Smith—who, half in a spirit of wag-gery, took up the cause of the illiterate driver of oxen, and started singing to a popular air some stanzas relating the story of his affair of the heart.  The song was taken up by the company and sung night after night by the camp fire:

> My name it is Joe Bowers
> I've got a brother Ike
> I came from old Missouri
> Yes all the way from Pike.

The ballad grew like a snow-ball rolled along the ground. It told the story of Joe's lucky strike in California, all intended for Sally; and then of the letter from his brother Ike containing the news that Sally had not been true to him; she had married a red-headed butcher.

> It told me more than that.
> It's enough to make me swear.
> It said Sal had a baby
> And the baby had red hair.

When the company went their several ways in California they taught the ballad to people all up and down the coast. "In 1856 it was printed in a cheap form in San Francisco and was sung by Johnson's minstrels at a hall known as the Old Melodeon.  Joe Bowers thus became the type of the unsophisticated Western miner, and Pike county became the symbol of the West."[30]

---

[30] Merwin, *Life of Bret Harte*, p. 59.  Russell Blankenship quotes Bayard Taylor: "The first emigrants that came over the plains were from Pike County, Missouri. . . . He is the Anglo-Saxon relapsed into semi-barbarism.  He is long, and sallow; he expectorates vehemently; he takes naturally to whiskey; he has the shakes all his life long at home, though he generally manages to get rid of them in California; he has little respect for the rights of others, but venerates the memory of Andrew Jackson."—*American Literature as an Expression of the National Mind*, pp. 439-41.

The author of a recent history of American literature, after pointing to the dialect in the language of the white people in *Tom Sawyer* as an example of Pike County dialect, says, "Probably the most effective use of the dialect to be found in our literature is in the books of Mark Twain."[31] He finds the language adequate for literary expression: "Whatever may be said for the bad grammar and garbled pronunciation used by the Middle Westerners, it must be admitted that their dialect was picturesque and swiftly expressive." Bret Harte, seeing its possibilities for poetry, put it into the mouth of his "Truthful James."[32] John Hay believed that his *Pike County Ballads* preceded Harte's *East and West Poems*. Both were probably taking advantage of a general humorous interest in the type.

Mark Twain identified himself with the region and its language in the "Explanatory" note prefixed to *Huckleberry Finn:* "In this book a number of dialects are used, to wit: the Missouri negro dialect; the extremest form of the backwoods Southwestern dialect; the ordinary 'Pike County' dialect; and four modified varieties of this last . . . done . . . with the trustworthy guidance and support of personal familiarity with these several forms of speech."

The tang to the humor of the Pike County dialect, as to the humor of Augustus Baldwin Longstreet's Georgia Crackers, comes from the contrast between the sophisticated onlooker and the illiterate speaker. In a democracy

---

[31] Blankenship, *op. cit.*, p. 440. Blankenship's statement that Mark Twain's "native language was the vernacular of Pike County" is to be doubted. While he doubtless dropped easily into the vernacular to insure his standing with Hannibal small boys and river men and western miners, he was probably enough in awe of his father to avoid it at home. John Marshall Clemens was the type of person who would cultivate precise language, and Mark Twain himself was sensitive to poor grammar. *Cf. Life on the Mississippi*, pp. 314-15.

[32] Blankenship, *op. cit.*, p. 439.

the superior man has no recourse but in a laugh; and the reader is drawn into an appreciation of the odd character. *The Jumping Frog* gets its peculiar quality from being the report of one oddity by another. The "original," Jim Smiley, is a highly interesting person to the "original," Simon Wheeler.

It was at Louisiana in Pike County, a stronghold of Virginians and Kentuckians, that contemporaries of Sam Clemens, turned Union men, threatened in 1865 to deal summarily with Frank P. Blair if he attempted to make his speech opposing the "test oath" of the "Drake Constitution." According to this "Constitution," no man could vote in Missouri until he swore that he had neither directly nor indirectly given aid to the Confederate cause. When his audience greeted him ascending the platform with the cry, "Throw the rebel out!" Blair "unbuckled a holster, laid two Colt revolvers on the speaker's desk, and said, 'I understand I am to be shot if I speak here today. Perhaps we would better attend to this ceremony now—.' " He then delivered his speech.[33]

It is locally believed that the phrase "gone up Salt River" originated in Pike County.[34] And Champ Clark,

[33] *Cf.* Mr. Richard E. Miller's picture in the Senate Chamber of the Capitol at Jefferson City: "Blair's Speech at Louisiana, Missouri, 1866." Description in *Report of the Capitol Decoration Commission*, Dr. John Pickard, ed. [Jefferson City, 1928].

[34] According to the Pike County legend coming down from the 1840's, "He's gone up Salt River" came to be applied humorously to the fate of a defeated candidate because of the habit of a citizen by the name of Jackson from Louisiana, the first county seat. When he was defeated for a town office, he moved up to the mouth of Salt River two or three miles away to get out of the neighborhood of those who had failed to support him. Undeterred by his failure, however, in 1845 he ran for the state legislature, and, when he was again defeated, moved farther up Salt River. In 1847 he ran for the same office again, and, again defeated, moved on up the river. As a result, when anyone asked, "Where's Jackson?" the reply would be, "He's gone up Salt River." The Missouri Argonauts took the expression with them to California, where it came to be used in the gold settlements with the same meaning. And when the forty-niners returned to their homes, they carried the expression with them to different parts of the world.—

Mark Twain's ally many years later in securing the passage of his copyright bill, was to make Bowling Green nationally known.[35] Champ Clark and Mark Twain both represented the region out of which they came: both had something of the Kentucky colonel, who was at the same time a "literary gentleman," lingering in their personalities, and both had the more democratic outlook that came from their pioneer upbringing.

If court was in session when the home-seekers reached Bowling Green, John Clemens had a chance to take stock of the region of which he was to be a citizen. It may be inferred that conditions were similar to those described by a traveler in Jefferson City in 1848:

The streets were unpaved, six inches deep with dust in summer, and knee deep with mud in the winter. Dust, dirt, and mud, . . . were everywhere perceptible. The houses were spattered with dry mud, the vehicles covered with thick layers of mud, . . . The session of Court attracted a considerable number of country people to the town, and these were principally collected about a miserable, naked-looking edifice made of mud in the form of brick, called the Court House, where a set of half educated, muddy-headed lawyers, made a muddle in attempting to make the "wrong side appear the better cause." A rougher set of citizens, whether regarded with reference to dress, manners or physical appearance, . . . could not be imagined. Bear-skin caps, Mackinaw blankets, leather leggings, old Bess rifles and hunting knives, entered into their dress and equipments. Tall, square-shouldered, broad-chested, stout men, made up of bone and gristle, they drank whiskey, chewed tobacco, and while waiting for the opening of

George A. Mahan in the *Columbia Missourian*, March 26, 1928. Apparently, however, the expression had an earlier origin. *Cf.* Wetmore's *Gazeteer of Missouri* (1837), p. 122: "The threat to row an antagonist up Salt River in the Western country, is understood to be equivalent to crossing a stray soul over the river Styx."

[35] *Letters*, II, 802.

the Court, engaged in . . . throwing heavy weights, jumping, wrestling, and boxing.[36]

But scattered through the rough crowd about the court-house would have been leaders, intelligent southern men, who appeared to be of a different sort. With these John Clemens perhaps talked about schools and churches to be built. His sons were to grow up among tradition-makers.

From Bowling Green the travelers may have turned to the northwest, off the Salt River Road, for the last twenty miles of their drive—unless they continued north twenty-five miles to New London, county seat of Ralls County, in order to take advantage of a better traveled river road to Florida. One or the other of these roads John Clemens would travel over often during the next four years, possibly taking turns with John Quarles, going to St. Charles or St. Louis with meat, eggs, and vegetables to trade for merchandise. Sam Clemens's first adventure into the world was doubtless as a child with his father on one of these "lagging, dragging" journeys. During the muddy season they would take their produce to Louisiana in Pike County, thirty miles to the east, or to Hannibal, twenty miles northeast, and thence down the Mississippi by river boat.

## §3

THE PICTURE of the Clemens family approaching Florida, Missouri, in 1835 in *The Boys' Life of Mark Twain* suggests the spirit of adventure with which they drew near

---

[36] J. L. Peyton, *Over the Alleghanies and Across the Prairies* (London, 1849), pp. 269-70. Cole County, in which Jefferson City is situated, was probably no further developed in 1848 than Pike County was in 1835, when its population was only half that of Pike County. Louisiana, on the Mississippi River in Pike— the river town for Bowling Green—had been a good deal of a place since about 1818.

the new home—John Clemens driving the "barouche" in which sat Mrs. Clemens with Benjamin, three years old, Margaret, five, and Pamela, eight. Orion, a boy of ten, and Jennie, the housemaid, were outriders on the extra horses.[37] Their kinspeople who greeted them on that June evening of their arrival were already successful in the new country. John Clemens had proved in Tennessee that he could prosper when conditions were favorable, and the little town of Florida was astir with enterprises needing only energy and coöperation to make them flourish. Mark Twain makes no mention of the fact that Mrs. Clemens's parents lived in Florida except that among his comments on his earliest memories of what happened in the "diminutive town," he says, "I believed that I remember helping my grandfather drink his whiskey toddy when I was six weeks old." Eugene Lampton, a first cousin and boyhood playmate of the Clemens children, who, as an old man, was minister in the Disciples Church at Madison in Monroe County, said, "Mark Twain was born in the home of his grandfather and mine—a little log cabin behind the store—and not in the house whose picture has been so widely circulated. The cabin was subsequently converted into the first church in Florida. . . ."[38] John Clemens was then thirty-seven years old. Sam[39] was born the thirtieth of November, after their arrival in early summer.

To a twentieth-century view, Sam Clemens's birthplace, with its log houses in the midst of a clearing and its streets knee-deep in mud in spring, would appear impos-

[37] *The Boys' Life of Mark Twain*, p. 25.

[38] T. V. Bodine, "A Visit to Florida," *Kansas City Star*, XXXII (May 19, 1912), 9 D.

[39] "As a boy he was plain Sam Clemens. As a youth he was Sam Clemens. As a miner and newspaper man in California he was likewise simply Sam Clemens."—William M. Clemens, *Biblio*, Aug., 1922-March, 1923.

sible for any but the hopeless ones described by William Faux. And the tourist who visits Florida today has his impression that Mark Twain grew up in "squalid, straggling towns in the Middle West" confirmed. With its primitive country store and improvised soft drink counter, it has reverted to type, and the monument to its favorite son makes the sight-seer sorry he came. While the Mark Twain State Park on a bluff above Salt River, to which the Clemens house has been moved, gives his imagination more to dwell upon, nothing gives him any conception of what the spirit of the village was in 1835, when, as the head of navigation, it was thought by the pioneers to be "a favorable point for the founding of a great commercial town." It was forty miles south of what was the official frontier line of the United States, and over two hundred miles east of it.[40] This meant that there was no longer any problem of protection from the Indians, that there would be social contacts, that it was possible for the man with a little capital, by purchasing a clearing and building a better type of house than the first crude cabins, to escape the initial hardships of pioneer life. The Lamptons were of the "better type of pioneer" described by Frederick J. Turner—a step beyond that represented by Lincoln's family[41] in general sophistication: "The backwoodsman of this type," he says, "represented the outer edge of the advance of civilization. Where settlement was closer, coöperative activity possible, and little villages, with the mill and retail stores, existed, conditions of life were ameliorated, and a better type of pioneer was found."[42]

The first store in the county and the first grist mill

[40] Harper's *Atlas of American History,* p. 38.
[41] *Rise of the New West,* p. 78.
[42] "Colonization of the West," *loc. cit.,* p. 315.

were in the immediate neighborhood of Florida. Situated at the forks of Salt River, eighty-five miles from the Mississippi, it had two grist mills by 1831, and a saw mill. By 1830, Hugh A. Hickman, who became owner of the oldest of these, ran boats loaded with flour to Louisiana and brought back sugar, coffee, and other staples.[43] Settlers within a radius of forty miles came there with corn to be ground and furs and produce to be shipped to St. Louis. When, therefore, Monroe County was subdivided from Ralls in 1831, Florida, seeming to its citizens to be the logical place for the county seat, laid itself out more formally, and Florida lots were advertised in papers out in the state. When John Clemens arrived, because he had had experience in locating a county seat he threw himself into the fight with such vigor that to this day his name is pronounced with asperity in Paris, the successful rival town.[44]

By 1837 the place had, besides three mills, four or five distilleries producing "about 10,000 gallons of whiskey annually and from one to 3000 gallons of brandy and gin." When sand and clay suitable for stoneware were discovered, a pottery was built. ". . . A potter, who hath power over the clay, is there making one vessel to honour, and another to dishonour, as a temperance devotee would insist; . . . vessels for milk, as well as jugs. . . ."[45] As most of the settlers raised hemp, "an extensive hemp manufactory" was built. All these enterprises depended, for

[43] Wetmore's *Gazetteer of Missouri* (St. Louis, 1837), p. 152.

[44] ". . . the thing by which he will be longest remembered in the county of Monroe resulted in its being deprived by legislative enactment of a row of its richest sections along the northern and southern borders." There follows the story of the compromise made necessary by the fight, when Paris was chosen for the county-seat instead of Florida.—Bodine, "A Visit to Florida," *loc. cit.*

[45] Wetmore's *Gazetteer of Missouri*, p. 120.

any large success, upon the establishment of a means of transportation. In 1831 an act of the state legislature, after declaring Salt River navigable as far up as Florida, and "free for all boats, rafts, and other vessels," had empowered anyone wanting to build a dam for a grist mill to receive from the circuit court of his county a writ of *ad quod damnum*. In January, 1837, the legislature authorized the Salt River Navigation Company to open books and receive subscriptions to the capital stock of the company. The name of John Clemens headed the list of sixteen commissioners from Ralls, Pike, and Monroe counties. The company was to have three years for organization and for the construction of the system of dams and locks necessary before it could operate.[46] In 1839 the time was extended two more years, but the possibility of securing a railroad for the region put an end to its interest in making Salt River navigable. In February, 1837, by another legislative enactment a board of commissioners was appointed to create the Florida and Paris Railroad Company and issue shares at fifty dollars each, the capital stock to be one hundred thousand dollars. Again John Clemens's name appears first of the nine men appointed.

The same month an act was passed incorporating the Florida Academy. The name of Edmund Damrell, who had built the first house in Florida, heads the list of trustees, which includes also the names of John Clemens and John A. Quarles.

There is no record in the scant history of the county of what came of all these plans, but the whirlwind of western development swept on to new frontiers, and all that Salt

---

[46] *Laws of the State of Missouri, 1836-1837*, pp. 229-34.

ERS,
*in the*

ne,
,

in an-
mplete
shment
d their
:eeding
ı Ame-
ɔn list,
ICES OF
ɔpulari-
aumber

the U-
ı fertile
cts, by
power-
ıeations
foreign
says on
s of cel-
origin-

# Salt River Navigation.

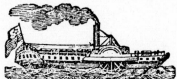

**N**OTICE is hereby given that pursuant to the provisions of an "act to incorporate the Salt River Navigation Company," the 15th day of January next, at the court house in the town of New London, Ralls County, is appointed by the Commissioners of said Company for holding an election; when and where "the Stockholders shall, by ballot, elect, from their own number, one President and seven Directors, to manage the affairs of said company, for one year, and until the election and qualification of their successors."

JOHN M. CLEMENS, ⎞
JOHN CISSELL, ⎟
JOHN J. LYLE, • ⎬ Commis-
HUGH MEREDITH, ⎟ sioners.
EDWARD DAMRELL,⎠

November 11, 1837.

☞Shareholders may "vote by proxy duly made in writing."

N
tec foi
& Sor
notes
all pei
make

*Dis.*
THI
tl
this d:
sons i
imme(
in wa

No
☞
Stand

SE

N
apart
mav c

SALT RIVER NAVIGATION. A NOTICE IN THE HANNIBAL
*Commercial Advertiser*, JANUARY 4, 1838.

River contributed to literature is contained in an ironical phrase. The student who attempts to recapture the spirit of the thirties in this section of Missouri, however, must feel the exhilaration and spirit of adventure that was in the air. And it is only from such a point of view that its significance as the setting in which Mark Twain's genius had its beginning can be properly understood. It belonged to the time of epic achievement in America, and to the part of the nation which caused Whitman to think of "a poetry that should in due time express and supply the teeming region"—"The pure breath, primitiveness, boundless prodigality and amplitude, strange mixture of delicacy and power, of continence, of real and ideal, and of all original and first-class elements, of these prairies, the Rocky mountains, and of the Mississippi and Missouri rivers—will they ever appear in, and in some sort form a standard for our poetry and art?"[47]

The point of view of the onlooker is to be distrusted; it betrays men into such misinterpretation as that of a recent writer who declared that "the cynical quality of Mark Twain's humor was the outcome of revolt against the poverty and repression of his early life in the little cabin in Florida, Missouri."[48] As Sam Clemens was only four years old when he left the town on Salt River, his memory of it was not of its period of high hope, but of its days of decline, when he returned for his summer vacations, as a lad of ten and thereabouts. He describes "the almost invisible village" in humorous vein, with its log church "twilighted by yellow tallow candles," but he had no bitter memories of the place, and it is to be doubted

[47] "Mississippi Valley Literature," *Specimen Days.*
[48] "Mark Twain as Exhibit A," *McClure's*, April, 1927.

whether the older members of the family had. Their life there had its compensations.

The "ameliorating condition" that made life among southern pioneers different from that of any other type of emigrant was that there were slaves to take the brunt of the rough work. What with butchering, and curing meats, and making soap, and spinning and weaving and sewing for a family of seven, and preparing Sunday dinners when all the Lamptons came home with them from preaching, everybody had enough to do; but Jane Clemens had more time to take her family to camp-meeting, and to tell them tales by the fireplace of her life in the good old state of Kentucky, because she had Jenny in the kitchen and Uncle Ned to keep the hearth fires burning. People in all the region had slaves; John Quarles, who lived on a farm four miles out from Florida, had thirty slaves.

Because Sam Clemens as a child had in John Quarles a hero of a different type from his somber, silent father and the visionary James Lampton, some account of the more successful pioneer will help to give an idea of the importance of his Florida years in developing the boy's character and imagination. "I have not come across a better man," Mark Twain wrote in later years, "I was his guest for two or three months every year . . . till I was eleven or twelve years old. . . . The life I led there with my cousins was full of charm, and so is the memory of it yet."[49]

Mark Twain often refers in his writings to the Quarles farm and the generous life there. In *Huckleberry Finn* and *Tom Sawyer, Detective* he models the farms he de-

[49] *Autobiography*, I, 96, 109, 110.

scribes on the place he loved as a child. The chief biographer of John Quarles believes his influence to have been so potent that Mark Twain came to look like him "with his big features, leonine head, and long gray hair. . . ." Though whimsical and kindly, John A. Quarles was a strong, virile, capable man with sympathy and imagination. . . . He had a certain potentiality and individuality of his own, . . . countless legends survive regarding him. His stories as a store-keeper in Florida, as a candidate for county judge, and later during the Civil War, as landlord of the old Virginia House in Paris, are still retold today.[50]

Another side of John Quarles must be mentioned in the account of the impression he made on his impressionable young nephew:

The question of human destiny [Mr. Bodine says], the why, the whence, the whither, was always with him. Unable to reconcile it with the accepted dogmas of his people, and driven by the promptings of a vigorous mind and a kindly heart, he became a "Universalist." What that meant during the days following the revival of Paulinian teaching in the valley country . . . we of today cannot appreciate. It was even worse than being an "Infidel," and often converted a man into a social pariah, though Judge Quarles did not suffer this fate, his natural kindness and his general usefulness as a man and citizen saving him from the common penalty.[51]

Sam Clemens, grown to be twelve years old, spending vacations by his uncle's fireside, can be trusted to have sensed the disapproval of his dereliction in religious matters. Jane Clemens, indeed, had probably forestalled his discovery by explaining its seriousness to him; but that the

[50] Bodine, "A Visit to Florida," *loc. cit.*
[51] *Ibid.*

generous man was such an object of censure would make him all the larger a hero to the young inquirer into the ways of life.  His father, too, refused to accept the Lamptons' religious convictions.  Men of the world, Sam would suspect, had special views that ordinary people could not share.  The point is of importance as a modifying circumstance for those critics to consider who have put undue emphasis upon the unrelieved Calvinistic elements in Mark Twain's early training.

But that was not the most interesting thing about John Quarles to the growing boy.  The stories he told about life in Tennessee made him forget everything else.  Mr. Bodine believes that Sam Clemens first became interested in the shot-eating frog from hearing his uncle tell about it in Florida.

"The Jumping Frog of Calaveras County" was originally a Tennessee amphibian and was brought to Missouri by Judge Quarles, the story along with many others . . . being weighed out with sugar and coffee while he was a merchant in Florida. . . . He was out hunting wild turkeys in the Tennessee woods and was overtaken by rain, being forced to seek shelter in a deserted negro cabin.  While sitting there alone he noted a toad hopping across the floor toward him, and to amuse himself and pass the time began to catch random flies and toss them into the ever open mouth of the frog.  When the flies gave out, he began to toss shot from his shot-pouch, one by one.  The frog made no fine discrimination but swallowed them as readily as he had the flies, with the result that the judge was soon out of shot.  Nothing else being offered, the toad . . . tried several times to move on, but the shot weighing him down, he finally gave up and sat blinking in settled despair.  A yellow jacket came sailing by about this time and catching it and stripping it of its wings . . . , the judge tossed it toward the toad.  The latter caught it and as it gulped down the live morsel, received a dig from the insect. In an instant, with one titanic effort, the toad expelled the wasp and with it all the judge's shot, enabling him to return home with a load in his gun and in no violation of the ancient superstition about hunters.[52]

With such a man as its directing spirit, John Quarles's farm was a place of blessed memory to the boy who was to be a city-dweller all his life. "It was a heavenly place for a boy, that farm of my uncle John's," he says. "The house was a double log one, with a spacious floor (roofed in) connecting it with the kitchen. In the summer the table was set in the middle of that shady and breezy floor. . . ." Not far away from the house was "a divine place for wading, and it had swimming pools, too, which were forbidden to us and therefore much frequented by us."[53]

Even the country school, three miles from the farm, had no unpleasant associations for Sam Clemens: "We attended the school with more or less regularity once or twice a week, in summer, walking to it in the cool of the morning by the forest paths, and back in the gloaming at the end of the day. . . . It is the part of my education which I look back upon with the most satisfaction."[54] It was on the farm, besides, that he learned to know the habits of animals and birds; there he had the close acquaintance of colored people which made him in after years one of their most eloquent defenders, and there he felt more intimately, perhaps, than ever again in his life, the spell of forest and prairie. Perhaps, as he said about optimists, observers are born, not made; but the free, joyous life of these vacation months, especially because he

[52] Bodine, "A Visit to Florida," *loc. cit.*
[53] *Autobiography*, I, 96, 97, 99, 109.
[54] *A Tramp Abroad*, chap. III.

was to be shut within the dingy walls of a newspaper office so young, must have had inestimable value in quickening his perception of the qualities of all living things. He speaks of "the far-off hammering of the wood-peckers" at the farm, "the muffled drumming of wood pheasants," and the "vast hawk hanging motionless in the sky, with its wings spread wide and the blue of the vault showing through the fringe of their end feathers." Something about the ways of birds interested Sam Clemens in a peculiar way. His mother, who was "cold toward bats," could not become reconciled to his insistence that she make their acquaintance. She simply couldn't learn to like "private bats." His impression of the handsome appearance and curious ways of blue jays stood him in good stead forty years later when he wrote the tale of Jim Baker's visitors from far and near. "It ain't any use to tell me a bluejay hasn't got a sense of humor," Jim declared. The owl, however, he was sure, couldn't see the point.[55]    In Florida Sam Clemens made the acquaintance of the black-bird. In his account of India, the land of wonders, Mark Twain paused through two pages to define his interest in that "Bird of Birds—the Indian crow":

In his straddling wide forward-step, and his springy sidewise series of hops, and his impudent air, and his cunning way of canting his head to one side upon occasion, he reminds one of the American blackbird. But the sharp resemblances stop there. . . . The black-bird is a perfect gentleman, in deportment and attire, and is not noisy, I believe, except when holding religious services and political conventions in a tree; . . .[56]

From the point of view of their fitness to be the medium for producing a culture, something must be said about

[55] *Ibid.*          [56] *Following the Equator,* II, 31-32.

the proximity of Florida and the Quarles farm to river, prairie, and forest. Except for casual mention in "A Campaign That Failed" and *The Gilded Age*, Salt River is not celebrated in Mark Twain's writings, but as it was quite as important to the place of his birth as "the shining reaches of the mighty Mississippi" were to Tom Sawyer's town; it is not insignificant that he who was to become the most celebrated historian of an American river should have gained his first impression of flowing water on its banks.

As an old man Mark Twain remembered "the prairie, and its loneliness and peace. . . . ," "a level great prairie which was covered with wild strawberry plants, vividly starred with prairie pinks, and walled in on all sides by forests." And he speaks of calling back "the solemn twilight and mystery of the deep woods, the earthy smells, the faint odors of the wild flowers, the sheen of rain-washed foliage, the rattling clatter of drops when the wind shook the trees . . . the woods in their autumn dress, the oaks purple, the hickories washed with gold, the maples and the sumachs luminous with crimson fires, . . ." On coon and possum hunts at night the "long marches through the black gloom of the woods" with the Negroes etched themselves on his imagination. On prairie chicken and wild turkey hunts they started in the morning while it was still dark; they "drifted silently after the hounds in the melancholy gloom. But presently the gray dawn stole over the world, the birds piped up, then the sun rose and poured light and comfort all around, everything was fresh and dewy and fragrant, and life was a boon again." The best of the hunt was getting home "very hungry, and just in time for breakfast."[57]

[57] *Autobiography*, I, 110-15.

Beyond the orchard, at the farm, were the Negro quarters and the tobacco fields. When darkness shut down on the outside world, or when a rainy day came, it was the Negroes that most delighted Sam Clemens—Aunt Hannah with her charms against witches and Uncle Dan'l, "faithful and affectionate good friend, ally, and adviser to the boy." He was the original of Jim in *Huckleberry Finn* and *Tom Sawyer Abroad:*

It was on the farm that I got my strong liking for his race and my appreciation of certain of its fine qualities. . . . I know the look of Uncle Dan'l's kitchen as it was on the privileged nights, when I was a child, and I can see the white and black children grouped on the hearth, . . . and I can hear Uncle Dan'l telling the immortal tales which Uncle Remus Harris was to gather into his book. . . . I can feel again the creepy joy which quivered through me when the time for the ghost story was reached . . . the last story of the evening and there was nothing between it and the unwelcome bed.[58]

This early friendship with Negroes in a more democratic western atmosphere must have been, in part, what made it impossible for Mark Twain to be whole-heartedly a southerner, in spite of all his southern tradition. It is to be noted, however, that the system of slavery brought to Missouri was of the earlier, more kindly sort. After the invention of the cotton gin had opened to planters the vision of an empire to be developed through the crops which could be handled by machine methods, the plantation system of the "black belt" became a different thing. The horror of being "sold down the river," which forms the leading motif of *Pudd'nhead Wilson*, and the description in the novel of the cruel methods of the overseer on

[58] *Ibid.*, pp. 100-15.

an Arkansas plantation, make the contrast between the Missouri system and that of the large cotton plantation apparent.

The southern element in Mark Twain's inheritance and training, often lost sight of because of the emphasis put upon his significance as a western writer, has constantly to be stressed in any attempt to account for his temperament and personality.[58a] It accounts largely for the breadth of his outlook and for a certain aristocratic freedom or ease which, with his drawl, was mistaken by his early lecture audiences—with his encouragement—for western boorishness. A more strenuous, northern atmosphere would not have furnished so favorable a climate for the germination of his humor or of his literary imagination. A comparison of the Missourian's vein with that of his Iowa neighbor, Hamlin Garland, makes the difference clear. Whatever the former touches that is local becomes generalized, of broad human significance; what the latter writes remains local.

For the attaining of this broader outlook, it may be said that the pioneer village of Florida, Missouri, was fortunately conditioned. It was bordered by great woods and prairies untouched by the hand of man. It was on the banks of a river which it looked upon with pride and hope; though "a small thing" it was their own, and might some day carry them out of the wilderness. There Sam Clemens had the freedom of the farm of his uncle John Quarles, a more generous-natured man than his father. He was in the midst of southern people who were more public-minded than many frontiersmen and among whom

[58a] Bernard De Voto, in his *Mark Twain's America* (1932), writes particularly well of this aspect of Mark Twain's environment.

it was possible for his thinking to follow, unthwarted, normal and wholesome lines. During the same period, his imagination was developed through association with old-time southern darkies; so that later he used characters he knew and stories which he first heard at this time in his life, as literary material.

§4

AFTER IT had become apparent that Salt River would never be made navigable, and Florida had lost the fight for the county seat, John Clemens, who was suffering one of his periodical declines of fortune, decided to take his family to Hannibal in Marion, the next county to the east. Certain events in the history of Marion County in the decade from 1830 to 1840 show that Albert Bigelow Paine's statement that Florida[59] belonged in that part of the West which was "unassembled," "undigested," and "comparatively unknown," while it may be relatively true, must be modified, at least, with certain concessions. These concessions are important when the region is considered as the habitat of Sam Clemens. If Florida was a favorable spot for the child's pre-school education, Marion County was a world in little, which must have expanded the boy's imagination with glimpses of the drama of the times.

As has already been pointed out, the region was developed by 1839 beyond the first pioneer stage. Marion County, organized in 1825, had a population, by 1840, of ten thousand, almost fifteen hundred of whom were slaves. It had twenty-four "primary and common" schools with 648 "scholars." Only eighty-seven of the white population, according to the sixth United States

[59] Florida is just over the border southwest from Marion County.

census, were illiterates.[60] Palmyra, the county seat, fifteen miles or so north of Florida, called itself the Athens
of the state. By 1839 it had two thriving newspapers,[61]
a female seminary, and at least one well-established
church.[62] It had regular stage connection with surrounding towns, including a river port. Politically and socially
it was the first town in northeast Missouri in the 1830's.

Until the Civil War Palmyra had a dramatic history.
Besides the abortive abolition movement to be described
further on, and the political ups and downs always vivid
in a southern community, the local history is picturesque
with stories of "Elopements Extraordinary" and affairs
of honor. The "Glover-Buckner Tragedy" involved two
families scattered through Pike and Marion counties. The
quarrel grew out of rivalry in a literary society. The
"challenge" followed, but in the end it was friends of the
principals in the quarrel that paid the price for their hot-
headed jealousy. Later a famous triangle affair was reported in Orion Clemens's paper with a story a page and
a half long. A St. Louis man, becoming suspicious of his
wife, who was visiting relatives in Palmyra, followed her
paramour up the river, intercepted letters passing between
the lovers, and shot down the interloper, a man of considerable prominence, in the hallway of the Palmyra
tavern. St. Louis papers sent reporters to attend the trial
that ensued. The murderer was acquitted, and his wife
returned home.

But social disturbances of this sort were no more characteristic of the country than movements to build churches

[60] 1840 Census, p. 407.
[61] The Palmyra *Spectator* was started Aug. 3, 1839.—*Missouri Historical Review*, XVII, 167.
[62] The Old School Baptist Church, 1821.—*History of Marion County*, p. 161.

and colleges. In addition to its more permanent cultural elements, Marion County was the seat of an experiment in education which has long since been forgotten, but which attracted some interest, nationally, in its day. In his *View of the Valley of the Mississippi, or the Emigrant's and Traveller's Guide to the West*, published in 1832, Robert Baird mentions two colleges in Missouri, one in St. Louis and the other "a new college under the control of Presbyterians . . . commencing operations at or near Palmyra, in Marion County."[63] The fortunes of this college must have been of considerable moment to the Clemenses, staunch Presbyterians, at a time when they no doubt expected to be able to send their sons to college. A preparatory school for the original college was established in the vicinity of Florida just over the border of Marion County.[64] The story of the rise and fall of Marion College is relevant here because of its connection with a movement which Mark Twain used as the basis of an autobiographical sketch late in his life. As an environmental item it cannot be neglected, because of its dramatic history. The story of the beginning of the school is told by a Missouri historian:

Rev. Dr. David Nelson, a Presbyterian minister, came to Missouri, from Kentucky, about the year 1829 or 1830, and settled thirteen miles northwest of Palmyra, in Marion County, where the land around and beyond was mostly government land, the location being on the border of the frontier settlements. . . . Soon after coming to Missouri he conceived the idea, or more probably fell in with the idea, of establishing a college in that part of Missouri, for the education of young men for the ministry.[65]

---

[63] P. 320.
[64] The "Lower" College not more than ten miles distant.
[65] F. A. Sampson, "Marion College and Its Founders," *Missouri Historical Review*, XX (July, 1926), 485.

The person who is thought to have made the original plan for the college was William Muldrow, founder of four towns in the district,[66] a hero-promoter beside whom Colonel Mulberry Sellers seems a very modest replica. Dr. Nelson and William Muldrow had associated with them Dr. David Clark. All were Presbyterians. "These three men made application to the Sixth General Assembly of Missouri, 1830-1831, for a college charter, which was granted January 15, 1831."[67] Their plan was to make it possible for the young men registered in the college to pay all their own expenses by developing the new land; it was somewhat like that afterward developed by the Presbyterian church at Berea, Kentucky, and at Park College, Missouri. F. A. Sampson describes William Muldrow as "one of the most remarkable men who ever lived in Missouri; a scheming man, of strong intellect, though uneducated, ever inventing some new project, often on a stupendous scale . . . visionary, . . . but his great energy had overcome many difficulties in other movements."[68] He had interested men of "means and great ability," like Dr. Clark and Dr. Ely, to come west. The trustees entered a large tract of land. Buildings were erected, and Marion College made a good start. .. . . . "the flavor of Attic salt was soon upon the speech, the manners, and the customs of the people in the neighbor-

[66] Marion City, West Ely, and Philadelphia, in Marion County, and New York, just over the border west from Philadelphia in Shelby County. Plans of these "cities" were made, showing streets and alleys, blocks and parks, churches, a college or female seminary, an opera house, and a model business district.

[67] F. A. Sampson, "Marion College and Its Founders," loc. cit., p. 486.

[68] William Muldrow anticipated the invention of the tractor. As the virgin prairie land was too stubborn to be broken up without heavy labor, the first settlers cleared the timber, where the soil was light loam. One of the legends of Muldrow is that he had half a dozen teams of oxen hitched to several plows that turned up a strip of prairie six feet wide.

hood," the local *History* assures us, "and Marion College assumed all the airs of Yale and Harvard."[69]   So assured of success did the founders feel that they located a preparatory or "lower" college, with Dr. Ely as president, fifteen or twenty miles south of the "upper" college.   Its residence hall, a brick house that must have been a rather elegant building for its day, is in good repair on a fine hill surrounded by fields and pastures today, and the tourist who is sufficiently interested to search out vestiges of the more vivid life of that early time is convinced that the founders of these colleges were justified in their faith in the land.   If they saw it just at sundown on a June day, the rich flats surrounded by a fringe of fine trees, they were satisfied that they need search no farther for a pastoral setting for college life.   Near the upper college William Muldrow laid out the town of Philadelphia; near the lower, West Ely.   Both are small inland villages on the map of Marion County still.

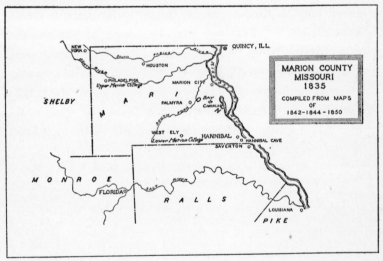

[60] *History of Marion County*, p. 228.

The first setback in the fortunes of Marion College came when it was discovered that Dr. Nelson and the other authorities were militant abolitionists.[70] At Quincy, Illinois, thirty miles away, was a college whose president was an ardent abolitionist. Two men representing the American Colonization Society came in 1836 to make Philadelphia the center of their activity—armed with tracts to educate the district in abolition principles. As Marion County was strongly pro-slavery a company of armed and mounted men was organized, which rode to Philadelphia, seized the two agents, and threatened to lynch them at once if they did not leave the country.[71] But Dr. Nelson, a man of deep convictions, read a paper from the Presbyterian pulpit in Philadelphia approving the movement to raise money and buy up slaves with the purpose of sending them to a colony in Liberia. Dr. John Bosley, a large slave-owner, attacked Dr. Nelson, and was stabbed, though not fatally, by William Muldrow, who is said to have prepared the paper for Dr. Nelson to read. Muldrow was arrested and sent to a prison in St. Charles, from which he was soon released; but Dr. Nelson was waited upon by a crowd of pro-slavery men of the county, who surrounded his house and demanded that he leave the state. As he was their guiding spirit, it was in the end a fatal blow to the colleges that he had to do so. "The anti-abolition crusade of 1835-36, the dissemination of anti-slavery tracts, the stabbing of Dr. Bosley by Mul-

[70] It does not appear from local histories that it was abolition zeal primarily that brought the missionary clergymen west, but the Marion County demonstration was a part of the movement that was taking form all over the nation. In 1833 Oberlin College was founded by abolition enthusiasts. Harriet Martineau, when she traveled in America in 1834-35, was convinced that slavery was "tottering to its fall."—*Society in America.*

[71] F. H. Sosey, "Palmyra and Its Historical Environment," *Missouri Historical Review,* XXIII (April, 1929), 363.

drow, and the boldly proclaimed emancipation opinions of
Dr. Nelson, all worked against the college."[72]    A Presbyterian minister from St. Louis became president, and it
seemed for a few years that it might survive: "The
number of students increased; commencements, the organization of Greek letter societies, and other activities of
colleges, with lectures by some of the ablest men of the
west, took place. Additional college buildings were erected,
and numerous cottages for the residence of students were
built."[73]    But the school finally went into the hands of a
receiver.

William Muldrow's real interest was in city-building,
and his favorite enterprise centered around Marion City,
which was to become the "metropolis of the West."   Dr.
Ely went east with Muldrow, with lithographed maps of
Marion City in colors, showing city lots, warehouses and
public buildings, and extensive plans for other cities and
colleges.

Col. Muldrow was a promoter of the first magnitude and a sales-
man of high order.   Rev. Ely was a wealthy and eminent divine
with a wide acquaintance in the East.   The two men had no
difficulty in interesting capitalists and those seeking homes in the
far West. . . . [They sold] $150,000 worth of lots in Marion
City and $35,000 worth . . . in Philadelphia.   Not only did they
make these outright sales but large sums of money were placed in
their hands to invest in wild lands all over the county by spec-
ulators who were convinced that the wonderful pictures that had

[72] "He located in Quincy and became president of Eels College, a strong
abolitionist institution."—*Ibid.*, p. 364.   "March 3, 1843, a band of anti-abo-
litionists assembled in a store in Palmyra and decided to burn the Eels abolition
college in Quincy.   They crossed the Mississippi River on the ice, partially accomplished their purpose, and returned home.   No arrests were ever made."—
*Ibid.*, p. 366.
[73] F. A. Sampson, "Marion College and Its Founders," *loc. cit.*, p. 487.

been painted by the two promoters spelled unbounded profit. One syndicate of capitalists, it was said, had placed $80,000 in Col. Muldrow's hands for investment, he to have a liberal per cent of the profits, and other large sums had been turned over to Rev. Ely. This money was honestly invested according to the belief of the two men.[74]

The plan did not stop at the development of cities and colleges. A railroad was to be built to connect Marion County with the outside world:

The year before [1834], the first railroad survey ever made in Missouri was started from Marion City. The levee [of the city] was commenced that fall, and work was again resumed on it the following spring. Muldrow's idea was to run the road to Philadelphia, thence west to Shelbyville, and eventually strike the Pacific coast, thus affording the new city direct commercial and social intercourse with the great West.[75]

The whole enterprise collapsed, however, with the panic of 1837-1840. In 1842 judgment was obtained against Marion College. The Masonic Lodge of the state eventually bought the buildings with 800 acres of land near Philadelphia and 470 acres near West Ely, and it was turned into a Masonic college.[76]

Other events besides the abolition movement helped to make Marion County think of itself as a unit. In 1832 it was called upon to send men to serve in the Black Hawk War in Illinois. In 1835, about the time the Clemens family came into the district, what came to be called the "Shelbyville War" was staged. A company of mounted men were sent from Marion to the county seat of Shelby

[74] F. H. Sosey, "Palmyra and Its Historical Environment," loc. cit., p. 367.
[75] F. H. Sosey, Robert DeVoy, pp. 18-19.
[76] F. A. Sampson, "Marion College and Its Founders," loc. cit., p. 487.

County, thirty miles away, to assist in defense against the Indians. It proved that a false alarm had been sent out as a result of a disturbance caused by whiskey drinkers. In 1837 Marion County furnished men for the state contingent in the Florida or Seminole War, and in 1837 what was known as the Iowa or "Honey War," growing out of the dispute concerning the Iowa boundary, drew forth men. Finally, a little later than the period under consideration, the "Marion Rangers" went forth to the Mexican War.[77] Much local spirit grew out of the excitement attending each event, and therefore each deserves at least a mention in the account of Sam Clemens's Missouri background.

Marion City, William Muldrow's gorgeous fabric in Marion County, has had two historians among English satirists. The first was Charles Dickens, who heard of the notorious city on his first lecture trip to the United States. In Eden, described in *Martin Chuzzlewit*, the British novelist subjects the "Metropolis of the Great West" to the touch of realism.

The young Martin Chuzzlewit, hoping to find a career for himself in domestic architecture, comes to St. Louis with his servant, Mark Tapley, and, in spite of warnings that convince the servant that they are following a will-o-the-wisp, invests what money they both have in Eden property. Scadder, the St. Louis agent of the Eden Land Corporation, pointing to "a great plan which occupied one whole side of the office," assures them that they are going

---

[77] *History of Marion County*, p. 210. The same exigencies, together with local fights connected with the fixing of boundary lines, gave many of these counties settled by spirited southern people considerable local pride. The "State of Pike" has already been mentioned. A little to the west, Callaway County, when the state failed to secede from the Union, was derisively called "the Kingdom of Callaway" because it contemplated separation on its own account.

to "A flourishing city . . . ! An architectural city! There
were banks, churches, cathedrals, market-places, factories,
hotels; stores, mansions, wharves; an exchange, a theatre;
public buildings of all kinds, down to the office of the
*Eden Stinger,* a daily Journal." After he has satisfied
himself that Martin and Mark are "Aristocrats of Natur',"
he lets them have "a little lot of fifty acres with the house
upon it" for one hundred and fifty dollars. They make
the trip up the Mississippi and find the place to be a
boggy, miasmic wood, where no human being can live in
health: "There were not above a score of cabins in the
whole; half of these appeared untenanted; all were rotten
and decayed. The most tottering, abject, and forlorn
among them was called, with great propriety, the Bank
and National Credit Office. It had some feeble props
about it but was settling deep down in the mud past all
recovery." A few hopeless, ague-stricken settlers were
marooned there, because they had no money to get away.
Martin, stricken with malarial fever, is valiantly nursed
by Mark, who in turn succumbs to its ravages. Their only
thought, when both are able to walk, is to return to England as soon as possible. Dickens shows up types of
people with their "Institutions," their booster, spread-
eagle patriotism, their suspicion of the mother country,
and their personal vulgarity. "We are the intellect and
virtue of the airth, the cream of human natur', and the
flower of moral force," the most noted person who visits
the strangers in Eden declares. When, on the steamboat
returning to St. Louis, Martin passes up the butter because
he sees a citizen cut into it with a knife he has just taken
from his tobacco-stained mouth, Elijah Pogram, "Member of Congress, one of the master minds of our country,"

exclaims, "Well! the morbid hatred of you British to the Institutions of our country, is as-*toni*shing!"

"Upon my life!" cried Martin in his turn, " . . . A man deliberately makes a hog of himself, and *that's* an Institution!"

"We have no time to ac-quire forms, sir," said Elijah Pogram.[78]

Dickens makes the only plain, rational American that Martin meets say, in New York, "I believe no satirist could breathe this air. If another Juvenal or Swift could rise up among us to-morrow, he would be hunted down." Every man in America swings backwards and forwards in a rocking-chair, or sits with his feet higher than his head, chews and spits tobacco, or "smokes away like a factory chimney," defends "nigger slavery," and worships a pistol-and-bowie-knife freedom. The satire is not at the expense of the West only, but of America. "This place," declared Mark Tapley in Marion City, "is a reg'lar little United States in itself."

The second satirist to use the story of Marion City to adorn a tale was a Missourian, writing half a century or so later than Dickens. The most important echo of this pre-Hannibal period in the writings of Mark Twain is in all probability in the character of Colonel Sellers, and in certain Missouri scenes in *The Gilded Age*.[79]  County

[78] *Martin Chuzzlewit*, chaps. XV, XVI, XXI, XXII, XXIII, XXXIII, XXXIV.

[79] In *Life on the Mississippi*, Marion City comes in for a passing note: "Marion City had gone backward in a most unaccountable way. This metropolis promised so well that the projectors tacked 'city' to its name in the very beginning with full confidence; but it was bad prophecy. When I first saw Marion City thirty-five years ago [1846] it contained one street and nearly or quite six houses. It contains but one house now, and this one, in a state of ruin, is getting ready to follow the former five into the river." It was not until after the Civil War that Marion City became one of the "ghost towns" of Missouri, for the

legends concerning the career of William Muldrow must
have contributed something to the character of the dweller
in aircastles; but as there is no mention of the Marion
County promoter either in Mark Twain's writings or in
his biography, to say that he was the original of Colonel
Sellers is scarcely warrantable.[80]  Colonel Muldrow was
so typical a figure in the story of land development in the
Middle West that any details from local tradition relating
to him, that held over in the memory of Mark Twain, in
all likelihood attached themselves to his impression of the
visionaries in his own family.

Mark Twain is, however, one of the historians of
Marion City. The story which reflects the spirit of
these early times is "A Scrap of Curious History," but it
does not touch upon the promoter's interest there. The
author represents the time as 1845 and himself as an
onlooker in the drama. The real time of the abolition
excitement reflected in the fictitious sketch was 1835-36,
as has been shown. The details of the Mark Twain story
are as follows: Robert Hardy, an abolition agent from
New England, was hanged in Marion City for aiding a
runaway slave from Palmyra to escape into Illinois. His
fate caused several young men to form a masked society
and declare themselves to be followers of "the martyr."
The house of a Presbyterian minister who had denounced
the movement was blown up, and he with it. When the
coroner's jury, thinking it safer not to fan the flames of

reason that it was the river port for the county seat, Palmyra.  Only a D. A. R.
marker shows today where it was situated.

[80] F. H. Sosey (*Missouri Historical Review*, XXIII, 361) says that Mark
Twain "secured his famous pen character, Colonel Sellers," from Marion City.
A. B. Paine says that the original of the character was James Lampton, his
mother's favorite cousin.—*Letters*, I, 12, 62.  See also the *Autobiography*, I, 89-
94.)

radical sentiment any further, pronounced that the minister came by his death through "the visitation of God,"
a young blacksmith in Marion City, "not to be robbed of
his glory," announced that he had committed the crime.
He, too, was publicly hanged.  The masked society then
grew and included "earnest, determined men," until the
Civil War put a stop to such local demonstrations.  Mark
Twain tells the story to illustrate how the chance for
"martyrdom gilded with notoriety" appeals to men's
vanity and makes them the instruments of reform.  "Such
things were happening all over the country.  Wild-
brained martyrdom was succeeded by uprising and organization.  Then, in natural order, followed riot, insurrec-
tion, and the wrack and restitutions of war.  It was bound
to come, and it would naturally come in that way.  It has
been the manner of reform ever since the beginning of
the world."[81]  "A Scrap of Curious History" is one of the
few Civil War records left by Mark Twain.  It belongs
in a class with "A Campaign That Failed" as a document
to support his disillusioned view of history.  In his later,
didactic vein, its humor is almost sardonic.  Men may say
what they will about fighting for disinterested devotion to
a principle, its drift is, but if you are in a position to know
the real facts, you discover that it is vanity that makes
martyrs.  In it one sees his sense that Marion County was
a little world whose dramatic struggles were as important
to its development as larger national affairs.  He compares what happened in Marion City to events following
the assassination of a president in the French Republic:
"In our village we had our Ravochals, our Henrys, our

[81] *Harper's Magazine*, CXXIX (Oct., 1914), 675.  Published with the note, "Written at La Bourboule-les-Bains, France, June, 1894."

Vaillants; and in a humble way our Cesario. . . . Fifty years ago we passed through, in all essentials, what France has been passing through during the past two or three years, in the matter of periodical frights, horrors, and shudderings."[82]

In Marion County, in other words, a miniature Civil War was staged between abolitionists and slave-holders, with the victory to the slave-holders. Strife of this kind, together with the necessity of furnishing contingents of soldiers for Indian and boundary-line wars made certain sections of northeast Missouri think of themselves as a world-in-little.

No just conclusion in regard to Mark Twain's life and art can be arrived at without an understanding of the heroic character of his early environment. Neither his biographer's account of it nor his *Autobiography* puts the reader in the way of forming a just conclusion, though he did not deprecate his childhood, or think of it as sordid. The matter of his inferiority complex has been much exaggerated. He came of proud stock at a time when it was putting its impress upon a new land—clumsily, to be sure, as is the way of all pioneering. He made his way socially

[82] The story illustrates Mark Twain's method of drawing upon his early impressions for the foundation of much of his fiction. Purporting to be autobiographical, it is fiction in all the details of the plot, but the local history shows that it preserves the spirit of a county struggle. F. H. Sosey, of the Palmyra *Spectator* (*op. cit.*, p. 362) comments ironically upon the authenticity of the "Scrap": "The story is fairly correct aside from the few minor defects that no murders were ever committed in Marion City, there were no legal or other hangings there, no houses were ever blown up by dynamite, there was no court house in the town. . . . Mark Twain never resided in Marion City. . . . The rest of the story is probably correct."

Mark Twain seems to have had Palmyra in mind as the scene of the story; he spoke of Marion City as the county seat. The traditional rivalry between Hannibal and Palmyra may have deterred him from commemorating Palmyra anywhere in his writings.

and professionally with the help of his wit, as many another genius has done.  If Dean Swift had had a bigger and better heart, their cases would be comparable in this respect.  His sensitiveness to social distinctions was a source of his strength because he was robust enough for it to give edge to his humor.  He belonged from the first among the important people of his community.

Carl Van Doren, in his review of Carl Sandburg's *Flame and Slag,* contrasts the conception of America gained by later emigrants to the West with the "epic sense of the American past" of the earlier stocks.  In the minds of the latter, he says,

there is the persistent image of the pioneer advancing from the seaboard, by forest trail and waterway, across lush prairie and naked plain, contending mightily, romantically, victoriously with aboriginal men and beasts, in the end settling peacefully down in farm, village, or thriving city to enjoy the Canaan he has thus won for himself and his children's children.  The air of this picture is fresh and pure, the earth green with grass, the roads fouled with nothing worse than mud; food may be had for the taking, shelter for the building, land for the seeking.  If there are hardships, they are relatively brief, yielding to enterprise and thrift in a decade or two at most.  If there are ugly aspects, they are largely unpreventable like frontier violence or ignorance, and they yield to solid contentment and popular enlightenment.  Ultimately these stocks inherit the earth, in the picture, . . .[83]

Such was the country that Mark Twain knew in his youth.  It was due to the epic quality of life in his earliest environment that he used the English language" as though it had never been used before" and that in his writings he could draw so largely from "all original and first class

[83] *Century,* CVI (Sept., 1923), 787.

elements." He came of a people who were girding themselves for heroic treks to the Mexican border and California. He knew both what was good and what was bad in a western town of heroic aspirations, and during his impressionable youth he was a spokesman, in a small way, for a country that was conscious of a heroic part to play in a nation committed to a manifest destiny.

# III

## CUB-PRINTER IN HANNIBAL

### §1

HANNIBAL, MISSOURI, in 1839 had a population of about four hundred and fifty, so that the advent of the Clemens family contributed to the size of the town about as largely as Sam Clemens's arrival did to that of Florida four years before. Part of the town site was still a dense forest of oak and other trees and thick shrubbery. The first house occupied by the family, on Bird and Hill streets, was far enough back from the river to escape high water—a distance of two or three city blocks.

The New Madrid earthquake in southeastern Missouri in 1812 was directly responsible for the location of the town. One Abraham Bird of New Madrid, in lieu of lands lost by him through the earthquake, was granted an "earthquake certificate," which enabled him to choose a tract of 640 acres in Marion County, and in 1818 the territorial government issued him a patent for the location of a town on his tract. In 1819 the town was plotted, and a sale of lots was held in St. Louis that year. Indians, whose wigwams occupied the surrounding hills, haunted the settlement, and in 1820 drove away "every citizen and sojourner of the place." But a mail service came through in that year, established over a post road from Louisiana to Palmyra, which had been in use fifteen years before John Clemens came to Missouri.[1]

[1] The *Missouri Gazette*, St. Louis, October 18, 1820, contained an advertise-

[ 76 ]

congress or
liscloses the
which have
rority of the
from Platts
aders are al-
by publica-

, in the stat-
alluded to in
entatives the
a completed,
of the road,
idges of the
it the other
made south
in like man-
ways. The
it is added
in the best

orth western
ot of the ra-
ias progres-
that is, with
king in all a
his road, the
ral says it is
et wide, the
swayed, and
The number
xty, and the
gth ; that on
ployed being
of timber in

roads which
Intel.

· Feb. 16.

and others meets with young, in thousands, all
over the country."

## LOTS FOR SALE, IN THE TOWN OF
# HANNIBAL.

THE undersigned have laid off a Town (which they
call *Hannibal*) at the mouth of Bear Creek, on the
west bank of the Mississippi river, about 25 miles above
the mouth of Salt River, and 15 miles below the mouth
of the two rivers.

HANNIBAL, it is believed, occupies the best site for
a town that there is on the Mississippi (any where above
St. Louis) being elevated above the highest floods, and
is secured by rocky shores; it is easy of access from
every direction, and commands an extensive view of
the river and surrounding country. There are two
springs of excellent water within the town; an excellent quarry of limestone, and is backed by one of the
most extensive tracts of rich and productive lands, that
there is in the Missouri territory; which tract of country is abundantly supplied with excellent timber, and is
well watered by springs, brooks and creeks, well
adapted for Mills, and will no doubt prove to be re-
markable-healthy from its elevated situated, &c. The
navigation of the Mississippi, above the mouth of Missouri, is known to be remarkably good for boats of the
largest description, the current being gentle and deep.

The town of HANNIBAL is laid off on a liberal plan,
the streets being wide; a very large street fronting the
river, and land given for wharfage. The proprietors
will also give plenty of Lands for public purposes.

*The sale of the above Lots will take place in St. Louis, on
the last day of APRIL, at the Auction Room of Thos.
F. Riddick.*

TERMS OF SALE—One fourth in 90 days, one fourth in
6 months, one fourth in 9 months and one fourth in 12
months, by giving notes with approved security.

Should any persons wish immediately to settle in the
above town, they can buy at private sale by applying
to either of the proprietors. Mechanics will meet with
good bargains.

STEPHEN RECTOR,
THOMPSON BAIRD,
THOS. RECTOR,
WM. V. RECTOR,
RICHARD GENTREY,
M. D. BATES,

} Proprietors.

March 17—42

R ENSH.
the Cl
complete a
sisting of
Plough
Straw I
Steelya
Bright
Sledge
Log Cl
Shovel:
Wire F
Shephe
Windo
Plough
Twille
Cloth,
Writing
An asse
With a

All of wh
Jan 30—3.

Spri
THE Sub
excelle
GOODS, c
Stripe:
Cotton

And a

Also, :

Irish t
Superl
The abo
by the pack
cularly invi

D

March 3

ONLY a
assort
disposed of
tail, by

ADVERTISEMENT OF HANNIBAL LOTS IN THE ST. LOUIS
*Enquirer,* MARCH 17, 1819.

In 1827 Hannibal consisted of five families; in 1830 it "numbered thirty souls." About this time the rivalry of Marion City, fifteen miles away, threatened to snuff out its flickering light. Its enemies there denounced it as a "frog-pond," a "grave-yard," and when, in 1835, "the stupendous scheme of Marion City was proclaimed from Maine to Georgia," the local history declares, " . . . the neighboring city seemed to realize the full destruction of Hannibal."[2] Finally, however, a few prudent people formed "The Hannibal Company," incorporated the town under trustees in 1838, and "sold property at low prices, chiefly to actual settlers."

By 1839 it had a thriving newspaper, and many business enterprises thought well enough of its prospects as the river port for a rich new farming area to put up their signs within its boundaries. A book-store had come to town:

TO THE READING COMMUNITY. As it is the intention of the subscriber to change his business from the Book selling to that of the Paper business and Book-binding exclusively, he proposes to sell out his entire stock of Miscellaneous Books at about cost and carriage. A list of the entire stock will be found in the Evening *Gazette* during the present winter.

B. L. Trumbull

Hannibal, Sept. 30, 1839.

Among the books advertised are works by Lady Blessington, Miss L. E. London, Miss Jane Austen, Bulwer, and Marryat, and "The Pickwick Papers, containing fifty illustrations and portraits."[3]

ment for bids for carrying mail: "From Louisiana by New London on Salt River and Hannibal to Palmyra, once a week, forty-eight miles."

[2] H. F. Conard, *Encyclopedia of the History of Missouri*, III, 165-69.

[3] *Hannibal Commercial Advertiser*, February 27, 1839. The *Advertiser* was founded in 1837. The *Hannibal Journal* was established the next year after the Clemens family moved to Hannibal, 1840.

John Clemens, always susceptible to the lure of new town sites, convinced that the town on the Mississippi had a better chance to grow than Florida on Salt River, was one of the actual settlers. The town prospered so steadily from the time of his coming that when he died, eight years later, its population was about twenty-five hundred. Coaches left with tri-weekly mail for Glasgow, on the Missouri River, and for Palmyra and St. Louis. During the months when the river was navigable, a daily mail came north from St. Louis. Tom Sawyer's ferryboat plied back and forth from the Illinois shore, whence a road led into John Hay's section of Illinois. It is doubtful whether Mr. Howells's description of the place as a "loafing, out-at-elbows, down-at-heels, slave-holding town" ever told more than half the truth about it. Though unkempt, as all new towns are, with its interest in land speculation in the county, its struggle for existence in competition with Marion City, its later competition with Palmyra, and its aspiration to secure a railroad, it had a rapid growth from the time it was incorporated.[4]

[4] "The population of the City is now about 3500. There are six organized congregations of Christians; one Masonic Lodge, and two Odd-Fellow Lodges; one Collegiate Institute; five common Schools; two Printing Offices, from which are issued weekly newspapers; fifteen Physicians; twelve Attorneys at Law; fourteen Wholesale and Retail Dry Goods Houses; five Forwarding and Commission Houses; two Hardware do.; one Iron Merchant; two Druggists; five Grocers; two Tinners and dealers in Stoves and Castings; two Drapers and Clothing Merchants; eight Tailors; one Hat Manufactory; three Saddle Shops; four Boot and Shoe Shops; two Watch Makers and Jewellers; one Sculptor; three House and Sign Painters; six Brick Yards; three Hotels; (one German,) two Livery Stables; two Steam Grist Mills, which turn out from 150 to 200 bbls. of flour every day; two steam Saw-Mills; two Confectionaries and Bakeries; five Cabinet Makers and Undertakers; eight Cooper Shops; which have made during the past season for the packing houses, an immense quantity of cooperage; twenty Carpenters; sixteen Brick-Layers; six Blacksmith Shops; four Slaughter Houses; several Packing Houses; one steam Distillery; eight Dram Shops; one Iron Foundry; one Tobacco Ware-House; two Rope Walks; one Carding Machine; one Tannery.

"During the slaughtering season about three hundred men were employed in the several slaughter and packing houses.

Mark Twain describes social levels in the town:

In the small town of Hannibal, Missouri, when I was a boy, everybody was poor, but didn't know it. And there were grades of society—people of good family, people of unclassified family, people of no family. Everybody knew everybody, and was affable to everybody, and nobody put on any visible airs; yet the class lines were quite clearly drawn and the familiar social life of each class was restricted to that class. It was a little democracy which was full of liberty, equality and Fourth of July, and sincerely so, too; yet you perceived that the aristocratic taint was there. It was there, and nobody found fault with the fact, or ever stopped to reflect that its presence was an inconsistency. I suppose that this state of things was mainly due to the circumstance that the town's population had come from slave states and still had the institution of slavery with them in their new home.[5]

It is impossible to realize in any accurate way what Sam Clemens's life in Hannibal was during the eight years after John Clemens took his family there in 1839 until his death in 1847. As autobiography, *Tom Sawyer* "half reveals and half conceals" the truth. The humorist "wrote of boy-life on the Mississippi because that had a peculiar charm" for him, he said; as a consequence it is pictured with the halo of romance. The literary discount necessary in taking any of Mark Twain's writings seriously —except as "unhistorical" history—is of two kinds. His habit of exaggeration for humorous effect forces the stu-

"From the first of September to the present time, one House purchased and received 30,000 bushels of wheat.—The number of bushels delivered in the City during this time was about 110,000. The quantity of Hemp received is about 200 tons; of Tobacco, 400,000 lbs.—One house has received 400 casks of Bacon,—near 13,000 hogs and 4,500 beef have been slaughtered. The number of steamboat arrivals during the last season was 1080—up and down, which discharged at this point freight for the great region of country lying around us—and carried away produce to the value of near $1,200,000."—*Hannibal Gazette*, Feb. 25, 1847.

[5] *Autobiography*, I, 119-20.

dent to be on his guard as much against understatement as overstatement. The best instance to illustrate the point is his story of his military experience, "A Campaign That Failed." It was written when Mark Twain was at the height of his power, and published in 1885, when he was in a humorously patronizing mood toward his early self. In a letter written in 1891, however, intended to convince some unknown correspondent that he had had experience of life at high pulse which could furnish him another kind of literary material than that which he used in his boys' stories, he said:

I was a *soldier* two weeks once in the beginning of the war, and was hunted like a rat the whole time. Familiar? My splendid Kipling himself hasn't a more burnt-in, hard-baked, and unforgettable familiarity with that death-on-the-pale-horse-with-hell-following-after, which is a raw soldier's first fortnight in the field—and which, without any doubt, is the most tremendous fortnight and the vividest he is ever going to see.[6]

The sentences sound as if he were anticipating Van Wyck Brooks's criticism. They are probably as much exaggerated a report of what the experience was to him as that in the burlesque episode. Both are expressions of different retrospective moods. But his nephew Samuel Moffett's account of this brief chapter in Mark Twain's life shows that it was not the irresponsible escapade the humorist first represented it to have been:

Brought up in a slaveholding atmosphere, Mark Twain naturally sympathised at first with the South. In June he joined the Confederates in Ralls County under General Tom Harris. His military career lasted for two weeks. Narrowly missing the distinction of being captured by Colonel Ulysses S. Grant, he resigned, ex-

[6] *Letters*, II, 541.

plaining that he had become "incapacitated by fatigue" through
persistent retreating . . . the official reports and correspondence
of the Confederate commanders speak very respectfully of the
work of the raw countrymen of the Harris Brigade.[7]

The case shows how difficult it is to come at the truth concerning Mark Twain's early life—lived at a time when
the members of his family were too entirely occupied with
the problem of managing to live, to keep any records.

It can be said, however, that during these eight years
he was comparatively free to educate himself—free to
lead his band north over Holliday's Hill, and, in the
enterprise of rolling down a boulder that threatened life
and property, come by sharper self-discipline than the
young Wordsworth experienced when he stole a boat to
row across Lake Windermere; free to play hooky and go
fishing up Bear Creek, or possibly explore the haunts of
the legendary bear for whom the creek was named—
though Sam Clemens could never have been an accomplished hunter or fisherman; free to wander off south of
town for a day in the cave, the endless passages of which
promised always new adventures; free to steal down the
roof in the middle of the night and join Tom Blankenship
to make a raid on a melon patch, or "get the low-down"
on the life of the town; most happily free to swim across
the great river and back again, to go off for a Saturday's
exploration of Glascock's Island, to haunt river boats that
lay at the wharf, and listen to the talk of river men. Ordinarily family and school watchfulness only served to make
these early attempts to satisfy his voracious curiosity more
real adventures; there were times, of course, when he had
to realize how fettered fast he was in his Hannibal world.

[7] Moffett, "Mark Twain: A Biographical Sketch," *The $30,000 Bequest*, p.
338-39.

A reminiscence in *A Tramp Abroad,* in which he recalls an incident connected with his first trip on the river, possibly accompanying his father on a business trip to St. Louis, shows that he was nervously aware of hazards in this early time of his life:

One evening on board a Mississippi steamboat, a boy of ten years lay asleep in a berth,—a long, slim-legged boy, he was, encased in quite a short shirt; it was the first time he had ever made a trip on a steamboat, and so he was troubled, and scared, and had gone to bed with his head filled with impending snaggings, and explosions, and conflagrations, and sudden death. About ten o'clock some twenty ladies were sitting around the ladies' saloon, quietly reading, sewing, embroidering, and so on, and among them sat a sweet, benignant old dame with round spectacles on her nose and her busy knitting-needles in her hands. Now all of a sudden, into the midst of this peaceful scene burst that slim-shanked boy in the brief shirt, wild-eyed, erect-haired, and shouting, "Fire, fire! *Jump and run, the boat's afire and there ain't a minute to lose!*" All those ladies looked sweetly up and smiled, nobody stirred, the old lady pulled her spectacles down, looked over them, and said gently:

"But you musn't catch cold, child. Run and put on your breast-pin, and then come and tell us all about it."

It was a cruel chill to give to a poor little devil's gushing vehemence. He was expecting to be a sort of hero—the creator of a wild panic—and here everybody sat and smiled a mocking smile, and an old woman made fun of his bugbear. I turned and crept humbly away—for I was that boy—and never even cared to discover whether I had dreamed the fire or actually seen it.[8]

The vivid part Sam Clemens's mother played in his early years is explained in his *Autobiography.* From her

[8] *A Tramp Abroad,* 90-91.

must have been derived what was most fanciful and unusual in the boy, his humor and sure satire, and his passionate hatred of cruelty. The "soldierly quality" of her
slender figure in the doorway as she defied a Corsican,
whose daughter she was protecting from his brutality, was
a vivid memory with Mark Twain. A sort of *noblesse
oblige* was only to be expected of one of Jane Lampton
Clemens's Kentucky blood. Her mother was a Casey—a
Montgomery-Casey.

. . . The Montgomerys and the Caseys of Kentucky had been
Indian fighters in the Daniel Boone period, and Grandmother
Casey, who had been Jane Montgomery, had worn moccasins in
her girlhood, and once saved her life by jumping a fence and
out-running a red skin pursuer. The Montgomery and Casey
annals were full of blood-curdling adventures, and there is to-day
a Casey County next to Adair, with a Montgomery County somewhat farther east.[9]

From Jane Clemens came Mark Twain's gayety and
charm. Writing about the spirit of the family before
Henry's death, Orion said, "My mother was as lively as
any girl of sixteen." There was sympathy and understanding between her and her truant son. ". . . Many
was the grave lecture commenced by Ma, to the effect that
Sam was misleading and spoiling Henry. But the lectures
were never concluded, for Sam would reply with a wit-
ticism, or dry, unexpected humor, that would drive the
lecture clean out of my mother's mind, and change it to
a laugh."[10] Two of her grandchildren, stirred by recent
strictures on the supposed tyranny she established over
her gifted son, have published an account of her as they

[9] A. B. P., I, 3.
[10] A. B. P., III, 1592, Appendix A.

remember her, of her broad humanity and her hatred of dullness.[11]

There is ample evidence that Sam Clemens had an almost devastating conscience. Besides the autobiographical stories of his boyhood suffering under its lashes, the mere count of the number of times the word conscience appears in Mark Twain's writings is evidence of how insistently that monitor had sought to establish its hold upon him. His "Carnival of Crime" story, written during the most successful period of his life, was his way of getting even with it, and is characteristic of his valiant and humorous manner of facing repulses throughout his life—just as he did his critics. His conscience was simply one manifestation of the excitable sensitiveness of his nature which made him an artist, and his Presbyterian up-bringing doubtless served to give force to its attacks; but that his mother ever exercised upon him unwholesome discipline is untenable to anyone who has read the full record with an open mind and a sense of humor.

From his conception of her character came his chivalrous regard for women. "She had no career," he wrote of her, "but she had a character, and it was of a fine and striking and lovable sort."[12] And his hearty taste for life came down from her, and the interest in people which was part of the secret of his personal magnetism. "She felt a strong interest in the whole world, and everybody and everything in it." Even Satan came in for a share of her sympathy; and Satan was Mark Twain's favorite mythological character.

It is a wholly attractive picture she makes in her early

[11] Doris and Samuel Webster, "Whitewashing Jane Clemens," *Bookman*, LXI (July, 1925), 531-35.

[12] *Autobiography*, I, 115.

Hannibal world, anxiously carrying off her small family to church, protecting them against the inroads of the measles, exercising her tongue upon her grave husband when he absent-mindedly neglected the children, tearfully defending slaves as human beings, meeting with a wise-crack a neighbor who expressed doubt about the final fate of her most problematical child. No one ever got the better of her—except that same child, who would conceal an occasional garter-snake in her work basket. We may be sure that she set her heels down firmly wherever she went, secretly conscious of the Clemens-Lampton claim to priority over many a more prosperous citizen. We may be sure, too, that life was never dull in her family.

## §2

DURING HIS earliest Hannibal years, the influence of Sam Clemens's father on his mind and temperament, though unrealized, must have been more potent than any of the records show. Because there has been a tendency among the later critics of Mark Twain to point to the record of John Marshall Clemens as a document in evidence of what the frontier failed to do for the young Sam Clemens, it is necessary to make it clear what kind of man the father was. Perhaps the main reason for the neglect of John Marshall Clemens as a positive factor in his son's life is that he was a business failure, and in the Gilded Age business failure was a crime. The boy remembered his father with a kind of aloof pity more than with pride. A sense of family failure, always poignant in an adolescent, developed in him a drive toward achievement. The father's "sunpain" was in part the cause of the son's success. But more important than this negative debt were certain unacknowledged debts of a positive sort. John Marshall Clemens was a superior man. Leaving out of account the fine sense of justice and integrity to which Mark Twain gave recognition in no uncertain terms, what was most reliable in the son's intellectual endowment came from his father. Furthermore, he was something more than a mere visionary; only half the truth is told about him when it is said that he was a man of over-large hopes. His was not a down-grade career; his frequent removals were usually into better situations.[13]  There are records to show that, wherever he took up his residence, he was effective as an influence in reclaiming the frontier from barbarism. It was due to just such southerners as he that within thirty years after the settlement of counties in northeast Missouri, roads, churches, schools, and libraries were established, and that people of that region developed a dignity, different from florid western inflation, justified by the attainment of a simple, rural culture. People lived their life there with gusto. If there were losses in standards of living on the frontier, there were also distinct gains. When the props of a more assured civilization were lacking, the Robinson Crusoe necessity of fending for themselves—less onerous in this region than on frontiers where there were no slaves—developed in early settlers an independence that often brought mental and physical regeneration. If this did not appear in the father, it was likely to come out later in the son.

And besides the more demonstrable legacies of a firm mental grasp and the ability to gain recognition for him-

[13] John Clemens was not a builder of aircastles in the sense that James Lampton was, though Mark Twain might have been defending both when he said ". . . he is human, and therefore in his reflective intervals he will always be speculating in 'futures.' "—*Following the Equator*, II, 187.

self and his community, two outstanding characteristics of
Mark Twain's personality must have come from his
father.  The first was his taste for publicity; the second
the pessimistic strain in his temperament.  If the ability to
stand publicity is a test of character, that test he did not
have to learn to stand up to; it was part of his birthright
as the son of a southern gentleman who was, throughout
his life, a man of affairs.  Furthermore, John Clemens
was not an optimist in the western sense of the term—
latterly so gravely disapproved.  His hope deferred
brought him heart-break in the end.  The son's unattain-
able hope was in direct line of development from the
father's disappointment, the logical outcome of his temperamental endowment.

John Marshall Clemens was born a Virginian of the
professional, slave-holding class, not the laboring, nor the
poor-white class.  His father, Samuel Clemens, "a man of
culture and literary taste," died in 1805.  When he "ad-
ministered the paternal estate in 1821" John Clemens received, as his share, "three negro slaves and a mahogany
side-board."  About the time of her second marriage, his
mother took her family to Adair County, Kentucky.
There, at Columbia, the county seat, John Clemens
studied law.  In 1823 he met and married Jane Lampton,
a good dancer, an accomplished horse-woman, a coquette
armed with unusual wit.  She had loved and quarreled
with one Dr. Barrett.  In a pique she married John Clemens, and they became wandering pioneers.  Their first
move was south to Gainesboro, in Jackson County, Tennessee, where, in 1825, their oldest son, Orion, was born.
After Fentress County was "erected," to the east, John
Clemens was one of the commissioners who located the

county seat at Jamestown.   The Clemens house was the
first built on the town site.   The young lawyer drew up
the specifications, extant in his handwriting, for the court-
house and jail.   He let the contract for them May 30,
1827, and became the first county court clerk.   Because
clients were slow in coming, as for many another lawyer,
frontier and otherwise, he eked out his income by setting
up a stock of merchandise in one room of his house.   When
land speculation caught his imagination, he bought sev-
enty-five thousand acres on one of the Tennessee "Knobs,"
about twenty miles south of Jamestown.   He was able to
pay five hundred dollars for the land, rationalizing his
interest as a desire to insure a fortune for his family.   He
was then thirty years old.   Pamela and Margaret Clemens
were born in Jamestown, and then about 1831, the family
made its third move, still in Tennessee, to Three Forks on
Wolf, in the Wolf River Valley—"the granary of Fentress county."   A year or so later the family moved a
fourth time, a little farther up the river to Pall Mall.
There John Clemens became postmaster.   A second son,
Benjamin, was born there in 1832.   In the Preface to the
*Tennessee Gazetteer* (1834) the author makes acknowledgment to John Marshall Clemens for information about
Fentress County.[14]   Apparently he was one of its "first
citizens"—known as "Squire" or "Judge."   He was prosperous in Tennessee until the financial crash of 1834.
" . . . in that storm my father's fortunes were wrecked.
From being honored and envied as the most opulent citizen of Fentress County—for outside his great landed
possessions he was considered to be worth not less than

---

[14] A. V. Goodpasture, "Mark Twain, Southerner," *Tennessee Historical Magazine,* July, 1931, p. 255.

three thousand five hundred dollars—he suddenly woke up and found himself reduced to less than one-fourth of that amount."[15]

The move to Florida, Missouri, was in answer to a fifth call of new lands. As has been shown, next to the Boone's Lick country, the Salt River district was the most promising out-state agricultural section at the time when Missouri came to statehood. It has been seen that John Clemens's name appeared among the trustees of the Florida Academy; that he was placed first on the boards of commissioners named in the acts of the legislature authorizing the formation of the Salt River Navigation Company, and the creation of the Florida and Paris Railroad Company. It was not a retrogression when he moved from Florida to Hannibal. He had not failed in the inland town from any but a financial point of view. The professional man's unwillingness to soil his hands with small thrift unfitted him for keeping store; but he had put Florida on the map of the state, so far as the powers that juggle the fate of town sites would permit. He appears, in documents of the time, to have been the first citizen there as at Jamestown: best fitted by native ability and training to plan intelligently for what the town needed. It was not through want of foresight or mistaken judgment on his part that Florida failed to live up to its promise. Unlike Marion City, it had an excellent natural situation. If railways had not come into Missouri, the project to make Salt River navigable would have been as laudable an enterprise as the state legislature originally believed it to be, and John Clemens's fight to make Florida the county seat of Monroe County would have been justifi-

[15] *Autobiography*, I, 5.

able.   Much experiment was necessary before the right way out of the wilderness could be found.   It was John Clemens's part to be one of the experimenters.   By 1839 Hannibal had proved its fitness to survive.   His belief that it would eventually become the chief commercial point of northeast Missouri caused him to take his family there.

Speaking of his findings in the files of early Hannibal papers, Mr. C. J. Armstrong, the leading student of Mark Twain in Hannibal, says:

These volumes show that John M. Clemens, the father of Mark Twain, filled a prominent and useful place in Hannibal.   Public meetings seem to have been the order of the day back in the late forties.   There were meetings to discuss prospective colleges, roads, railroads, a city charter, a court of common pleas and the secession of Hannibal from Marion County and its annexation to Ralls County.   At these meetings Judge Clemens takes a prominent part, is sometimes chairman, sometimes secretary, always on some committee.   He was secretary and later president of the Hannibal Library Institute.[16]

He was on committees to appraise property,[17] on committees to draft resolutions.[18]   The report of a "Committee on Roads" signed "John M. Clemens, Ch'm," obviously written by him, shows that his ability to write clear English must have been what brought him many of these offices.   In 1843 he had been chief among the founders of the "Hannibal Library Institute."   There is some evidence, also, that his had been the original idea for securing the Hannibal and St. Joseph railroad.   The fullest account of the early history of the town contains

[16] *Hannibal Courier-Post*, March 20, 1931.
[17] *Hannibal Gazette*, Jan. 21, 1847.
[18] *Ibid.*, Nov. 26, 1846.

the following: "As early as 1837 John M. Clemens had appeared as a corporator in a chartered railway company, and as he figured as chairman of the organizing meeting in Hannibal, held in his office in 1846, for the creation of what became the Hannibal & St. Joseph Railroad, it may be concluded that he, if not original promoter, was one of the prime movers of the enterprise."[19]

It is no slight evidence of John Clemens's intellectual endowment that in communities where free-thinking was taboo, and in a Calvinistic family circle, he remained a free-thinker. In 1897, possibly with a tardy desire to do his father justice, Mark Twain wrote: "My father was a refined and kindly gentleman, very grave, rather austere, of rigid probity, a sternly just and upright man, albeit he attended no church and never spoke of religious matters, and had no part nor lot in the pious joys of his Presbyterian family, nor ever seemed to suffer from this deprivation." The next sentences explain, perhaps, why the tribute was tardy: "He laid his hand upon me in punishment only twice in his life, and then not heavily; once for telling him a lie—which surprised me, and showed me how unsuspicious he was, for that was not my maiden effort. He punished me those two times only, and never any other member of the family at all; . . ."[20] In an early sketch entitled "A Memory"[21] is another mention of his father, which explains more definitely the relation of the two to each other:

When I say that I never knew my austere father to be enamored of but one poem in all the long half century that he lived, persons who knew him will easily believe me; when I say that I never

<hr>

[19] Conard, *op. cit.*, p. 167.  [20] *Following the Equator*, II, 28.
[21] *The Galaxy*, X (Aug., 1870), 286-87.

composed but one poem in all the long third of a century that I have lived, persons who know me will be sincerely grateful; and finally, when I say that the poem which I composed was not the one which my father was enamored of, persons who may have known us both will not need to have this truth shot into them with a mountain howitzer before they can receive it. My father and I were always on the most distant terms when I was a boy—a sort of armed neutrality, so to speak.

There follows an account of his father's reading *Hiawatha* "with the same inflectionless, judicial frigidity with which he always read his charge to the jury." The comment makes it clear why the father, with his judicial mind, appeared unattractive to the eager, imaginative boy, and why the memory of the stern old man was painful in after years.

That he was not a heartless man, however, is seen in a letter dated January 7, 1842, part of which is reprinted by Albert Bigelow Paine. He was writing from Tennessee, whither he had gone in the hope of collecting some old debts and of raising money on the Tennessee land. He had succeeded in neither. His debtor was not able to pay: "It seems so very hard upon him to pay such a sum that I could not have the conscience to hold him to it." His inability to push his debtors to the wall kept him down. Mark Twain says, speaking of his father's election to office in 1847: ". . . we were about to be comfortable once more, after several years of grinding poverty and privation which had been inflicted upon us by the dishonest act of one Ira Stout, to whom my father had lent several thousand dollars—a fortune in those days and in that region."[22]  John Clemens was unfitted by nature either

[22] *Autobiography*, II, 274.

for small gains or for the high-handed get-ahead methods required for business success. Further on in the letter mentioned above, anxious, as always, about what his family would think of him, he accounted, also, for his failure to sell a slave he had taken along with him, and he was troubled about what he would do when he returned home: "The future, taking its complexion from the state of my health or mind, is alternately beaming in sunshine or overshadowed with clouds; but mostly cloudy."[23] These might be the words of his distinguished son writing fifty years later. The effective expression of his mood is significant as showing the source of Mark Twain's ability as a writer.

Something may be said, perhaps not inappropriately at this point, in attempt to modify the impression conveyed by certain recent commentators upon Mark Twain's life who have said that it was to be expected that the humorist would be a "biological failure" because he came from a "loveless" household. John Clemens was a silent man. The atmosphere in the Clemens family was doubtless austere and somewhat formal. In an account of his pre-monitory dream of Henry's death, at his sister Pamela's home in St. Louis, Mark Twain speaks of their shaking hands with each other when they said goodnight.[24] That was some years after John Clemens's death. As a family, they seem to have preferred the nice formalities. But Mrs. Clemens, Albert Bigelow Paine said, "confided to a neighbor that, . . . her husband had been always warmhearted, with a deep affection for his family . . . he had never returned from a journey without bringing each one some present, however trifling."[25] The affection which

[23] A. B. P., I, 43.    [24] *Autobiography*, I, 308.    [25] A. B. P., I, 74.

they were shy about showing to each other they seem to have bestowed upon pets. "We had nineteen cats at one time, in 1845," Mark Twain said.[26] Theirs was a household of rather stern ideals, where the boy had to exercise his wits to maintain his independence, but the accounts of it are not unattractive.

The records indicate that the visionary tendency of John Clemens, as already pointed out, has been a good deal exaggerated. When seen in the milieu of the fabulous forties, he appears almost conservative. Albert Bigelow Paine says that as a *young* man he was "somewhat too optimistic and visionary." Though Judge Driscoll in *Pudd'nhead Wilson* becomes a half-melodramatic caricature as the story progresses, he comes nearer suggesting the personality of John Clemens than any other of Mark Twain's creations: ". . . about forty years old, judge of the county court. He was very proud of his old Virginian ancestry. . . . He was fine and just and generous. To be a gentleman—a gentleman without stain or blemish—was his only religion. . . . He was respected, esteemed, and beloved by all the community . . . [his family] were Presbyterians, the Judge was a free thinker."[27]

The student is confirmed in his impression that Mark Twain's memory of his father was unreliable by Mr. Armstrong's discovery in one of the contemporary Hannibal papers that John Clemens, at the time of his death, in March, 1847, had not yet been elected clerk of the "surrogate court." Mark Twain put a good deal of emphasis upon the promise of better fortunes at the time of

---

[26] *Autobiography*, I, 119.    [27] *Pudd'nhead Wilson*, p. 3.

his father's death because of the newly acquired position[28] but the *History of Marion County* says, "At the time of his death Judge Clemens had announced himself as a candidate for clerk of the circuit court."[29] "The first announcement of his candidacy," Mr. Armstrong says, "is in the *Hannibal Gazette*, Nov. 5, 1846. In both *Journal* and *Gazette* this announcement is carried up until the time of his death. The election for the office of clerk of the circuit court took place on Monday, August 2, 1847."[30] John Clemens died March 24, 1847. The issue of the *Gazette* for March 25, 1847, contained the following obituary:

Died in this city, on yesterday, the 24th inst., after a protracted and painful illness, John M. Clemens, Esq., in the 49th year of his age. . . .

Judge Clemens has been for many years a citizen of northeastern Missouri, and of Hannibal. He has been honored by several public stations, which he filled with credit to himself and advantage to the community. He was noted for his good sense and clear, discriminating mind. These, added to a high sense of justice and moral rectitude, made him a man of uncommon influence and usefulness. His public spirit was exercised zealously and with effect upon every proper occasion. His efforts to establish a library and institute of learning in our city were such as to entitle him to all commendation, and his untimely death is felt on this

[28] A. B. P., I, 72. "He was elected by a heavy majority, and it was believed he could hold the office as long as he chose." The papers show where Mark Twain's idea of a "heavy majority" came from. The *Hannibal Gazette*, Jan. 21, 1847, p. 2, col. 4: "We are authorized to announce John M. Clemens, Esq., as a candidate for the office of Clerk of the Circuit Court of Marion County at the next *August* election." The *Hannibal Journal* for Feb. 11, 1847, p. 2, contains a communication from a citizen who signs himself Senex: ". . . so far as I have heard, his candidacy meets with general approbation. I believe that no doubt is entertained of his election. . . . [His] clerical skill, business habits, and moral character qualify him, in an eminent degree for the performance of its duties."

[29] P. 294.

[30] "New Light Thrown on Early Life of Mark Twain by Discoveries of Dr. Armstrong in Old Paper Files," *Hannibal Courier-Post*, March 20, 1931.

account as well as many others as a loss to the whole community. He who devotes his energies to the diffusion of learning and intellectual enjoyments is not without his reward, even in death. There are many amongst us, who during life, will linger with no common delight on the memory of him who contributed so much to their purest pleasures. As a good and useful citizen, a lover of his kind, and an honest man, John M. Clemens will hold a place in the recollection of all who knew him.

There followed the conventional obituary verses.

The issue of the *Journal* for March 25 contains the following notices: "The members of the Hannibal Library Institute are requested to attend the funeral of *John M. Clemens*, Esq., this afternoon, with the usual badge of crepe on the left arm. S. Cross, Sec'y." A month later the *Gazette* noted the necessity of filling out the quota of delegates to the Whig Convention at Fayette. "The death of *Judge Clemens* leaves one vacancy."[31]

Ill health made John Clemens appear older than he was. But his pride kept him erect to the last. He never appeared whipped—"did not retreat from his moral and intellectual standards, . . . he was never intimidated by the rougher element, and his eyes were of the kind that would disconcert nine men out of ten. . . . Absolutely fearless, he permitted none to trample on his rights."[32] While that which gave charm to Mark Twain's personality came, doubtless, from his mother, the solid background of uprightness that won admirers for him abroad, where many another American was merely the wonder of a day, the passion to avoid hypocrisy, the substratum of melancholy in his bearing as he grew older, came from his father. His constant defense of his mother seems almost

---

[31] *Hannibal Gazette*, April 29, 1847.    [32] A. B. P., I, 8.

to have been undertaken to correct what may have been the local impression, and his own childish impression, that the title of the family to distinction lay in his father: "My father was a justice of the peace, and I supposed he possessed the power of life and death over all men, and could hang anybody that offended him. This was distinction enough for me as a general thing; . . ."[33]

Like his illustrious son after him, in the larger world, John Marshall Clemens, in his little world, threw himself into the stream of life where the current was strongest. ". . . the more deeply and urgently and organically you feel the pressure of society the more deeply and consciously and fruitfully you become yourself," said a recent critic of American civilization.[34] John Clemens's struggle in a frontier world was a worthy antecedent chapter in the career of his son.

Mark Twain, then, received from his father his capacity for public life. From his father came his consistent integrity, together with a logical and at the same time merciful mind. From his father came a steady purpose to try for a finer type of success than that which he saw about him—the mood which brought on his break with the optimistic temper of the Gilded Age.

## §3

BY THE SIDE of his father's bier, Sam Clemens promised his mother that he would live to be like him, "a faithful and industrious man, and upright." The family were of the old-fashioned breed. The next three years, from 1847 until 1850, when he began work with his brother Orion on

[33] *Life on the Mississippi*, p. 35.
[34] Van Wyck Brooks, *America's Coming of Age*, p. 92.

the *Hannibal Journal*, is the interval during which least is known of the boy's life; no autobiographic records reveal anything about them. Since it has become clear that Joseph P. Ament did not take his *Missouri Courier* to Hannibal until 1848—more than a year after John Marshall Clemens's death, there is an uncertainty as to when the boy began his career as printer. It was so fixed a memory of Mark Twain's, however, that he dropped out of school immediately after his father's death and that his mother believed the best place where he could become self-supporting, and at the same time continue his education, to be in a newspaper office,[35] that the assumption seems justified that he worked either on the *Journal* or the *Gazette* from the spring of 1847 until the summer of 1848. The better theory is that he went to work on the *Gazette* and that after Mr. Ament bought it the boy proved to be so intelligent that he was formally taken on as an apprentice when the *Courier* and *Gazette* were consolidated.

Joseph P. Ament had bought the *Missouri Courier* in Palmyra in 1841. Established in 1832 on sound Jacksonian principles, it was the oldest Democratic paper in the state. When Hannibal outgrew Palmyra, and it became apparent that it would be the eastern terminus of the new railway through North Missouri, Ament bought the *Gazette*, also Democratic, and merged the two papers, keeping the older title.

Mark Twain left only a slight account of his earliest master. His cellar contained a supply of potatoes, which could be drawn upon to make up for inadequate provision at table; and his cast-off clothes fitted apprentices poorly.[36] He was seemingly of the unimaginative type of

---

[35] A. B. P., I, 76.                    [36] *Autobiography*, II, 276-85.

newspaper man who conducts his paper primarily as a political organ. But he seems to have had the intelligence to value his young apprentice for abilities that complemented his own. The evidence is that the lad's development under his tutelage was rapid: "When he had been with Ament little more than a year Sam had become office favorite and chief standby. Whatever required intelligence and care and imagination was given to Sam Clemens."[37] The boy became "a sort of sub-editor" and "during the last year of the Mexican War, when a telegraph-wire found its way across the Mississippi to Hannibal . . . he was given charge of the extras with news from the front; and the burning importance of his mission, the bringing of news hot from the field of battle, spurred him to endeavors that won plaudits and success."[38] Although the only impression of Mr. Ament's character left in the memory of Mark Twain, so far as Albert Bigelow Paine's account or the *Autobiography* shows, was of his niggardliness, newspaper comments at the time when he sold the *Courier* appear to be greater expressions of respect than mere editorial courtesy demanded. The notice in the St. Louis *Intelligencer* is only perfunctory. It appears in the issue for November 30, 1853: "The Hannibal *Courier* has changed hands. Mr. Joseph P. Ament, who has long and ably conducted it, has sold out. . . . The *Courier* is the oldest Democratic paper in the state." But the comment that Orion and Sam Clemens printed in the *Journal*, coming from a paper of rival politics, sounds positive. After the customary notice, it reads: "Mr. Ament's ability made him an efficient supporter of his party principles, while his courtesy, and uniformly manly

[37] A. B. P., I, 77.   [38] *Ibid.*, I, 78.

course, procured him many friends among his opponents. We heartily wish him success wherever he may bend his steps, and in whatever business he may undertake—except making proselytes to his party."[39]    It appears that, as editor, Mr. Ament had discovered a chance to partake of party spoils. The *Whig Messenger* for December 1, 1852, contained a farewell notice when he went East:

We understand that this gentleman, who, for the past eight or ten years, has conducted the Courier newspaper with marked ability, leaves the West in a few days for Richmond, Virginia, where he will spend the winter, and in March next will proceed to Washington to accept an honorable and lucrative employment. . . . This we are glad of, for no man in Missouri more justly deserves the respect and gratitude of his party than Mr. Ament.

He returned "with health improved and in fine spirits." He had secured the appointment as Receiver in the Land Office in Palmyra. In a half-column editorial about "our old friend" which repeats its former eulogy, the *Journal* says,

General Pierce's appointment of this gentlemen to the office of Receiver, was welcomed with much gratification by the Democratic party of this section, and we may say of the whole State; for, as a citizen of Hannibal, we have a right to say with some degree of pride, that his paper was acknowledged by all parties, to be the ablest Democratic paper in the State.

As a clever man, and a man of strict integrity, the Whigs also were as much pleased with his appointment as any Democratic appointment that could have been made.

Although he has given us some hard raps for what he was pleased to call our "rabid whiggery," yet we are willing to render justice to a political opponent.[40]

[39] *Hannibal Journal*, Nov. 25, 1852.
[40] *Ibid.*, April 28, 1853.

## §4

MORE IMPORTANT than his association with Joseph P. Ament were Sam Clemens's three or four years with his brother Orion, according to his biographer's account, on the Hannibal weekly *Journal*. It is as impossible to discover accurately when the boy left the *Courier* office as when he began work as printer; but it was probably, as Albert Bigelow Paine says, when Orion bought the *Journal*. If so, he worked for Joseph P. Ament from 1848 until 1851, instead of the two years of his apprenticeship merely, continuing with him for a year after his brother returned from St. Louis.

Orion Clemens was fourteen years old when the family moved to Hannibal. Nothing is known of his education, but he was such a reader that he was not reliable help in his father's business.[41]   He was consequently apprenticed in the *Journal* office, and by the time he was seventeen, as he was "a very good journeyman printer," he secured work in St. Louis to help support the family. He seems to have looked upon the trade at this time merely as a means to further his education: "Printing was a step downward, for it was a trade, and Orion felt it keenly. A gentleman's son and a prospective heir of the Tennessee land, he was entitled to a profession."[42]   He must have remained in St. Louis six or eight years. Sometime during those years, as he had never given up the ambition to be a lawyer, he read law evenings in the office of Edward Bates, who, when he became a member of Lincoln's cabinet, secured Orion's appointment as secretary of the Territory of Nevada. In 1850, or somewhat earlier, he

41 A. B. P., I, 27.                    42 *Ibid.*, I, 28.

Lenoir Rhyne College
LIBRARY

returned to Hannibal because he felt that he was needed at home.[43]

"A periodical ambition of Orion's," Albert Bigelow Paine says, "was to own and conduct a newspaper. He felt that in such a position he might become a power in Western Journalism." "Once his father had considered buying the Hannibal *Journal* to give Orion a chance, and possibly to further his own political ambitions. Now Orion considered it for himself. The paper was for sale under a mortgage, and he was enabled to borrow the $500 which would secure ownership."[44]

But this account of Orion Clemens's newspaper career is corrected in several details by items in the files of newspapers recently recovered.[45] In September, 1850, he started a weekly Whig newspaper of his own, which he called the *Western Union*. The issue of November 1, 1850 (Vol. I, No. 6), reads: "The editor will yield a place in its columns . . . to news . . . in the range of politics, history, general literature, science, or the mechanic arts." The State

[43] *Ibid.*, I, 84.

[44] *Ibid.*, I, 85. In the *Missouri Statesman* (Columbia, Mo.), for Feb. 1, 1850, appears the notice, "The Editor of the Hannibal *Journal*, having determined to go to California in the spring, offers that paper and his city property for sale at a great bargain."

[45] Somewhat imperfect files of the *Whig Messenger* (weekly), the *Tri Weekly Messenger*, the *Hannibal Courier*, the *Western Union*, the *Hannibal Journal* (weekly), and the *Hannibal Daily Journal*, 1848-1853—from the estate of William T. League, grandson of the editor of the *Messenger*, presented by Miss Nettie A. League of Hannibal, Missouri, 1926 and 1927. It was not thought, until these were rescued from Miss League's attic, that any papers of the period were extant. A. B. Paine (*op. cit.*, I, 91) says, "No contributions of this time have been preserved. High prices have been offered for copies of the Hannibal *Journal* containing them, but without success." It was through the enterprise of Mr. C. J. Armstrong of Hannibal that the papers were discovered and secured for the State Historical Library of Missouri.

Besides the papers referred to above, a fairly complete file of the *Hannibal Gazette* (Nov. 5, 1845-May 4, 1848) has recently been acquired by the same library. Mr. Ament merged the *Gazette* with the *Missouri Courier* in 1848.

Historical Society of Missouri possesses an imperfect file, making a thin bound volume, which represents this first venture of his. Then early in the spring of 1851 he bought the *Hannibal Weekly Dollar Journal*, and combined the two under the name *Hannibal Journal and Western Union*. It was possibly at this time that he took both Sam and Henry into his office,[46] and for a time the paper prospered: "He started full of enthusiasm. He worked like a slave to save help: wrote his own editorials, and made his literary selections at night. The others worked too. Orion gave them hard tasks and long hours. He had the feeling that the paper meant fortune or failure to them all; that all must labor without stint."[47]

In February, 1852, he abandoned the double title in favor of the name *Journal*, possibly because he had started as apprentice on the older paper. In the issue of October 2, 1851, Orion had announced that he hoped to start a magazine, a monthly periodical devoted to "miscellanies, Poetry, Literature, and Political news," but there is no record that the plan came to anything. In May, 1852, he announced a plan to start a tri-weekly *Journal*, but the issue of June 17 contains the notice, "Not having yet succeeded in obtaining sufficient advertising and subscription patronage to make the publication of a tri-weekly safe, I shall postpone the undertaking for the present—to be resumed in 'the better time coming.'" In March, 1853, three months before Sam left Hannibal, however, Orion started the *Hannibal Daily Journal*, which had seven months of intermittent life. Notices in other periodicals in the state congratulated him upon his "handsome little

[46] *Cf.* C. J. Armstrong, "Mark Twain's Early Writings Discovered," *Missouri Historical Review*, XXIV (July, 1930), 487.

[47] A. B. P., I, 85.

sheet"; the *Lagrange Missourian* commented upon the enterprise of Hannibal, which "now boasts of three week-lies, one tri-weekly, and one daily paper."[48]

Orion Clemens was at that time twenty-eight years old. There are a good many evidences that he occupied an honorable position in the town. It was announced that he was to speak in the Baptist church.[49] He had succeeded his father as one of the stockholders in the Hannibal Library Institute.[50] When he sold the *Journal* to the other Whig newspaper in the town, it published in the issue of September 27, 1853, the following editorial under the title "Orion Clemens, Esq.":

The public have already been informed that the above named gentleman, a short time since, sold to us his printing establishment in this city, and that the Hannibal Journal, heretofore so ably conducted by him, has ceased to be published. Whither he will go is unknown to us. Kind and obliging to all, Mr. Clemens did not deserve to have a single enemy. Industrious and attentive to his business, a good practical printer, a ready writer, an honest man, Mr. Clemens merits and we believe enjoys the respect and confidence of all who know him. His talents as a writer will command the respect of the community, and his integrity will win for him the confidence of the people wherever he goes. May his future success be equal to his merit.[51]

[48] Quoted in the *Hannibal Daily Journal*, April 4, 1853.

[49] "ADDRESS: Our Citizens are hereby informed that Mr. O. Clemens will address the meeting at the Baptist church to-night.—D. T. Morton."—*Hannibal Daily Journal*, Sept. 5, 1853.

[50] "LIBRARY NOTICE: A meeting of the stockholders of the Hannibal Library Institute will be held on TUESDAY evening, April 5th, at early candle light. . . . O. Clemens."—*Hannibal Daily Journal*, March 29, 1853.

[51] Hannibal *Tri-Weekly Messenger*, Sept. 27, 1853. See Mr. Fred W. Lorch's study in the *Palimpsest*, "Orion Clemens Number": "The Tradition" (353-57); "Molly Clemens's Note-book" (357-364); "Literary Apprenticeship" (364-72); "Adrift for Heresy" (372-81); "The Closing Years" (381-387); "Comment" (387-88), Oct., 1929. When passing years have sufficiently dulled personal feeling so that the heirs to the Clemens estate feel that they can release for publication

The following report has not yet been laid before a public meeting of Stockholders; but it is deemed proper to publish it now, without that formality, that it may at once meet the eye of all the stockholders, and all who may feel interested in this very important institution.

**Report of the Committee**

or

**THE STOCKHOLDERS OF THE HANNIBAL LIBRARY INSTITUTE.**

The Committee appointed at the meeting of the stockholders of the Hannibal Library Institute, held 5th of March, for the purpose of examining into the condition of the Library, and suggesting means for its improvement, present the following report:

The Library was organized under a regular charter in the year 1844, and for a time it appeared to be in a flourishing condition, the number of Stockholders being 70, and of books, as appears by the catalogue, amounting to 425. But within the past two or three years, many of the original Stockholders having removed to other places, little attention has been bestowed upon its no directors have been elected, and no librarian has been appointed. The annual dues have not been collected, and no new books purchased. The number of stockholders in the city and vicinity is comparatively small, and, with few exceptions, they have ceased to make use of the books.

The books in their cases are now in the office of Dr. D. T. Morton. Some few of them have probably been lost, and some are probably now out in the possession of Stockholders, and will be recovered. There remain, however, a large number of excellent volumes, sufficient to form the nucleus of a good library, by the exertion of the public spirit which it is believed may be excited, by a little effort, in its favor.

The committee suggest that a meeting of Stockholders be held at an early day, after sufficient notice, to elect Directors, and effect a reorganization, when all the shares of those long in arrears, and who continue to neglect payment, can be declared forfeited to the Company, and resold. The propriety of issuing new shares for sale at a moderate price will be presented as a question for consideration. By this means, it is believed, the benefits of the Library can be largely extended, and its annual revenue increased, so that all desirable new issues of works of a proper character can be procured. As these questions—the selection of a proper room and other matters—will all come before the meeting, it is hoped the stock holders who wish to preserve their shares and continue their connection with the institution, will be prompt in attendance.

In connection with this important subject, the committee is endeavoring to procure some lectures on interesting literary subjects, which will call the attention of the citizens generally to the advantages of a Public Library. Due notice will be given of them in course, with as little delay as possible.
                            Z. G. DRAPER,
                            O. CLEMENS,
                            H. MEREDITH.

CONCERNING THE HANNIBAL LIBRARY INSTITUTE. FROM THE
*Hannibal Weekly Journal*, MARCH 31, 1853.

In no connection does Mark Twain's humor appear to poorer advantage than when it is vented upon Orion Clemens. As soon as he had his first taste of success, Sam assumed a rôle of mentor toward the "gentle and melancholy" older brother—apparently with his encouragement, which gave license to his humor. As the whole record now appears—in his description of Orion in his *Autobiography,* supplemented by his letters about him, especially those to William Dean Howells—it sounds too much like sport at the expense of a helpless creature. Nor do any of the records left by Orion Clemens during his Hannibal years justify the picture of him drawn by a Chicago writer in the "Note," "A Celebrated Village Idiot,"[52] though he was the type of man who suffers necessarily when dragged out into the garish light where only that which can maintain itself in the economic struggle is valued. He failed with the *Hannibal Journal* after Sam left him, but he was notable for his industry and integrity, and he was the main support of the Clemens family for over ten years. His history, however, is important only in so far as it has added something to the document of his brother. "Following the life of Mark Twain, whether through his letters or along the sequence of detailed occurrence, we are never more than a little while, or a little distance, from his brother Orion."[53] It has been said that Sam Clemens's association with his brother was of value chiefly because he learned from him how not to conduct his life; but he made his start as a writer under Orion's

the Autobiography which Orion Clemens wrote at the instigation of Mark Twain (A. B. P., II, 674-77), it will be a valuable addition to the Sam Clemens source-book.

[52] J. O. Bennett in *The Adventures of Thomas Jefferson Snodgrass* (ed. Charles Honce).

[53] *Letters,* I, 352.

censorship. The same trait that made him turn to people all his life for fortification may account to some extent for his frequent returns to his brother's roof, but his letters show that there must have been a peculiar sympathy between the two men. From his father and Joseph P. Ament Sam Clemens learned how to be a man among men, but some lack of imaginative sympathy kept him aloof from his father, and Ament's political methods aroused his satire. It was a certain fineness in Orion Clemens, doubtless, that lay at the bottom of the attachment between the two. It is probably not an exaggeration to say that the greatest single influence in Mark Twain's life was his older brother, lasting through the publication of *Roughing It*.

# IV

## SUB-EDITOR ON THE *HANNIBAL JOURNAL*

### §1

THE RECOVERY of the Hannibal papers published from
1839 to 1853 makes it possible to discover how extensive
Sam Clemens's experiments in writing were under his
brother Orion's tutelage, and something about how extensive the literary interests of his region were. The
writings in the *Hannibal Journal* that can be ascribed to
Sam Clemens, with greater or less degree of certainty,
may be grouped under four heads. The first group in-
volves an altercation with a rival editor in Hannibal, who
seems to have drawn down upon himself the young humorist's shafts of ridicule. The second represents a more
ambitious exercise. Under the *nom de plume*, W. Epaminondas Adrastus Blab, Sam Clemens appears to have experimented with feature story writing. The third group
of youthful writing centers around the famous "To Mary
in H—l" poem. The fourth comprises three columns of
miscellaneous squibs, each headed "Our Assistant's Column." Apparently Orion Clemens, because he realized
that he could ill afford to lose his brother from the *Journal*, dignified him with the title of Assistant Editor. All
but the second of these groups of writings can be identified
by means of the story, "My First Literary Venture,"

which was written about the time *Innocents Abroad* was
published—around 1870.[1]

In this autobiographical sketch Mark Twain relates the
events of what he calls his "week" as editor of the *Hannibal Journal*. As a matter of fact, those events included
two separate adventures in editorship, about eight months
apart, and were apparently the first expressions of the
youth's restless energy becoming conscious of itself and
impelled inevitably to break out of the narrow limits of its
small-town routine.[1a] Albert Bigelow Paine refers to this
as his first writing. According to the account in Chapter
XVIII of the biography,[2] the *Journal* was so seriously in
danger of failing that Orion Clemens made a trip to Tennessee to try to raise money on the great tract of land
which his father had so confidently left to the family. He
entrusted Sam with the office in his absence, and the only
benefit that came from the journey was that it started the
boy on a literary career. The Hannibal papers of the
time that are available[3] show that while many of the details in "My First Literary Venture" were consciously
modified to make a good story—and some, doubtless, had
suffered modification in the memory of Mark Twain after
twenty years—they are, in the main, authentic. The first
items in the chronological list of his work are:

[1] The sketch was written sometime before April, 1871. The Merle Johnson
*Bibliography of Mark Twain* shows that "My First Literary Venture" appeared in:
*The Galaxy*, April, 1871; "Practical Jokes," 1872; *Sketches New and Old* (1875),
pp. 93-95; *Sketches* (1880), pp. 138-141.
   See also Mark Twain, *Editorial Wild Oats* (1905), pp. 3-11.
   [1a] In this "week" Mark Twain includes the woodcut, "Local Resolves to Com-
mit Suicide," *Hannibal Journal*, Sept. 16, 1852; the "snappy footnote," to "To
Miss Katie of H—l," in the issue of May 6, 1853; and the parody on "The Burial
of Sir John Moore," in the issue of May 23, 1853.—*Sketches New and Old*
(1903), pp. 110-12.
   [2] A. B. P., I, 89-93.
   [3] See above, p. 102 n.

1851

Edited the Hannibal *Journal* during the absence of the owner and editor, Orion Clemens.

Wrote local items for the Hannibal *Journal*.

Burlesque of a rival editor in the Hannibal *Journal*.

Wrote two sketches for the *Saturday Evening Post* (Philadelphia).

*To Mary in H—l*, Hannibal *Journal*.

1852-53

*Jim Wolfe and the Fire*—Hannibal *Journal*.

Burlesque of a rival editor in the Hannibal *Journal*.

1853

Wrote obituary poems—not published.

Wrote first letters home.

It will be seen that some of these dates can be corrected from data in the newspapers recently brought to light.

§2

THE FIRST of Sam Clemens's editorial ventures involved a joke he played upon the local editor of the *Tri-Weekly Messenger*, a rival Whig paper in Hannibal. The account of the escapade in "My First Literary Venture" is as follows:

I was a printer's "devil" and a progressive and aspiring one. My uncle had me on his paper (the *Weekly Hannibal Journal*, two dollars a year, in advance—five hundred subscribers, and they paid in cord-wood, cabbages, and unmarketable turnips), and on a lucky summer's day he left town to be gone a week, and asked me if I thought I could edit one issue of the paper judiciously. Ah! didn't I want to try! Higgins was the editor on the rival paper. He had lately been jilted, and one night a friend found an open note on the poor fellow's bed, in which he stated that he could no

longer endure life and had drowned himself in Bear Creek. The
friend ran down there and discovered Higgins wading back to
shore. He had concluded he wouldn't. The village was full of
it for several days, but Higgins did not suspect it. I thought this
was a fine opportunity. I wrote an elaborately wretched account
of the whole matter, and then illustrated it with villainous
cuts engraved on the bottoms of wooden type with a jackknife—
one of them a picture of Higgins wading out into the creek in his
shirt, with a lantern, sounding the depth of the water with a
walking stick. I thought it was desperately funny and was densely
unconscious that there was any moral obliquity about such a
publication.[4]

The author's introduction of himself as an employee of his
"uncle" makes it apparent that he is consciously taking
literary liberties with facts, but, so far as the story can be
pieced out from the papers in the files, the publication of
the woodcuts here referred to was the culmination of a
journalistic scrimmage carried on through several issues
by the city editors of the *Tri-Weekly Messenger* and the
*Hannibal Journal*, which, in its origin, had nothing to do
with Higgins's romance. It must have started somewhat
as follows. In July, 1852, when a mad dog caused some
disturbance in Hannibal, the city editor of the *Messenger*,
a bachelor recently come from the rival town of Quincy,
Illinois, published among his "Miscellaneous Matters,"
signed "Local," a warning that citizens take precautions
against the danger.[5] In August he published a rather

_____
[4] "My First Literary Venture," *Sketches New and Old*.
[5] The *Tri-Weekly Messenger*, July 24, 1852, "*Miscellaneous Matters* by the 'Local' ":

"*Mad Dogs:*—On Thursday a calf, belonging to Mr. John Lacy, was bitten by
a mad dog, and was afterwards killed to relieve it from misery. We make mention of this that citizens may be on their guard against this distressing malady,
and that proper precautions may be used to prevent any serious consequences resulting from carelessness on the part of those who have dogs in their possession."

flippant note about the fate of dogs appearing on the streets without collars.[6]

There is no indication that the *Journal* took any notice of the first warning, but after the second squib, it must have published, as coming from a correspondent, some sort of mock-serious suggestion that all dogs should be exterminated—signed "A Dog-be-deviled Citizen." This was apparently answered by some other paper in the town, possibly the *Courier*,[7] defending dogs. The two furnished the *Messenger* "Local" a chance to exercise his editorial irony, for the August 24 *Messenger*, under the heading "Two Richmonds in the Field!—any chance for a Richard?" says:

In our cotemporaries [*sic*][8] of last week dogs are commented upon in a masterly manner both pro and con. . . . "A Dog-be-deviled Citizen," [he says] must be a man of nervous temperament. . . . The faithful dogs . . . [defend] the property of citizens; then surely, if music be their humor, they may be permitted to engage in vocal concerts, leaving it to the option of nervous gentlemen to place cotton in their ears ere they retire to their pillows.

The other answer had evidently been signed "Many Citizens," and had protested against the cruel method of putting dogs to death. "Local" suggests a more humane method:

[6] *Ibid.*, August 17, 1852:
"The Dogs are beginning to suffer for their want of good manners in appearing on the streets without collars, and it is now a common occurrence to see their canine lordships humbled to the earth through the fact of their being minus a neck-band."
[7] The two available issues of the *Courier* for August, 1852, contain no hint of the affair.
[8] Spelling, grammar, capitals, and punctuation in the excerpts taken from the papers are reproduced just as they appear. "A Dog-be-deviled Citizen" is printed in different places with various methods of capitalization.

With how much more *éclat* would the doomed brutes make their exit from this terrestrial globe if they were gently led to the place of execution by the proper officials, decked in all the grandeur of a little "brief authority"—their dogships placed in a chair, the band put around the neck, a few prayers in *hog-Latin* mumbled over their future welfare, and then with a sudden twist of the screw, be launched into the breathless expanse of the future.[9]

The *Journal* must have printed an answer from its correspondent, the "Dog-be-deviled Citizen," identifying the city editor of the *Messenger* with "the canine race," in his tendency to bite back. The August 26 issue of the *Messenger* contains further advice from "Local," hinting his suspicion that the correspondent of the *Journal* was a fellow-editor:

His hypochondric [*sic*] symptoms are obtaining so complete a mastery over him that even his fellow being seems "transformed into a beast"—dog, of course. . . . He prefaces his notice with "friend Local," which surely implies that he is sunk as deeply in the mire as ourself.[10]

The *Journal*, it seems, bided its time. In order to understand the provocation for the woodcut it is necessary, at this point, to finish out the story from the account in "My First Literary Venture." The rival editor, one gathers from the papers, was conspicuous in the town as a stranger and a bachelor—probably also for his florid style of writing. So that, when he threatened to kill himself because of a disappointment in love, and then lost courage for the deed, the secret interest in the matter throughout the town was a thing that could be reckoned upon. Orion Clemens had left Sam in charge of the week's issue of the

[9] The *Tri-Weekly Messenger*, August 24, 1852.
[10] *Ibid.*, August 26, 1852.

'LOCAL,' disconsolate from receiving no further notice from 'A Dog-be-Deviled Citizen,' contemplates Suicide. His 'pocket-pistol' (i. e. the *bottle*,) failing in the patriotic work of ridding the country of a nuisance, he resolves to 'extinguish his chunk' by feeding his carcass to the fishes of Bear Creek, while friend and foe are wrapt in sleep. Fearing, however, that he may get out of his depth, he *sounds the stream with his walking-stick.*

---

The artist has, you will perceive, Mr. Editor, caught the gentleman's countenance as correctly as the thing could have been done with the real *dog*-gerytype apparatus. Ain't he pretty? and don't he step along through the mud with an air? 'Peace to his *re*-manes.'

'A Dog-be-Deviled Citizen.'

Scott Mass Meeting.

FROM THE *Hannibal Daily Journal*, SEPTEMBER 16, 1852.

*Journal.* The sixteen-year-old editor *pro tem.* saw his chance to make the paper "spicy," and retaliated upon his ambitious rival with the first of the woodcuts referred to in the sketch, and in Albert Bigelow Paine's biography.[11] In a very crude way "Local" is cartooned with the head of a dog, wading anxiously out into the stream with a lantern in one hand and a cane in the other. The reader is left to guess at his safety-first motive. The bottle referred to in the explanatory note is close at hand.[12]

### "LOCAL" RESOLVES TO COMMIT SUICIDE.

'Local,' disconsolate from receiving no further notice from 'A Dog-be-Deviled Citizen,' contemplates Suicide. His 'pocket pistol' (i.e. the *bottle,*) failing in the patriotic work of ridding the country of a nuisance, he resolves to 'extinguish his chunk' by feeding his carcass to the fishes of Bear Creek, while friend and foe are wrapt in sleep. Fearing, however, that he may get out of his depth, he *sounds the stream with his walking-stick.*

The artist has, you will perceive, Mr. Editor, caught the gentleman's countenance as correctly as the thing could have been done with the real *dog*-gerytype apparatus. Ain't he pretty? and don't he step along through the mud with an air? 'Peace to his *re*-manes.'

'A Dog-be-Deviled Citizen.'

The *Messenger* "Local" commented upon the woodcut with great sarcasm, and the *Journal* a week later published two more woodcuts under the heading "Pictur' Department"—with which the Dog-be-Deviled Citizen announced his intention of drawing off:

### "PICTUR" DEPARTMENT.

"Local" discovers something interesting in the *Journal,* and becomes excited.

[11] A. B. P., I, 89-90.          [12] See illustration facing p. 112.

["LOCAL," determined upon the destruction of the great enemy of the canine race, charters an old swivel (a six pounder) and declares war. *Lead* being scarce, he loads his cannon with *Tri-Weekly Messengers*.]

"LOCAL" is somewhat astonished at the effect of the discharge, and is under the impression that there was something the matter with the apparatus—thinks the hole must have been drilled in the wrong end of the artillery. He finds, however, that although he missed the "DOG-BE-DEVILED CITIZEN,"* he nevertheless hit the man "who has not the decency of a gentleman nor the honor of a blackguard," and thinks it best to stop the controversy.

MR. EDITOR:
I have now dropped this farce, and all attempts to again call me forth will be useless.

A DOG-BE-DEVILED CITIZEN.

* Who walks quietly away, in the distance, uninjured.

The "Pictur' Department" (see illustration facing page 116) is in column 3 of the editorial page of the September 23 *Journal*. In column 2 is an editorial which appears to have been written by Orion Clemens upon his return:

### THE DOG CONTROVERSY.

"In justice to the editor of the Journal, we would take this occasion to remark, that we believe him innocent of intentionally doing us an injury, and absolve him from all censure."

We find the above in the local column of the Tri-Weekly Messenger. The local editor of the Messenger is a young man, recently come amongst us, with a design of occupying a respectable position in society, by industry and by propriety and straight-for-wardness of conduct; rightly estimating the value placed by good men upon these properties of character. . . . The jokes of our correspondent have been rather rough; but originating and perpetrated in a spirit of fun, and without a serious thought, no attention was expected to be paid to them, beyond a smile at the local editor's expense.

There can be no doubt that the woodcuts are those referred to in "My First Literary Venture." Whether Mark Twain's literary imagination, two decades later, invented the story of the jilting, does not become clear, but "Local" commented upon the "Dog-be-Deviled Citizen," after the first engraving appeared, as "a writer who has not the decency of a gentleman nor the honor of a blackguard." This must have had some deeper provocation than a mere editorial fencing bout. In his final comment upon the "gross and insipid personalities" of the "picture gallery furnished in the Journal this morning," he dismisses them as "the feeble eminations [sic] of a puppy's brain." The file of the Journal contains no "elaborately wretched account of the whole matter," but a lingering memory of "Local's" thrust at his youth doubtless suggested to Mark Twain the dénouement of the episode:

Higgins dropped in with a double-barrelled shotgun early in the forenoon. When he found that it was an infant (as he called me) that had done him the damage, he simply pulled my ears and went away; but he threw up his situation that night and left town for good.[13]

§3

THE SECOND section of what seem to have been the first experiments of Sam Clemens in getting out a newspaper comprises four "feature stories." Three of them appear in the same paper with the first of the woodcuts described above. If the September 16, 1852, issue of the Journal

---

[13] "My First Literary Venture," Sketches New and Old.

was the trial sheet of the young editor, these seem to have been the main part of his attempt to prove that he was equal to the task of filling it up.  It is to be remembered that he had not yet reached his seventeenth birthday when he strove in this way to reach up to the stature of editor; that he had served two years' apprenticeship under Joseph P. Ament on the *Hannibal Courier*, where he had charge of the circulation, was printer's devil, and even served as local editor in an emergency; that when Orion Clemens bought the *Journal*, he "felt that together they could carry on the paper and win success."[14]  The first woodcut appears halfway down on the second column of the page. Occupying almost all of the third column and half the fourth is the first of the stories.  It is entitled "A Historical Exhibition" and is introduced by a note that was probably written by Orion Clemens when Sam at some time or other offered him the sketch for publication.  The editor absolves himself from responsibility if the effort of his "young friend" should fall rather flat with his patrons. The second is entitled "Editorial Agility."  It also has an introductory note in which the contributor is referred to as a "youngster."[15]

The September 16 issue of the *Journal* also contains the third "feature story," the account of a drunken brawl on Holliday's Hill, signed W. Epaminondas Adrastus Perkins.  It must be taken with the later experiments as

[14] Albert Bigelow Paine, *The Boys' Life of Mark Twain*, pp. 43-47; and A. B. P., I, chapters XV and XVII.

[15] These notes seem to identify the two stories with those referred to in *The Boy's Life of Mark Twain*. "He liked the taste of print," the author says, and tells of two anecdotes that were accepted by *The Saturday Evening Post*. "When they appeared he walked on air. This was in 1851." Then, "Orion printed two of his sketches in the *Journal*, which was the extent of his efforts at this time. None of his early work has been preserved."—*The Boys' Life of Mark Twain*, p. 47.

ournal, we
rk, that we
ly doing us
eensure.
uxin of the
il editor of
ently come
pying a re-
stry and by
of conduct;
y good men
. Having
igs towards
e, of course,
n a commu-
w obstacles
ie may have
indent have
and perpe-
ut a serious
o be paid to
editor's ex-

received a
by Messrs.
groceries,
8 Charles
arance it is
r it. It is
t is known
in the ma-
nd is there-
as well as
f its great
public as it

iolitan has
. Tredway,
"Jefferson
intly a man
dertakes to
l indefinite
ms.

" LOCAL " discovers something interesting in the *Journal*, and becomes excited.

["LOCAL," determined upon the destruction of the great enemy of the canine race, charters an old swivel (a six pounder) and declares war. *Lead* being scarce, he loads his cannon with *Tri-Weekly Messengers*.]

" LOCAL " is somewhat astonished at the effect of the discharge, and is under the impression that there was something the matter with the apparatus—thinks the hole must have been drilled in the wrong end of the artillery. He finds, however, that although he missed the " DOG-BE-DEVILED CITIZEN,"* he nevertheless hit the man " who has not the decency of a gentleman nor the honor of a blackguard," and thinks it best to stop the controversy.

MR. EDITOR:

I have now dropped this farce, and all attempts to again call me forth will be useless.

A DOG-BE-DEVILED CITIZEN.

FIRE AT
Smith and N
cy, were b
One of thes
be worth at
an insurance
of wheat we
which the fi
ment, insure

Mr. Myei
section of tl
upon the ne
company hav
whole capita
pany shall be
to lay the an
in the affirm
Another a
Devol, to str
and insert, "
and grants co
remain a pub
Treasury, on
amendment v
34. Variou:
all of which
Mr. Gordo
section, impo
and personal
Before comii
It will be
to pass the S
ny from und
probably be p
House adjo

[FI

J

no

Mr. Gord
amendment w
object of whi
the cash value
on which a ta
Mr. Hunte
provement m:

FROM THE *Hannibal Daily Journal*, SEPTEMBER 23, 1852.

conscious attempts to lose nothing of the story in the telling. But the fourth and last of the W. Epaminondas Adrastus Blab stories is a different kind of fun-making and, in places, is distinctly suggestive of the Mark Twain vein. It is possible that the first two were earlier experiments that had been laid aside by Orion Clemens until they should be needed to fill out an issue of the paper. The last story accounts for the change of the name Perkins, signed to the sketch of the previous week, to the name Blab:

## BLABBING GOVERNMENT SECRETS.

The people generally seem to think that the present extra session of the State Legislature was convened for the purpose of transacting this Railroad business, and I hasten from a sense of duty to my fellow-citizens, to correct this wrong impression; their ignorance on this subject shows that they have paid very little attention to the proceedings of the Legislature.— Now this is just the way of it: I didn't like my surname; as for the handles to it,—they did *very* well; *I* wouldn't care if I had twenty more like 'em; but the surname didn't suit; and although the Legislature is not, I believe, accustomed to change people's surnames, I nevertheless wrote to Gov. King, who is a particular friend of mine, requesting him to call the session and make the wished-for alteration, and leaving the selection of the new name to his own refined taste and judgment. Well, the request was granted: the Legislature was convened; my title was altered, shortened, and greatly beautified—and all at a cost of *only a few thousands of dollars to the State!*—These Democratic Legislators work cheap, don't they, Editor?

This new cognomen suits me, and I hope it meets with favor in the eyes of the inhabitants of this great Union; and if Congress takes the matter up and changes it back the way it was, the villainous President that signs the documents and makes it a law will never get *my support*—No, sir! not if he's NEVER elected again! As for Queen Victoria and Lord Derby, they may cut up as much as they like—it's none of their business.

Blab—Blab—sounds pretty—makes good jingle—it's just the thing—the Blab's were ancestors of mine, anyhow. The first Blab lived in Adam's time, and had a little falling out with that distinguished gentleman about a tin cup, . . . but Adam was no more respectable than Blab—he never had a mother! at least people said so, and folks of that character don't stand very high nowadays. However, if it hadn't been for that little difficulty, a Blab would have been President instead of John Quincy Adams! Despite all these things, the Blabs have been somewhat distinguished, anyhow; honorable mention was made of one of them in a book that was never published, and another one was hung last week for his rascality, and I'm glad of it; for he was a Democrat and ought to have been hung long ago. I go in for hanging all the Whigs and Democrats, and then the only Blab that ever went unhung would stand a chance—a slim one, too, I reckon, for then that great military hero you mentioned sometime since— I believe you call him Ensign Jehiel Stebbings—would step in. It's no go.

W. E. A. B.

"The first Blab lived in Adam's time" brings to mind the sentence from the *Autobiography* of Mark Twain: "Back of the Virginian Clemenses is a dim procession of ancestors stretching back to Noah's time."[16] "As for Queen Victoria and Lord Derby, they may cut up as much as they like" has a Mark Twain flavor. The reminder that Adam "never had a mother" and that "folks of that character don't stand very high nowadays" might have come from the *Burlesque Biography* written in 1881. The reference to one of the Blabs that was "hung last week for rascality"

---

[16] *Autobiography*, I, 82.

makes one think of the account of one of the Twains who went to "one of those fine old English places of resort called Newgate. . . . While there he died suddenly."[17]

A note underneath the "Pictur' Department" in the September 23 *Journal* seems to be the boy's bow to the public after this first adventure as editor-in-chief.

### FOR THE JOURNAL.

*Mr. Editor:*

I believe it is customary, nowadays, for a man, as soon as he gets his name up, to take a "furrin" tour, for the benefit of his health; or, if his health is good, he goes without any excuse at all. Now, I think my health was sufficiently injured by last week's efforts, to justify me in starting on my tour; and, ere your hebdomadal is published, I shall be on my way to another country— yes, Mr. Editor, I have retired from public life to the shades of Glascock's Island!—and I shall gratify such of your readers as have never been so far from home, with an account of this great island, and my voyage thither.

W. Epaminondas Adrastus Blab.

### §4

The third group of writings which the recent recovery of the *Hannibal Journal* has brought to light grew out of the publication of the verses "To Miss Katie of H—l" ("To Mary in H—l"). For many years these verses have been looked upon as the chief product of Mark Twain's youthful pen. His biographer's account of them is brief:

The embryo Mark Twain also wrote a poem. It was addressed "To Mary in Hannibal," but the title was too long to be set in one column, so he left out all the letters in Hannibal, except the first and the last, and supplied their place with a dash, with a

[17] "A Burlesque Biography," *The $30,000 Bequest and Other Stories*, pp. 197-98.

startling result . . . Orion returned, remonstrated, apologized. He reduced Sam to the ranks.[18]

The incident is elaborated in "My First Literary Venture" with some differences:

Next I gently touched up the newest stranger—the lion of the day, the gorgeous journeyman tailor from Quincy. He was a simpering coxcomb of the first water, and the "loudest" dressed man in the State. He was an inveterate woman-killer. Every week he wrote lushy "poetry" for the *Journal* about his newest conquest. His rhymes for my week were headed, "To Mary in H—l," meaning to Mary in Hannibal, of course. But while setting up the piece I was suddenly riven from head to heel by what I regarded as a perfect thunderbolt of humor, and I compressed it into a snappy foot-note at the bottom—thus:

> We will let this thing pass, just this once; but we wish Mr. J. Gordon Runnels to understand distinctly that we have a character to sustain, and from this time forth, when he wants to commune with his friends in h—l, he must select some other medium than the columns of this Journal!

The paper came out, and I never knew any little thing to attract so much attention as those playful trifles of mine. For once the *Hannibal Journal* was in demand—a novelty it had not experienced before . . . actually booked the unparalleled number of thirty-three new subscribers.[19]

The real facts of the publication of the poem seem to have involved a second attempt of Sam Clemens to fill the editor's chair in the absence of the editor, and to attract the interest of the public. There seems to be no doubt that the events related in "My First Literary Venture" cover two separate adventures, one on the weekly *Journal* and the other on the *Hannibal Daily Journal*, which was started by Orion, in connection with the weekly, March 8,

[18] A. B. P., I, 90. Also noted in III, 1674.
[19] *Sketches New and Old.*

1853. The poem itself appears on the editorial page of the daily for May 6, 1853, with the note, "Written for the 'Daily Journal'," and is reprinted in the weekly *Journal*, May 12, 1853. It is signed "Rambler" and is in the most approved style of Hannibal newspaper verse of the day. Its title is "Love Concealed," its sub-title "To Miss Katie of H—l," not "Mary in H—l."[20]

### LOVE CONCEALED.

#### TO MISS KATIE OF H—L

Oh, thou wilt never know how fond a love
    This heart could have felt for thee;
Or ever dream how love and friendship strove,
    Through long, long hours for mastery;
How passion often urged, but pride restrained,
    Or how thy coldness grieved, but kindness pained.

How hours have soothed the feelings, then that were
    The torture of my lonely life—
But ever yet will often fall a tear,
    O'er wildest hopes and thoughts then rife;
Where'er recalled by passing word or tone,
    Fond memory mirrors all those visions flown.

For much I fear he has won thy heart,
    And thou art but a friend to me;
I feel that in thy love I have no part,
    I know how much he worships thee!
Yet still often will there rise a gleam of hope,
    Wherewith but only time and pride can cope.

Hannibal, May 4th, 1853.          RAMBLER.

[20] *Letters*, I, 28. A letter written from Philadelphia, October 26, 1853, to his brother Orion ends, "Tell me all that is going on in H—l." Mr. Paine adds the note: "H—l . . . he had first used in the title of the poem which he had published a few years before, during one of Orion's absences. . . . The poem had no great merit, but under the abbreviated title it could hardly fail to invite notice. It was one of several things he did to liven up circulation during the brief period of his authority."

On the same page is the note in the Editor's column: "The editor left yesterday for St. Louis. This must be our excuse if the paper is lacking in interest." It may be taken as the seventeen-year-old[21] editor's bid for the attention of the patrons of the paper.

In the editorial column of the next issue of the paper, May 7, is printed what purports to be the letter of a correspondent:

Mr. Editor:

In your yesterday's paper I see a piece of poetry addressed "To Katie in H—l" (hell).—Now, I've often seen pieces to "Mary in Heaven," or "Lucy in Heaven," or something of that sort, but "Katie in Hell," is carrying the matter too far.

*Grumbler.*[22]

The May 8 issue is lacking from the file in the Missouri State Historical Society Library, but the May 9 *Journal* contains the following in the editor's column:

FOR THE DAILY JOURNAL.

Poor Grumbler! are you so ignorant as not to be able to distinguish "of" from "in"? Read again—see if it is not "of" H—l (Hannibal), instead of "in" Hell. Now, did you suppose that there was another such idiot as yourself in the city of Hannibal, one who, like yourself, would as soon address a person in "hell" as upon earth, you are widely mistaken. Poor fellow, I much fear that some Lunatic Asylum will have to mourn the absence of a fit subject until you are placed in a straight jacket and sent there.—From the remotest depths of my heart I pity you, nor will I condescend to notice you, for it ill becomes a rational man to engage in a controversy with one who has placed upon his shoulders a head without eyes, brains, or sense. Now, Grumbler,

[21] Sam Clemens's birthday was November 30.
[22] Quoted in the May 12, 1853, *Weekly Journal.*

lingly

153.

nerry
lower
Queen
nother
d ev-
ildren
>r the
an il-
me or
aven't
. His
en he

Louis.
cking

r!!
g (of
hap-

Then ye who linger o'er the tomb
Of the inanimate, immortal Clay.
Mourn not, but look beyond the gloom
To where his spirit soars in endless day.

HOLLY.

Written for the "Daily Journal."

## LOVE CONCEALED.

### TO MISS KATIE OF H———L.

Oh, thou wilt never know how fond a love
This heart could have felt for thee;
Or ever dream how love and friendship strove,
Through long, long hours for mastery;
How passion often urged, but pride restrained,
Or how thy coldness grieved, but kindness pained.

How hours have soothed the feelings, then that were
The torture of my lonely life—
But ever yet will often fall a tear,
O'er wildest hopes and thoughts then rife;
Where'er recalled by passing word or tone,
Fond memory mirrors all those visions flown.

For much I fear he has won thy heart,
And thou art but a friend to me;
I feel that in thy love I have no part,
I know how much he worships thee;
Yet still often will there rise a gleam of hope,
Wherewith but only time and pride can cope.

Hannibal, May 4th, 1853.          RAMBLER.

SAM CLEMENS'S FIRST POEM. FROM THE *Hannibal Daily Journal,*
MAY 6, 1853.

to suj
*all* of
rum—
poor
cheek
plies
has of
sell h
she th
the ba
cause
See
the s
"ther
have
and s(
munit
quarr
Th(
thoug
say, v
it. H
you w
that p
and g
There
of del
looks
that s(
to his
keeps
Do

one word of advice (and I leave you to the torture of your ig-norance)—don't, for the sake of your friends, (if any you have) expose yourself any further. I am done with you, so I wish you a safe arrival at that place for which only you are a fit subject—the Lunatic Asylum.

*Rambler.*

The May 10 issue replies with another letter:

*For the Daily Journal.*

### TO RAMBLER.

Must apologize. I merely glanced at your doggerel, and natur-ally supposing that you had friends in "H—l," (or *Hannibal*, as you are pleased to interpret it.) I just thought you seemed to need someone to take care of and give you advice, and considered it my duty, in a friendly way, to tell you that you are going too far. However, you turned it off into Hannibal, very well, and I give you credit for your ingenuity.

You "will not again condescend to notice me," you say. Cruel "Rambler!" thus to annihilate me, because I cannot appreciate your poetry!

Resp'ly
Your Friend
and Admirer
*Grumbler.*

In the *Hannibal Daily Journal,* May 12, a new cor-respondent comes upon the scene:

*For the Daily Journal.*

Mr. Editor:

Several articles have recently appeared in the *Daily Journal,* over the signature of "Rambler" (truly appropriate).

It is really amusing to every intelligent and intellectual mind, to see how consequential some coxcombs are. The parlor is too remote a place, and not conspicuous enough to reveal the overflowing affections of the H-e-a-r-t.  So the obscure (yes too ob-scure) columns of the public press are resorted to, by the venerable writer, as being in keeping with, and a more appropriate way of infusing the sentiments of an all loving h-e-a-r-t into the mind of one of the misses of the city of Hannibal. . . . It is desired, that the world should awake from its slumbers, and learn that there is one loving heart extant.  "Vanity of Vanities!" such may be the custom from whence he hails, but I can assure Mr. "Rambler," that the above course will never win the affections and admira-tion of the young misses in this latitude; such a course is not con-genial to their nature.

Peter Pencilcase's Son,<br>John Snooks.

Hannibal, May 12, 1853.

In the May 13 issue Rambler answers this attack:

*For the Daily Journal.*

Mr. Editor:

In your paper of yesterday I find that I have attracted the notice of a ———— fool.  I had fondly hoped that I would not again be troubled with that class of individuals.  But alas for me! I was doomed to be disappointed.  Here, now, comes poor pitiful "Snooks," charging upon me.  I am wholly unable to compre-hend his "pitiful" article.  It has been subjected to criticisms of several and none have been able to make "sense" of anything he has said.  He calls me a "Cox-Comb."  I will not say that he belongs to that long-eared race of animals that have more head and ears than brains.  It is the custom from whence I hailed for a man to act just as I have, without having every "puny puppy" that runs the streets, whining at his heels.—His piece is couched in exceedingly bad taste.

*Rambler.*

The May 13 *Journal* contains also an editorial note which may be the departing bow of the editor *pro tem.*, or it may be Orion Clemens's note that he has returned and is taking over the editor's chair: "Rambler and his enemies must stop their 'stuff.' It is a great bore to us, and doubtless to the public generally."

If we accept the statement of his biographer that Sam Clemens wrote "To Mary in H—l" *(sic)*, and take Mark Twain's word for it that he wrote the "snappy foot-note" to it, we must infer that the altercation was staged by the boy to revive interest in the paper. It appears from the evidence in the bound volumes of the papers that the editors of the *Messenger* were more progressive than Orion Clemens. They published a business directory of their advertisers, and were more enterprising in securing locals. It must have been disturbing to Sam that the other Whig paper, which they regarded somewhat as an interloper, should be outstripping them. Albert Bigelow Paine's emphasis upon the down-hill condition of the *Journal* indicates that the humiliation of it stayed in Mark Twain's memory.[23] Furthermore, the boy was restive probably because he was having to expend his energies in hard routine work.[24] Now he had a chance again to try his hand at amusing the public. His former effort had been successful, perhaps, from his point of view; so he may have invented a second battle of words. He himself, one can imagine, was both "Rambler" and "Grumbler," as well as "John Snooks," whom he seems to have intended to be identified with himself. In a column which his brother allowed him to edit a week or so later is a squib signed "Rambler." "Peter Pencilcase's Son, John Snooks" belongs in a class with his other experiments with pen names.

[23] A. B. P., I, 89.          [24] *Ibid.*, I, 85.

The fiction of "Rambler" as a "gorgeous journeyman tailor," a "simpering coxcomb," if fiction it was, may have been invented first by Sam Clemens to cover the fact that he was dabbling in poetry, and may have lingered in the memory of Mark Twain after a lapse of seventeen years. In the John Snooks letter the phrase "venerable writer" may have been inserted to avert suspicion that he was writing poetry. "Puny puppy" in "Rambler's" answer to the letter seems to hark back to his battle with "Local" and to be the boy's way of assuming to himself a part in the fiction.    There is the alternative, of course, of taking "Rambler" as a real correspondent of the *Journal* and a real journeyman tailor from Quincy, and the rest as the young editor's joke at his expense.    But if Mark Twain's statement in "My First Literary Venture" that he was the critic of the poem—"Grumbler"—and his biographer's statement that he wrote it—that he was "Rambler"—can both be accepted without literary discount, it would almost justify the conclusion that Mark Twain had an adolescent verse-writing period in the spring, a year or more after he was awakened by the page out of the "Life of Joan of Arc."    If so, he did not think enough of it to have it recorded in his biography further than to acknowledge satirically three attempts.    Two other poems and some feature stories signed "Rambler" are of interest from this point of view.    It is impossible to identify the "obituary poems" referred to on page 4.

If May 6-13 was Sam Clemens's second week as editor of the *Daily Journal*—it is in the May 13 issue that the last reply of "Rambler" appears, along with the note calling off the controversy—it seems safe to assign to the youngster another contribution on his last editorial page. In the first column is this note:

All our red headed friends should read the article over the signature "A Son of Adam." We like the racy humor of his style of writing, and invite him to continue his correspondence for this paper.

For the Journal.

In the next column is printed the following:

### "Oh, She has a Red Head"

Turn up your nose at red heads![25] What ignorance! I pity your lack of taste. . . .

What gives to the bright flowers of the field—those tinted by nature's own hand—the power to charm the eye and purify the mind of man, and his thoughts to heaven, but the softening touches of the all-admired red!

Unless the delicate blushes of the rose mingled upon the cheek of youth—though the features be perfect in form and proportion, and the eye beam with celestial sweetness, no one will pronounce their possessor beautiful.

And the flag under which the proud sons of American sires find protection in every nation under heaven, is rendered more conspicuous and beautiful by red which mingles in its sacred "stars and stripes."

The Falls of Niagara are never seen to advantage, unless embellished with the rainbow's hues.

The midnight storm may howl, and the thunder loud may roar; but how are its grandeur and beauty heightened but by the lightning's vivid flash?

[25] "The color of Mark Twain's hair in his early life has been variously referred to as red, black, and brown. It was, in fact, as stated by McMurry, "sandy in boyhood, deepening later to that rich mahogany tone known as auburn."—A. B. P., I, 77.

Mrs. Thomas Bailey Aldrich, *Crowding Memories* (p. 151): "Mr. Clemens was at this time thirty-one or two years old . . . head covered with thick, shaggy, red-colored hair."

Most animals are fond of red—and *all children,* before their tastes are corrupted, and their judgments perverted, are fond of red.

The Romans anciently regarded red hair as necessary to a beautiful lady!

Thomas Jefferson's hair was red—and Jesus Christ, our Savior—"The chief among ten thousand, and altogether lovely," is said to have had auburn hair—and, although it is not stated in so many words, I have but little doubt that Adam's hair was red —for he was made of "red earth" (as his name indicates); and as the name Adam was given to him *after* he was made, it is pretty clear he must have had red hair! And the great probability is that Eve's hair was red also, she being made of a 'rib' from Adam, who was made of a lump of "red earth."

Now Adam and Eve before they sinned, are generally supposed to have been the most lovely and beautiful of creation, and they, in all probability were both "red headed."

But you, O ye deteriorated black-headed descendants of an illustrious stock! have no more taste than to glory in the evidence of your departure from original beauty! I'm ashamed of you; I don't know but you'll repudiate your ancestry, and deny you are descended from Adam next.

A Son of Adam.[26]

# §5

ALBERT BIGELOW PAINE says that Orion afterwards accused himself because he did not see that if he had allowed Sam a freer hand on the *Journal,* the youth might have made the paper successful.[27] It appears that after his return from St. Louis he did encourage the boy to continue editorial work. The note recommending the writer of the apology for red heads may have been written by Orion

---

[26] *Cf.* the "Blabbing Government Secrets" sketch, pp. 117-18 above.
[27] A. B. P., I, 90.

Clemens in pursuance of this policy. Whether the "unparalleled number of thirty-three new subscribers" motivated the innovation, or whether he became convinced that he was on the eve of losing the boy if he did not give him more recognition, he introduced a new feature into the *Daily Journal* for May, 1853—"Our Assistant's Column." In it, seemingly, Sam Clemens makes his début as a columnist. Into it the seventeen-year-old editor put raps at rival editors, comments on local happenings, especially when they offered him a chance for a pun, notices of spiritualistic activities, bits of satire upon woman's foibles and ambitions, "selected material," containing curious facts and matters of useful information. In it he found humorous vent for his rage at the cruelty of a drunken brute and for his interest in what was going on in New York, in the records of river boats, and in everything connected with the fortunes of parties bound for California. The "Assistant" appears in only three issues of the paper. The three columns form the fourth section of what seem to be genuine Mark Twain juvenilia.

From the *Hannibal Daily Journal*, May 23, 1853, page 3:

## OUR ASSISTANT'S COLUMN

*Small Pox.*—Two cases of this disease were put ashore here yesterday from the Jeannie Deans. They were both children— one five, and the other seven years of age. They will most probably die. Immediately after landing, they were conveyed out of the city, and therefore, as to the disease spreading, there need be no alarm whatever.

The cases were children of German immigrants just arrived from the old country; they stopped but a day or two in St. Louis.

*Woman's Rights and Man's Rights.*—On Saturday night, one Mr. Jaques got drunk and proceeded to show his utter contempt for all such new-fangled humbugs as "Woman's Rights," and his own peculiar and exalted ideas of "Man's Rights" by unmercifully beating and maltreating his wife and children, and disturbing the peace generally. Quite a forcible illustration.

But the "People's Rights" should be cared for; and the gentleman ought to be ducked, ridden on a rail, tarred and feathered, and politely requested to bundle up his "duds" and make himself scarce.

_____

*More Borrowing.*—The McDonough (Ill.) Independent has copied the article contributed to this paper by "B. H. W.," entitled "A Triplet Table," without giving the credit. It's a hard matter to learn you "Suckers" manners.—This is the first offense of the 'Independent,' however, and we don't want to "hurt your pheelinks"—but sir, some of you cotemporaries over there on the other side of the drink would steal the Declaration of Independence and palm it off for original matter, if they had half a chance!

_____

The weather is rather warm—ladies have commenced the usual amusements of the season, viz: fainting, fanning, slopping about in the mud, &c.,—fat, lazy "niggers" begin to sweat and look greasy—chills no longer considered an affliction.

_____

It is cowardly to carry weapons of any kind—especially a "brick in your hat."

_____

Several negroes got to quarreling in the street yesterday, and went out of town to have a set to, but were separated before much damage was done.

_____

["The Burial of Sir Abner Gilstrap . . ." Parody of "The Burial of Sir John Moore." Reproduced and discussed on pages 135-39 below.]

*Delaine and Love.*—The Local of the Albany Transcript states that no man under thirty-five can sit beside nine yards of delaine without becoming afflicted with the palpitation of the heart.

From the *Hannibal Daily Journal*, May 25, 1853, page 3:

## OUR ASSISTANT'S COLUMN

The Assistant Editor of the Messenger has put in his opinion about the editorial-pilfering affair—thinks we are afraid somebody will steal our little squib about the weather—supposes it was original, &c.

Come, now, Mr. Assistant, you're inclined to be facetious. You ought never to bite till you're bitten—and we fear that will not be soon, for we haven't discovered any thing in your department of the paper worth stealing for some time. Never speak when it's not your "put-in." Remember that, you are young and inexperienced, and need a little friendly advice occasionally, and we give it freely and without charge.

---

The St. Louis Spirit World is driving ahead at the old nine days' wonder. The spirits seem very fond of writing, and keep the people posted on all the important events that transpire in the celestial world.

---

Miss Lucy Stone is lecturing on Woman's Rights in Philadelphia. Wonder if she wouldn't like to cut wood; bring water; shoe horses; be a deck hand, or something of that sort? She has a right to do it; and if she wants to carry a hod, we say, let her alone.

---

Interesting ruins of ancient cities have lately been discovered in Mexico. One of the cities is three miles in length. Ruined temples and other edifices, human skeletons, mines, etc., have been found. The search for wonders is to be continued. This is interesting news for the antiquarian.

---

The man who was delighted with such unspeakable joy, has been removed to the deaf and dumb asylum.—[Ex.]

And the man that "Struck Billy Patterson," who has lately been heard from, has not checked his pugilistic propensities. He is now preparing to strike—for higher wages.

---

## DOMINICAN REPUBLIC—QUARREL WITH THE CLERGY—SANTANA VICTORIOUS

The Dominican Republic has been violently agitated with a quarrel between the Chief thereof and the Archbishop of St. Domingo.

The latter refused to take the oath of fealty, and said he would exile himself before he would "take an oath to that heretical constitution."

The President gave him promptly his passport, ordered a national vessel to bear him away, and furnished him with funds to support him. "Sir," said he to the Archbishop, "I have always been and am very religious—very Catholic. But the clergy must be kept aloof from politics. They have threatened to disturb the State; this must not be." Thereupon a decree was issued "disposing of the Archbishop."

On second thought, however, the ecclesiastic concluded to yield to the civil authority, and made a declaration of his fealty to the Republic, with great pomp, on the 4th of April.

---

It is estimated that considerably upwards of ten thousand cattle alone have crossed the river at St. Joseph, destined for California. How many have crossed at other points, we have not understood. But it is very certain an immense amount of stock will cross the plains, this spring, cattle, sheep, horses, and mules. The number of cattle it is supposed will exceed *one hundred thous-*

*and head.*  Persons can now readily account for the high prices of beef and stock.—[St. Joseph Gaz.]

---

The grass on the other side of the river is said to be getting very good now.  Many of the emigrants are now on their winding way, having bid adieu for a while to busy scenes of civilization, to try the realities of a life upon the uninhabited plains, save by the red man and the game.  They are in search of what a wise man once said is the root of all evil—gold.  We wish them a safe journey and prosperous time.—[St. Joseph Gaz.]

From the *Hannibal Daily Journal*, May 26, 1853, page 3:

## OUR ASSISTANT'S COLUMN

The Courier says we have been advocating mob law.  Nonsense!  A fellow who whips his wife is not a man, and therefore can be excused properly from a "ride on a rail," because "cruelty to animals" is objectionable, and not because it is "mob law."

---

We are unable to furnish the usual amount of reading matter to-day, on account of the sickness of a principal hand, and the press of job-work.

---

*The Next World.*—A man writing in the Spiritual Telegraph says he was so unfortunate several years since, as to fall off a bluff near the Ogeechie River, one hundred feet high, and was very agreeably astonished to find himself in heaven, or at least imagined himself there!  He thought it a beautiful piece of territory, with hills, valleys, flowers, &c.  He struck down a winding path and presently came to a river, which he explored with one of the celestial inhabitants, and after seeing divers queer sights, he suddenly came to himself on a pile of rocks, under the bluff.  This is a hard story; for tumbling off a precipice one hundred feet high, and landing on a bed of stones, with no other

damage than a few hours' insensibility is a right tough yarn.—
We are not astonished that such a fall as he got knocked him
out of this world and into another; but that the gentleman ever
got back to tell about it is what we wonder at!

---

From fifteen to twenty thousand persons are continually con-
gregated around the new Crystal Palace in New York city, and
drunkenness and debauching are carried on to their fullest extent.

---

## QUICKEST TRIP OF THE SEASON

The Die Vernon arrived here this morning at 45 minutes
past 5 o'clock—left St. Louis this last evening at 4 o'clock!
Where is the *Messenger's* report of the Jeannie Deans' quick
trip? The Jeannie on that quick trip left St. Louis at 15 minutes
past 4 o'clock, and arrived here at 40 minutes past 6 o'clock next
morning. Now the *Messenger* was misinformed, or just wanted
to blow. Which was it, Mr. Messenger? Come out; you are
beaten badly.

Die Vernon's time,    13 hours, 45 m.
Jeannie Deans' time,  14 hours, 20 m.

---

When Jennie Lind was in the United States it was said she
intended to expend large sums of money in establishing schools
and other useful institutions in Sweden; and since she has been
in her native country it has been declared that she has fulfilled
her promises; but the Berlin correspondent of the Literary
Gazette says it is all a hoax—she has done nothing of the kind;
and is not near so liberal as she "used to was."

---

The office of Corporation Attorney of New York City pays
well. The fees of this official for the yr. 1852 were over twenty
thousand dollars! Who wouldn't care to take the gentleman's
place?

# HANNIBAL JOURNAL.
## DAILY.

VOLUME I.     HANNIBAL, MO.: FRIDAY EVENING, MAY 6, 1853.     NUMBER 47.

## FRESH FANCY AND STAPLE GOODS!!!
RICH AND BEAUTIFUL!!!

### SPRING AND SUMMER STYLES.
COLLINS & BREED,
MAIN STREET, HANNIBAL, MISSOURI.

Martin & Brother,
No 118 Main St. St. L. tts
No. 113 Broadway, New Yo k.

NEVER FAILING REMEDY!!!

HOLLOWAY'S OINTMENT.

SPALDING & ROGERS'

### CIRCUS COMPANY,
ON BOARD THE

### FLOATING PALACE,
WILL Exhibit in HANNIBAL, on Tuesday the 17th day of May, Performance at 2 and 1-2 O'clock, P. M.

A Great Reduction in the Prices of
## DRY-GOODS!!
And in all the different Kinds of Goods usually kept in Hannibal!!

Wholesale or Retail!

LARGE LOT OF CLOTHING.

SPRING TRADE. 1853.
WEBSTER, MARSH & CO.,
Wholesale Clothiers,
No. 80, Main Street St. Louis, Mo.

THE INDIAN CHIEF
THIS NEW HOME,

TRIPLETT, McFADIN & CO.,
Commission and Forwarding Merchants,
ST. LOUIS, MO.

E. M. MOFFETT,    THOS. S. MILLER.
Wholesale Grocer and Commission Merchant,
CORNER LEVEE AND HILL STREET,
HANNIBAL, MO.

DR. M. F. BROWN.

PAGE OF THE *Hannibal Journal* AS IT APPEARED ABOUT THE TIME
SAM CLEMENS PUBLISHED THE "ASSISTANT'S COLUMN."

Dan Rice's Hippodrome and Menagerie will be in Louisville on the 31st of this month.[28]

The means of identifying the columns as Sam Clemens's work lies in "The Parody on the Burial of Sir John Moore," which appears at the end of the first column, and which, in "My First Literary Venture," Mark Twain says that he wrote. After the episode of the woodcuts, the author says:

Being satisfied with this effort, I looked around for other worlds to conquer, and it struck me that it would make good, interesting matter to charge the editor of a neighboring country paper with a piece of gratuitous rascality and "see him squirm."

I did it, putting the article into the form of a parody on the "Burial of Sir John Moore"—and a pretty crude parody it was too.

From the files of the *Hannibal Journal* it appears that the parody was not invented merely to satisfy the young editor's ambition to furnish his patrons with interesting reading; but that it was the outcome of a quarrel of several months' duration. The town of Bloomington in Macon County, Missouri, in 1850 the county seat, was a place of sufficient importance to aspire to secure the Hannibal and St. Joseph Railroad through its boundaries. Much political maneuvering seems to have preceded the location of those early lines, and Bloomington had lost the fight. The newspapers of all the towns interested were active in the controversy. Bloomington had two newspapers, the *Journal* and the *Republican*. The editor of the *Bloomington Republican*, one Abner Gilstrap, who was something of a

[28] Mr. Willard S. Morse, 526 Adelaide Drive, Santa Monica, California, has embodied in a privately printed book from photostatic copies of Sam Clemens's Hannibal *Journal* writings all the pieces described in this chapter and in Mr. C. J. Armstrong's "Mark Twain's Early Writings Discovered," *Missouri Historical Review*, XXIV (July, 1930), 485-502.

fire-eater, had charged certain Hannibal business men, responsible, as he thought, for the success of Hannibal and the slight to Bloomington, with having bribed the railway authorities, by holding out to them a vision of immense profits to be realized from the sale of new town lots. Abner Gilstrap was a candidate for the legislature, and his political opponents made the most of his quarrels. The *Bloomington Journal* reprinted with satisfaction attacks of other newspapers upon its rival. The *Hannibal Journal* was not more deeply implicated, apparently, than the other Hannibal papers, both Whig and Democrat; but the wit of the young editor had got his squibs quoted in other newspapers of northern Missouri, and Abner Gilstrap had thrust back in his May 11 issue with some sort of Dialogue between the *Bloomington Republican* and the *Hannibal Journal*, apparently in verse. The May 20 *Journal* contains three notices of the Dialogue. The *Bloomington Journal* is quoted: "The editor of the Republican has had a fit of 'Ass-tericks' since he wrote that dialogue between the Hannibal Journal and himself, which lasted some time." In a longer article the "circus-man who presides over the *Republican*" is quoted as objecting to the liberty that his rival papers have taken with his name:

The uncourteous, undignified course which the editors of the Chronicle and Hannibal Journal have pursued, of using the individual name of editors is adopted by the Bloomington Journal. "Our Friend Abner," "Poor innocent Abner." This is not tolerated by the *Rules Editorial*.

But he will defend himself "even to the kicking over of skunks." What the *Hannibal Journal* first attacked, he says, was "selected matter," inserted in the paper by the foreman.   The editor knew nothing about it till the paper came out.   The last of the three notices quotes the "devil" of the *Republican* as assuming responsibility for errors in the Dialogue:

Many errors occur in the reading matter, and particularly in the Dialogue between the Hannibal Journal and Bloomington Republican.  Our devil says he done that on purpose, and pleads justification as follows:

And now at this day comes the Devil in propria persona; and, for plea, says, that he has been tampering with the mental and moral condition of the editor of the Hannibal Journal, and having a perfect right to do so, drawn from long and established usage, he avers, and so charges, that the Editor of the Bloomington Republican, had no right to interfere, nor in any way to expose his operations, wherefore he prays judgment, &c.

Devil.

The *Hannibal Journal* appends a comment:

We don't know which is the more incomprehensible, the absurd paragraphs indicted [*sic*] by Mr. Gilstrap, himself, or the mysterious ones of *The Devil*, his master, who, it seems, has at last come to the assistance of his faithful servant, the Editor of the Republican.

There is no way of proving that the altercation up to this point was conducted by Sam Clemens.   Orion may have begun the quarrel, but three days later, in his column in the *Journal*, the young editor printed the parody.   He was leaving Hannibal; so he would bury Abner Gilstrap. The "Iron Horse," of course, refers to the fact that the railway had been the neighboring editor's undoing.   The note prefacing the lines is quoted with them:

We have pondered long and well over the Bloomington Republican's mysterious rhymes in that paper of the 11th, but can't discover what the editor was driving at, or what he intended to mean, and don't suppose he knows himself.  We could guess better at the meaning of Egyptian hieroglyphics than his verses.— However, will reply with a random shot of some sort:

The Burial of Sir Abner Gilstrap, Editor of the Bloomington "Republican."

———

Parody on "The Burial of Sir John Moore."

———

Not a drum was heard, nor a funeral note,
    As his corpse to the ramparts we hurried;
Not a soldier discharged his farewell shot,
    O'er the grave where our hero we buried.
            —Burial of Sir John Moore.

Not a sound was heard, nor a funeral note,
    As his carcass through town we hurried;
Not e'en an obituary we wrote,
    In respect for the rascal we buried.

We buried him darkly, at dead of night—
    The dirt with our pitchforks turning;
By the moonbeams' grim and ghastly light,
    And our candles dimly burning.

No useless coffin confined his breast,
    Nor in sheet nor in shirt we bound him;
But he lay like an Editor taking his rest,
    With a Hannibal Journal round him.

Few and *very* short were the *prayers* we said,
    And we felt not a pang of sorrow;
But we mused, as we gazed on the wretch now defunct—
    *Oh! where will he be tomorrow?*

The "Iron Horse" will snort o'er his head,
   And the notes of its whistle upbraid him;
But nothing he'll care if they let him sleep on,
   In the grave where his nonsense hath laid him.

Slowly, but gladly we laid him down,
   From the field of his fame fresh and gory;
We carved not a line, we raised not a stone,
   To mark where we buried a tory.[29]

Less than a week after the last "Assistant's Column" appeared in the May 26 issue of the *Journal*, Sam Clemens left for St. Louis with the purpose of making money enough to buy a ticket for New York. At the top of the editor's column in the May 27 issue is the notice, "*Wanted!* An Apprentice of the Printing Business. Apply soon."

Orion Clemens seems to have missed his assistant sorely. He failed to get out the *Daily* through most of June, and in August he announced that a minister in the town would act as editor. Toward the last of September, 1853, he sold the *Journal* to William T. League.

## §6

THESE EARLY writings will not suggest the need of any new rating of Mark Twain. It is doubtful whether anything critical or original could be discovered that would much affect the judgment that Albert Bigelow Paine's biography and the twenty-five volumes of his writings in the Harper edition have put the world in the way of making. But when taken in their context in the *Journal*, these records do give the impression that Sam Clemens's town

[29] The *Hannibal Daily Journal*, May 23, 1853 (also in the May 26 *Weekly Journal*).

was somewhat more of a place in 1850-53 than the critics
have given it credit for, and that it had lived pretty well
up to its promise of five years before. It had five newspapers in the early fifties: the *Missouri Courier*, a Democratic weekly, the weekly and the tri-weekly *Whig
Messenger*, the weekly and the daily *Hannibal Journal*.
It had building restrictions: within a certain area buildings must be of brick. It was as much interested in the
building of plank roads to surrounding towns as it now is
in the building of hard roads:

> Plank roads are the order of the day among our friends of
> the *"little village of Hannibal,"* above us. They are projecting a
> plank road across the Schnai Carte Bottom in Illinois, to connect
> with Pittsfield and Griggsville. They are also about extending
> the New London Road through Ralls County [Mo.] and are
> also projecting another to Philadelphia, in the western part of the
> county of Marion. Such enterprise is not only commendable but
> must result in great good to the country generally. . . .[30]

In the town were manufactured "omnibuses, carriages,
gigs, and wagons." Boat-building was its proudest enterprise: "BOAT BUILDING AT HANNIBAL: Two very large
steamboats are now being built at the boatyard above this
city. One of them is said to be within a foot or two of the
largest boat on the river."[31] An "anatomical boot and
shoemaker" appealed to the public for patronage, and
"Antagonistic Dentistry" was apparently the latest word
in that profession. The "Daguerrean artists" must have
pursued a thriving business, from the number of their advertisements. Brainard and Lambert had "lying in Bear
Creek at the foot of Main Street" their "Floating Daguer-

---

[30] Quoted from the *Louisiana Record* in the *Hannibal Daily Journal*, March 22,
1853, p. 2.
[31] *Western Union*, May 15, 1851.

rean Gallery." Leer and Arbogast, "tobacconers," must have been patronized by Sam Clemens: "Leer and Arbogast are the true friends of the 'Devil.' We do not make this astounding assertion unprepared to make it good. The 'imps of darkness' belonging to this office were presented by these gentlemen with a fine bunch of 'Princeps' a few days since.[32] Another *Journal* squib is evidently a thrust at a rival dealer who wrote verses.

*You will please insert this card in your paper:* A Reward of 500 cigars for the man, woman, or child, wise man or wild man, simpleton or anything of the kind; the above reward is offered to anyone who will this modern Lord Byron find, who scribbled a piece of would-be poetry in the Tri-Weekly Messenger of Tuesday last. Our reward cigars are a lot of Missouri tobies, just received from the country, for a dead horse, in other words, a bad debt. We think Mr. Barnum will give a handsome price for this Lord Byron, with his poetry pasted on his forhead.

Yours respectfully,

Leer and Arbogast.

Hannibal was also a church town. There was a first and a second Presbyterian church, and the North and South Methodist churches, besides the Christian, Baptist, and Episcopal congregations. A problem discussed in the newspapers was whether the Catholic church should be admitted.[33]

Schools were as enthusiastically supported as churches. The development of a stable state of society depended upon these institutions. There was the Marion Female Seminary in the basement of the Christian Church, and the Reverend Daniel Emerson started the English and

[32] *Journal*, July 1, 1852.

[33] Lyman Beecher's *A Plea for the West* (1835) represents the attitude expressed in these discussions.

Classical School in the basement of the Presbyterian Church. Besides, there was Miss McDonald's School and the Hannibal Female Academy. Miss Horr, who had been selected for Sam's first teacher, was honored with an editorial note of approval still.

The "cotillion parties in the city hall" were conducted with a good deal of formality.

The town had frequent minstrel shows:

*Alabama Joe!*—J. A. North's celebrated troupe of Ethiopian Minstrels gave two of their unique and select concerts at "Bower's City Hotel," to fashionable audiences on Monday and Tuesday evenings. After the exhibition on the last night, the ladies and gentlemen remained at the Hotel, and whiled away a few hours in the fascinating pleasures of the "mazzy dance." The troupe left yesterday for Keokuk.[34]

The "Floating Palace," a show-boat, came occasionally to the wharf. "The furor attending the exhibition of the 'Palace'," its advertisement assured the public, "falls short of that excited by Jenny Lind only." The "performance" of the Nightingale Operatic Company, it was promised, would be "recherché." There were, besides, balloon ascensions, steamboat launchings, Dan Rice and his Hippodrome, entertainments by the Histrionic Association, by Professor Barton "the Wizard of the West," "Spirit Rappings," political speeches reported at full length, and lectures advertised by the Kentucky Colonization Society, the American Tract Society, the Prohibitionists, the Hannibal Medical Society, and the Hannibal Library Institute.

There is a good deal of evidence in these papers—in the advertisements, in "fillers" down the columns, in the political speeches quoted, and in the accounts of town

[34] *Journal*, Dec. 20, 1849.

activities—that Hannibal had a more distinctly literary atmosphere than towns in Missouri have today. The fillers were of three kinds. There are many anecdotes from Greek mythology and many references to such classical writers as Cicero and Demosthenes. There are allusions of various sorts to current writers of note. Thackeray's opinion of America is quoted, and Dickens's account of the origin of *Pickwick Papers*. Captain Marryat's death is noticed, and there is a comment about the sum Hawthorne received for writing his biography of Pierce, and on his appointment as consul to Liverpool. There is much comment on Harriet Beecher Stowe, with notices of books written in answer to her "blackmanity." Hints about Daniel Webster's devotion to the bottle, much reference to Byron, Bulwer-Lytton, Macaulay, and "the everlasting Mrs. Trollope." And, lastly, eighteenth-century writers receive much notice. Samuel Johnson is the favorite. It almost appears that if a column was short of material an inch or two, Sam or Orion Clemens turned through Boswell for an anecdote to fill it out. Besides, there are frequent allusions to Young, Goldsmith, Pope, and Burns; less frequent, to Boswell, Sir Isaac Newton, Hogarth, Dr. Bentley, Bolingbroke, Hannah More, Gray, and Cowper. There are more anecdotes about Franklin than about any other eighteenth-century American. It appears to have been in better form to quote from an eighteenth-century writer than from more recent authors.

The admiration for Goldsmith, Young, Pope, and Gray is shown, also, in imitations of their style. Not only was there an evident town interest in books, but verse-writing was as much the vogue then as now. E. H. Turner, tobacconist, appears as something of a town laureate.

The *Whig Messenger* published his verses—usually of the Country Churchyard type:

> Here pensive silence spreads her noiseless wings,
> And o'er my soul a sweet enchantment flings.

The *Messenger* reported also that Mr. Turner was collaborating with Mr. John Woodward on a "three-act domestic drama," and the same paper announced a poetry contest:

> TO POETS: Our carrier authorizes us to offer an elegant morocco-bound Annual for 1853, and a volume of the Tri-Weekly Messenger, for the best New Year's Address, of not less than one hundred lines. Manuscripts to be submitted to the editor for decision. Offers to be handed in by the twentieth of December.

The *Journal*, not to be outdone in encouraging the Muse, proposed, the next spring, to print in the new *Daily* writings of the young women of the female academies—from *The Bouquet* and *The Mignonette*, their school papers.

> THE BOUQUET.—A very pleasant, as well as useful custom in two of our schools. Once in every two weeks a small manuscript pamphlet is publicly read. This pamphlet is made up of contributions from the scholars. If the three lovely editresses of the periodical published at Miss McDonald's school will give their consent, we should like to print some extracts from that as well as from the "Bouquet," of which we have obtained the use through the kindness of Misses Smith and Patrick. From this we extract the first *local* article, because our readers will be best pleased with writings bearing such unmistakable evidence of originality.[35]

The local editor of the *Whig Messenger,* the next month, after a visit to Miss McDonald's school, reported in a one-fourth column eulogy, having heard "the recital

---

[35] *Hannibal Daily Journal,* April 15, 1853.

of the 'Mignonette'." It emulated the *Journal*, apparently: "We shall from time to time give our readers extracts from this paper." The verses of the young women appear in all the Hannibal papers over such pen names as "Inez," "Imogene," "Blanche"; "Lilly" published a political apologue on Whig and Democrat.

There can be no doubt that Sam Clemens, after his adolescent awakening when he discovered the story of Joan of Arc,[36] had a verse-writing period which he probably kept secret, and which he did not think enough of to record in his biography further than to acknowledge satirically three attempts. At any rate, two other poems besides his lines "To Miss Katie of H—l," signed "Rambler," take on interest beyond their merit. Both appeared a day earlier than "Love Concealed" and are in the same vein. One is in the *Hannibal Courier* of May 5. The other is in the *Daily Journal* of the same date and is quoted in the weekly *Journal* of May 12.

The literary antiquarian is tempted, of course, to assign to Sam Clemens almost any verse in these *Journals* that appears over an assumed name. It is all of a kind. Love's sorrows is a theme that is rung in all changes. The youth shied at being known as a poet, however, as his device for printing "Love Concealed" shows—with his reference to it as "doggerel" and to himself as the "venerable writer." It was probably not known in the town who "Rambler" was.

And at the same time, while he was publishing these romantic effusions, he seems also to have been interested in comic verse. The May 7, 1853, issue of the *Journal*, which, as has been said, he put out in Orion's absence,

[36] A. B. P., I, 81.

contains the following without the customary notice, "Clipped":

Married in Podunk on the 3rd ultimo, by the Rev. D. Willis, Mr. H. Hoe with Miss Anne Handle, all of that city.

> How useless an Handle without any Hoe,
> And useless a Hoe without any Handle;
> No better a winter without any snow,
> Or a candlestick minus a candle.

> But here, joined in one, the Handle and Hoe
> With life's rugged journey, smooth over,
> And each prove a helper in this world below,
> Till death shall hoe both to another.

The lines in the *Journal* that the reader most desires to associate with Sam Clemens, purport to be quoted. They would appear to be an early use of the "tall talk" of the river, anticipating a passage in *Life on the Mississippi*.[36a] A notice is quoted from the *Palmyra Whig*[37] suggesting that the railroad be built from Palmyra to Quincy "by the time Hannibal finishes the cut-off." "The above reminds us," the *Journal* says, "of the desperate resolutions of a young gentleman whose 'gal' had slighted him. He expressed his feelings as follows:

> "I'll flog the *Young Earthquake*,
> The earth I will physic
> Volcanoes I'll strangle,
> Or choke with the phthisic."

---

[36a] See *Life on the Mississippi*, chap. III.

[37] Sam Clemens's comments on other North Missouri newspapers frequently called forth such retaliation as that from the *Paris Mercury*, quoted in the May 13, 1853, *Journal*, before Sam left, June 1. It may be that Orion's rebuke, together with the memory of others of the same kind, motivated the boy's leaving. He frequently mentioned newspapers that stole from the *Journal* without acknowledgment. The *Mercury*, after quoting his reference, said, "The above very courteous tid-bit was perpetrated by some indiscreet youth or ill-bred scamp in the office of the *Journal*, during the editor's absence in St. Louis. . . . Mr. Clemens owes it to us to retract. . . ."

All this was merely the sort of thing "which all human beings churn out in their youth," as he said of Mary Baker Eddy's verses,[38] but it has, nevertheless, some significance in connection with a view of Mark Twain that has developed since his death—the view that, along with his firm and persistent realism, there was a romantic strain in his temperament which accounts for many of the contradictions in his mind and writings. In this early verse-writing his romantic vein found abortive expression. That it was abortive was due in part, doubtless, to the disillusioned mood of his father and of the more careful thinkers among the pioneers in his community, but there is another hint that cannot be neglected in this connection.

In a speech at the time he was made a member of the Author's Club in London, when Sir Spencer Walpole spoke in commendation of his writings, Mark Twain said that there are "certain heredities that come down to us which our writings of the present day may be traced to. I, for instance, read the *Walpole Letters when I was a boy*.[39] I absorbed them, gathered in their grace, wit, and humor, and put them away to be used by-and-by. One does that so unconsciously with the things one really likes."[40] "When I was a boy" may refer to his Hannibal days, or to the days of his *Wanderjähre*, or to his River days. If it could be discovered that the Library Institute possessed the letters of Horace Walpole, or that they were available at the Sign of the Big Book, the chief bookstore in Hannibal, it would offer a large range for surmise. During the last half of Mark Twain's life his adventures in reading were intimately related to his real life, but he appar-

[38] *Christian Science*, p. 106.
[39] My italics.            [40] *Speeches*, p. 215.

ently had interests during his early years which he could not trust the people around him to share. An interest in the letters of Walpole, with their rational and sophisticated outlook, would help to account for the repression of Sam Clemens's romantic instinct. The youthful editor *pro tem.* spoke of himself humorously as a "rational man." The author of *Tom Sawyer* and *Huckleberry Finn* was due to have a more extended romantic period than we have any record of in the case of Mark Twain. An interest in the Walpole letters would account, also, for a certain quaintness in his personality and in his literary style, the suggestion of the earlier century.

There is only slight evidence in the local papers that the region had a part in the humor of the 1830-1860 development described by Franklin J. Meine.[41]  The inference would rather be that because it was sub-literary such writing was thought unworthy of a place in sheets devoted to important political affairs. Such books as Longstreet's *Georgia Scenes* (1835), Thompson's *Major Jones's Courtship* (1844), and Hooper's *Adventures of Captain Simon Suggs* (1845) were doubtless lying about the printing office or on the counters of the town book-stores, and would be a challenge to Sam Clemens to try his hand in

---

[41] Franklin J. Meine, Introduction to *Tall Tales from the Southwest.* "Tall Talking," however, was as popular a type of frontier diversion in Missouri as elsewhere. The term is the title of a squib in the November 19, 1846, *Hannibal Gazette:* "I defy the buzzing of the professional insect who has just sat down, and I defy his futile attempts to penetrate with his puny sting, the interstices of my impervious covering." A hundred miles away in Missouri a pioneer woman had gained the title of the Great Interrogator because of her habit of calling to every passerby, "What's the news?" When she called to a neighbor, "What's the news of the Indians?" he replied, "Very, very bad, Madam, . . . Tecumseh and his Indians have put handspikes under Lake Michigan, and are going to upset it and drown us all."—*Columbian Missourian,* Jan. 20, 1932.

their manner.[42]    But it was not until he offered the Snodgrass letters for publication three years later that he really
gave himself over to the experiment.  His *Journal* feature stories were really a more nearly regular kind of
writing, though they were exceptional in the Hannibal
papers.  "Blabbing Government Secrets" has the more
formal tone of the New Orleans letters described in the
next chapter.  But one cannot know what the young
printer was reading—was probably taking pride in reading
because no one else in town knew of it.  "The Dandy
Frightening the Squatter" incident, discovered by Franklin J. Meine, might have been suggested by the fight between the batteauxman and the West-country waggoner,
with its description of creatures "half horse, half alligator"
in Paulding's *Letters from the South* (1817).[43]

In all these Hannibal records the contrast that gave
much of the zest to early American humor is apparent, the
contrast between the shrewdly intelligent better thinkers
that came into the new country—especially southern professional men—the men who gave form and stability to
the new communities, and the mass of more irresponsible
men, women, and children who lived on the illusion.  The
intense evangelical individualism fostered by the early
churches gave the latter class recognition.  The only recourse of the more solid men, whose part it was to fight
through to order in business and government in the new
community, was in humor.  They left poetry and religion
to the other class.  Sam Clemens, when he was seventeen

[42] In the September 25, 1851, *Journal* a letter from the "Head of Salt River,"
with the distorted spelling used a little later for humorous effect to represent the
rustic illiterate, is signed Timothy Twinkleman. If one could attribute it to Sam
Clemens, it would antedate "The Dandy Frightening the Squatter," discovered by
Franklin J. Meine.
[43] II, 74-78.

years old, was at a stand between these two classes. One strain in his family put the emphasis upon the dream. His observation of the world from the *Journal* office, as his early writings show, had made him intensely aware of the significant predominance of political and economic factors: these were the things that ruled the world. The example of Orion, "a dreamer and a reader," a failure in business, confirmed the impression that there was a difficult choice to be made between the "tough-minded" and the "tender-minded" attitude. Already, with his finely sensitive mind, he was resorting to humor, as his *Journal* writings make evident, to maintain himself in the main stream—as he continued to do throughout his life.

# V

## WANDERJÄHRE, 1853-1861

### §1

IN HANNIBAL, when conditions in the *Journal* office became irritating and when Orion Clemens was intolerant of
his editorial pranks, three lures beckoned Sam Clemens
away. All three of these were noticed frequently in the
"Assistant's Column," reproduced in the preceding chapter. There was the Crystal Palace Fair in New York, at
which Hannibal was to be represented by a bale of hemp
and two barrels of flour, and there was always the river,
with its "Die Vernon" and its "Jeannie Deans" making the
fast time of thirteen or fourteen hours between St. Louis
and Hannibal. Then there were parties passing through
Hannibal on their way west. "Several California teams
passed through here this morning. Messrs. T. W. Bun-
berry, A. J. Price, and Sam'l Fry started this morning
with a good, light wagon and four yoke of fine oxen."[1]
"Two hundred Mormons went up the Mississippi yesterday on the Jeannie Deans. They were bound for Salt
Lake."[2] In his *Autobiography* Mark Twain gives a
glimpse of his feeling in 1849, when one of his fellows, a
lad of twelve, started away with gold-seekers: "I remember the departure of the cavalcade when it spurred Westward. We were all there to see and to envy. And I can

---

[1] *Hannibal Daily Journal,* May 18, 1853.
[2] *Ibid.,* May 2, 1853.

still see that proud little chap sailing by on a great horse.
. . . We were all on hand to gaze and envy when he returned, two years later, in unimaginable glory—for he had
traveled."[3]  Each of the three lures, in its turn, was to
pull Sam Clemens away from his literary calling.  The
first led to what may be called the third formative period
of his early years—to his travels as journeyman printer.

When, writing the year before his death, Mark Twain
said, "To me the most important feature of my life is its
literary feature,"[4] he indicated the only profitable point of
view for his critic and his biographer.  Every other aspect
is of importance, now that his life-span is seen in perspec-
tive, only as it contributes to his career as writer.  The
youthful experiments described in the last chapter are immensely important as Mark Twain's first attempt to find
himself in a literary career.  It is now evident, however,
that they were abortive; unlike the juvenilia of such
writers as Byron and Tennyson, they served only to make
their author turn elsewhere, to prepare for a new start in
life.  The best evidence that they were premature lies in
the first letters that he wrote back home after he reached
New York.

In June, 1853, he had left the *Journal*, and said to
his mother that he was going to St. Louis to visit his sister
Pamela.  His purpose from the first, however, had been
to try his fortunes in New York.  He worked on the
*Evening News* in St. Louis merely long enough to make
the money to pay his expenses thither.  The letter he
wrote to his mother on his arrival is dated August 24.[5]

    [3] *Autobiography*, II, 183.
    [4] "The Turning Point of My Life," *What is Man? and Other Essays*, p. 136.
    [5] The two letters reprinted here antedate the letters published by Albert Bige-
low Paine in *Mark Twain's Letters*.  The first was discovered in the files of the

Orion published it in the *Journal*, but the fact that he found it necessary to preface it with an apologetic note suggests why Sam had felt that he could not continue longer under his brother's restraint.

The free and easy impudence of the writer of the following letter will be appreciated by those who recognize him. We should be pleased to have more of his letters:

New York,

Wednesday, August 24th, 1853.

My dear Mother: You will doubtless be a little surprised, and somewhat angry when you receive this, and find me so far from home; but you must bear a little with me, for you know I was always the best boy you had, and perhaps you remember that people used to say to their children—"Now don't do like O. and H. C.—but take S. for your guide!"

Well, I was out of work in St. Louis, and didn't fancy loafing in such a dry place, where there is no pleasure to be seen without paying well for it, and so I thought I might as well go to New York. I packed my 'duds' and left for this village, where I arrived, all right, this morning.

It took a day, by steamboat and cars, to go from St. Louis to Bloomington, Ill.; another day by railroad, from there to Chicago, where I laid over all day Sunday; from Chicago to Monroe, in Michigan, by railroad, another day; from Monroe, across Lake Erie, in the fine Lake palace, "Southern Michigan," to Buffalo, another day; from Buffalo to Albany, by railroad, another day; and from Albany to New York, by Hudson river steamboat, another day—an awful trip, taking five days, where it should have been only three. I shall wait a day or so for my insides to get settled, after the jolting they received, when I shall look out for a sit; for they say there is plenty of work to be had for *sober* compositors.

*Journal* by Mr. Roy King of the State Historical Society of Missouri, and reprinted in the *Missouri Historical Review*, October, 1930. The second I discovered and reprinted in *Modern Language Notes*, 1927.

The trip, however, was a pleasant one. Rochester, famous on account of the "Spirit Rappings" was of course interesting, and when I saw the Court House in Syracuse, it called to mind the time when it was surrounded with chains and companies of soldiers, to prevent the rescue of McReynolds' nigger, by the infernal abolitionists. I reckon I had better black my face, for in these Eastern States niggers are considerably better than white people.

I saw a curiosity to-day, but I don't know what to call it. Two beings, about like common people, with the exception of their faces, which are more like the "phiz" of an orang-outang, than human. They are white, though, like other people. Imagine a person about the size of F——— J———'s oldest boy, with small lips, full breast, with a constant uneasy, fidgety motion, bright, intelligent eyes, that seems [sic] as if they would look through you, and you have these *things*. They were found in the island of Borneo (the only ones of the species ever discovered,) about twenty years of age. They possess amazing strength; the smallest one would shoulder three hundred pounds as easily as I would a plug of tobacco; they are supposed to be a cross between man and orang-outang; one is the best natured being in the world, while the other would tear a stranger to pieces, if he did but touch him; they wear their hair "Samson" fashion, down to their waists. They have no apple in their throats, whatever, and can therefore scarcely make a sound; no memory either; what transpires to-day, they have forgotten before to-morrow; they look like one mass of muscle, and can walk either on all fours or upright; when let alone, they will walk to and fro across the room, thirteen hours out of the twenty-four; not a day passes but they walk twenty-five or thirty miles, without resting thirty minutes; I watched them about an hour and they were "tramping" the whole time. The little one bent his arm with the elbow in front, and the hand pointing upward, and no two strapping six footers in the room could pull it out straight. Their faces and

meeting at the

d.

MORTON.

the Journal.

ier, who signs
bjects to being
the following
prietors of the

ial attention to
d come out and
" creeter," and
kull and cross
er.

f the above is
f the Courier,
: to produce the
the "creeter?"
they are taking
l? Is it true?
Or rather, are
worthy citizens
there two more
d on over and
f applying the
r Law to this
ail and attempt
re just entering
ling against ad-
? What would
>
acquainted with
for this attack?
his community
? Has it one

been here out a few months from Boston, and
his wife and child are also among the victims.

### LETTER FROM NEW YORK.

The free and easy impudence of the writer of
the following letter will be appreciated by those
who recognize him. We should be pleased to
have more of his letters :

NEW YORK, }
Wednesday, August 24th, 1853. }

MY DEAR MOTHER: you will doubtless be
a little surprised, and somewhat angry when you
receive this, and find me so far from home; but
you must bear a little with me, for you know I
was always the best boy you had, and perhaps
you remember the people used to say to their
children—"Now don't do like O. and H. C—
but take S. for your guide!"

Well, I was out of work in St. Louis, and
did'nt fancy loafing in such a dry place, where
there is no pleasure to be seen without paying
well for it, and so I thought I might as well go
to New York. I packed up my "duds" and left
for this village, where I arrived, all right, this
morning.

It took a day, by steamboat and cars, to go
from St. Louis to Bloomington, Ill; another day
by railroad, from there to Chicago, where I laid
over all day Sunday; from Chicago to Monroe,
in Michigan, by railroad, another day; from
Monroe, across Lake Erie, in the fine Lake
palace, "Southern Michigan," to Buffalo, another day; from Buffalo to Albany, by railroad,
another day; and from Albany to New York,
by Hudson river steamboat, another day—an
awful trip, taking five days, where it should
have been only three. I shall wait a day or so
for my insides to get settled, after the jolting
they received, when I shall look out for a sit;
for they say there is plenty of work to be had
for sober compositors.

In what wil
duction, be
importance
increase mo:
We are |
the prospec
cheering th
have an add
sippi for its
When the c
interior do
other.—[St

☞ A p
ded a week
ing the mut
on Jenning:
(near this |
for life: *
stating that
of the priso
his executic
summoned
the occasio.

ARRI
Co

W. C.
Elija !
Mrs.
Dr. H
Richa
John '
A. B.
R. P.
P. J. |

Total c
195—of fc

FROM SAM CLEMENS'S FIRST TRAVEL LETTER AS IT APPEARED IN THE
*Hannibal Journal*, SEPTEMBER 8, 1853.

eyes are those of the beast, and when they fix their glittering orbs on you with a steady, unflinching gaze, you instinctively draw back a step, and a very unpleasant sensation steals through your veins. They are both males and brothers, and very small, though I do not know their exact height. I have nothing else to write about, and nothing from here would be interesting anyhow. The Crystal Palace is a beautiful building—so is the Marble Palace. I can find nothing better to write about. I will say something about these in my next.[6]

The second letter, written a week later, appeared in the *Journal* with a more approving preface:

The following letter is some encouragement to apprentices in country printing offices, as it shows that it is practicable to acquire enough knowledge of the business in a Western country office to command the best situations West or East. There are a great many who suppose that no mechanical business can be learned well in the West.

New York, Aug. 31, 1853.

My dear Mother: New York is at present overstocked with printers; and I suppose they are from the South, driven North by yellow fever. I got a permanent situation on Monday morning, in a book and job office, and went to work. The printers here are badly organized, and therefore have to work for various prices. These prices are 23, 25, 28, 30, 32, and 35 cents per 1,000 ems. The price I get is 23 cents; but I did very well to get a place at all, for there are thirty or forty—yes, fifty good printers in the city with no work at all; besides, my situation is permanent, and I shall keep it till I can get a better one. The office I work in is John A. Gray's, 97 Cliff street, and next to Harper's, is the most extensive in the city. In the room in which I work I have forty compositors for company. Taking compositors, press men, stereotypers, and all, there are about two hundred

[6] *Hannibal Journal*, Sept. 8, 1853.

persons employed in the concern. The "Knickerbocker," "New York Recorder," "Choral Advocate," "Jewish Chronicle," "Littell's Living Age," "Irish ————," and half a dozen other papers and periodicals are printed here, besides an immense number of books. They are very particular about spacing, justification, proofs, etc., and even if I do not make much money, I will learn a great deal. I thought Ustick was particular enough, but acknowledge now that he was not old-maidish. Why, you must put exactly the same space between every two words, and *every line must be spaced alike.* They think it dreadful to space one line with three em spaces, and the next one with five ems. However, I expected this, and worked accordingly from the beginning; and out of all the proofs I saw, without boasting, I can say mine was by far the cleanest. In St. Louis, Mr. Baird said my proofs were the cleanest that were ever set in his office. The foreman of the Anzeiger told me the same—foreman of the Watchman the same; and with all this evidence, I believe I *do* set a clean proof.

My boarding house is more than a mile from the office; and I can hear the signal calling the hands to work before I start down; they use a steam whistle for that purpose. I work in the fifth story; and from one window I have a pretty good view of the city, while another commands a view of the shipping beyond the Battery; and the "forest of masts," with all sorts of flags flying, is no mean sight. You have everything in the shape of water craft, from a fishing smack to the steamships and men-of-war; but packed so closely together for miles, that when close to them you can scarcely distinguish one from another.

Of all the commodities, manufactures—or whatever you please to call it—in New York, trundle-bed trash—children I mean—take the lead. Why, from Cliff street, up Frankfort to Nassau street, six or seven squares—my road to dinner—I think I could count two hundred brats. Niggers, mulattoes, quadroons, Chinese, and some the Lord no doubt originally intended to be white, but the dirt on whose faces leaves one uncertain as to that fact, block up the little, narrow street; and to wade through this mass of human vermin, would raise the ire of the most patient person that ever lived.  In going to and from my meals, I go by the way of Broadway—and to *cross* Broadway is the rub—but once across, it is *the* rub for two or three squares.  My plan— and how could I choose another, when there *is* no other—is to get into the crowd; and when I get in, I am borne, and rubbed, and crowded along, and need scarcely trouble myself about using my own legs; and when I get out, it seems like I had been pulled to pieces and very badly put together again.

Last night I was in what is known as one of *the* finest fruit saloons in the world.  The whole length of the huge, glittering hall is filled with beautiful ornamented marble slab tables, covered with the finest fruit I ever saw in my life.  I suppose the fruit could not be mentioned with which they could not supply you.  It is a perfect palace.  The gas lamps hang in clusters of half a dozen together—representing grapes, I suppose—all over the hall.

P.S.  The printers have two libraries in town, entirely free to the craft; and in these I can spend my evenings most pleasantly. If books are not good company, where will I find it?

Both letters are unsigned, but there can be no doubt that they belong with the two earliest letters in the two-volume collection.  The first of those, the fragment to his sister Pamela, describes the Crystal Palace according to the promise of the first letter.  The editor's note, in connection with the letters to Pamela, is that in New York "he was working in the printing office of John A. Gray and Green on Cliff street," which facts are noted in the *Journal* letter.[7]  The first of the two closes with the words: "You ask me where I spend my evenings.  Where would you suppose, with a free printers' library containing more than 4,000 volumes within a quarter of a mile of me, and

[7] *Cf. Autobiography*, II, 287.

nobody at home to talk to?"[8] data similar to those in the postscript of the *Journal* letter. In the first letter to his sister he says that four times a day he walks "a little over a mile"; and in the letter published in the *Journal* the writer tells his mother that his boarding house is "more than a mile from the office." The young printer refers, furthermore, to his experience on the St. Louis *Evening News*.

Written two months before he was eighteen years old, these two letters represent a youth of a good deal of dignity, interested in seeing the sights and intensely conscious of his ability to fend for himself. When he had leisure evenings he could find amusement in books. There are in the letters in embryo the same elements that went into the *Quaker City* letters fifteen years later. His imagination plays around what he observes: "the 'forest of masts,' with all sorts of flags flying, is no mean sight." Later he would have caught himself up for using so conventional an image, but his reference to himself as the model of the family, and the description of the "trundle-bed trash" of New York anticipate his later habit of finding a humorous point of view of his own that was a sort of anti-mask to the conventional view. Most of both letters, however, is given over to curious facts and useful information—in this as in his letters to his sister—an element which persisted throughout his writings, but which he learned in time to manage more casually. On the other hand, he was doing the kind of thing he had promised in the Blab letter written for the *Journal* a few months earlier: "I shall gratify such of your readers as have never been so far from home, with an account of this great island, and

[8] *Letters,* I, 22.

my voyage thither." It is tempting to take the sentence as an evidence that he was already thinking of himself as an embryo Lemuel Gulliver.

A tendency, which became the habit of his lifetime, is noticeable in both letters—to find satisfaction in concrete things. It is indicative of what may be called the chief motive force of this third formative period—an avidity to know what is interesting about the world. In his own column in the *Hannibal Journal* he had quoted curious facts he had gleaned from exchanges. His letters show that he is now checking up on what he has learned, and taking stock of the world on his own account. His passion to understand man he became conscious of later—so far he had "got him out of books."[9] His love of useful information took its rise, apparently, in something more than the youthful vanity evident in these letters; it seems to have been connected with his passion for freedom in that already he trusted his intellect to secure for him the liberty he craved. Such common maxims as "Knowledge is power" and "The truth shall make you free," much quoted in contemporary papers in the Middle West, would have seemed to his compositor eye at this time to contain the deepest of wisdom. All his life he loved generalizations, though he distrusted them unless they could be supported with "perpendicular fact." Later he would see the ironical implications on the reverse side of such easy maxims.

§2

THE LETTERS to his mother written from New York at the end of the summer make it clear how far the youth had to go before he could attain the freedom to be him-

[9] "The Turning Point in My Life," *What is Man? and Other Essays,* p. 137.

self. They are stiff with the consciousness of what is expected of him. His Hannibal efforts to find himself had not carried him far. In New York he was a mere compositor. He tried in Philadelphia to get some verses published in the *Ledger*, but they were "not received with approval."[10]

Nevertheless, his Philadelphia letters show that he was bent upon such practice exercises as he knew that Orion would approve of for publication. His letter to his mother must have been written with that in view. Not having heard yet that the family had moved away, he wrote his next letter, dated October 26, 1853, to Orion in Hannibal, apparently expecting that it would be offered to one of the Hannibal papers for publication.[11] But by that time his brother had moved to Muscatine, Iowa. The letter was forwarded to him, and he published it at once in his new paper, the *Muscatine Journal*, as "Philadelphia Correspondence." A University of Iowa thesis reprints parts of it omitted by Albert Bigelow Paine from his edition of Mark Twain's *Letters*. They are his most ambitious piece of writing, yet discovered, before the *Snodgrass Letters*. His account of a detail of his journey from New York surpasses any of his Hannibal writings of the early part of the year in vividness of narration:

I came here from New York by way of the Camden and Amboy railroad—the same on which the collision occurred some time since. I never thought of this till our train stopped, "all of a

[10] A. B. P., I, 98.

[11] A sentence in the conclusion, "I intend visiting the Navy Yard, Mint, etc., before I write again." (*Letters*, I, 28), appears to be a bid for an invitation to write travel letters. It may be said, in this connection, that, probably as a result of this early ambition of his, Mark Twain's letters throughout his life sound as if they might have been written with an eye on an ultimate publisher. As early as 1880, in a letter to one of his best friends, he inserted the clause, "somebody may be reading *this* letter 80 years hence."—*Letters*, I, 385.

sudden," and then began to go backwards like blazes. Then ran
back half a mile, and switched off on another track, and stopped;
and the next moment a large passenger train came round a bend
in the road, and whistled past us like lightening! Ugh! ejac-
ulated I, as I looked to see if Mr. C's bones were all safe. If we
had been three seconds later getting off that track, the two loco-
motives would have come together, and we should no doubt have
been helped off. The conductors silenced questions by not answer-
ing them.[12]

As a whole, the letter gives an excellent idea of the most
notable features of Philadelphia: Fairmount Park, the
Water Works, handsome "private dwellings," the omni-
bus service, Girard College, and the places sacred to the
memory of Franklin. "I took a squint at The House of
Refuge, (which we used to read about at Sunday
School)."[13]   He comments on the best type of stone for
columns—"sombre red granite." His imagination is alert:
"To see some of . . . the huge blocks [of granite] lying
about . . . carries one, in imagination, to the ruined piles
of ancient Babylon."[14]   He is extending his horizon and
his powers in terms of what he learned in Hannibal. His
experience there, it is apparent, did more than make a
good compositor of him; he is a good traveler. Nor is he
satisfied with observing the externals of things. He
searches out books to learn more about them. ". . . if you
will get a back number of Lady's Book, you will find a
better description of the Works than I can give . . .
George Lippard, in his 'Legends of Washington and his
Generals,' has rendered the Wassahickon sacred to my

---

[12] F. W. Lorch, "Mark Twain in Iowa," *The Iowa Journal of History and
Politics,* XXVII (July, 1929), 413.
[13] *Ibid.,* p. 412.          [14] A. B. P., I, 100.

eyes, and I shall make that trip, as well as one to German-town soon."[15]

He liked Philadelphia.[16]  The whole letter shows that he was feeling freer than he did in New York in the summer.  He was interested most of all in the State House and "Independence Bell."  He had seen something in New York which should have a place in Independence Hall—a flag which was

the personal property of Washington, and was planted on the Battery when the British evacuated New York.  After that it was not used until the laying of the corner stone of the Washington monument.  Then this faded and tattered, though time-honored relic of "the days that tried men's souls" was taken to Washington and unfurled to the breeze at the ceremony.[17]

His feeling for a public occasion is here seen for the first time: when the multitude saw the flag that had waved "defiance to the British," he says, "a shout went up that would have sent the blood from the cheek of a tyrant."[18]

The most suggestive point in his report of this patriotic demonstration, however, is his quotation from Tom Paine's *The American Crisis*, "These are the times that try men's souls"—not as if simply dropping into a convenient, ready-made phrase, which it would be to-day, but with its original, living connotation still fresh upon it. The sentence might merely have aroused his imagination when he read in the *Legends of Washington and His Generals* that it was the battle-cry of the American troops crossing the Delaware and at Trenton, just as places mentioned there were "sacred" to him.  But he was drowning his homesickness at this time with reading—to supplement

[15] Lorch, *op. cit.*, p. 412.
[16] "I like this Philadelphia."—*Letters*, I, 27.
[17] Lorch, *op. cit.*, p. 413.        [18] *Ibid.*

his travels. There is the chance that he turned to Paine's apology for the American Revolution—even that his interest carried him on into *Common Sense* and the *Rights of Man*. The fact, which he had doubtless discovered by this time, that Washington, Jefferson, and Franklin all held much the same liberal views as Paine, would also touch his imagination. In Philadelphia he had his interest in Franklin as well as in Washington deepened. Suggestions concerning Tom Paine's relation to Franklin might motivate his interest. All these things were follow-ups of lines of interest he had acquired in Hannibal. Franklin was much quoted in papers in the Middle West in the forties; and a squib entitled "Tom Paine's Bones" was offered as propaganda against atheism. Sensitiveness about such free thinkers as his father and his uncle John Quarles would insure his interest in such a squib.

The shout of the democratic masses in America, described in his Philadelphia letter, as fitted to send the "blood from the cheek of a tyrant" seems to echo Paine's sentence, which would have delighted Mark Twain at any time of his life, "Tyranny, like hell, is not easily conquered." Sam Clemens was at the stage of his life when he wanted authority to think for himself. His biographer notices the change, but does not account for it: "We have somehow the feeling that he had all at once stepped from boyhood to manhood, and that the separation was marked by a very definite line."[19] A way to account for the change lies in the theory that his reading in Paine had given him his first glimpse of what seemed to him a worthy ideal of life and thinking different from that approved in his Hannibal world. As a representative of

[19] A. B. P., I, 96.

the latter, Orion Clemens's authority had become too repressive to be tolerated. The right to freedom voiced by Paine would have brought balm to his soul: " . . . the harder the conflict, the more glorious the triumph. What we obtain too cheap, we esteem too lightly: it is dearness only that gives every thing its value. Heaven knows how to put a proper price upon its goods; and it would be strange, indeed, if so celestial an article as FREEDOM should not be highly rated."[20] Such lines as these would captivate the youth and prepare the ground for seeds of an independent philosophy of life. Lines from the *Rights of Man*, read at this impressionable time of his life, may have contained the seeds that flowered forty years later in *A Connecticut Yankee in King Arthur's Court*. "Every age and generation must be as free to act for itself *in all cases* as the age and generations which preceded it. The vanity and presumption of governing beyond the grave is the most ridiculous and insolent of all tyrannies. Man has no property in man."[21] "I am not afraid," wrote the seventeen-year-old, shortly before he left New York. "I shall . . . endeavor to be (and shall be) as 'independent as a wood-sawyer's clerk'."[22]

But Sam Clemens was not yet ready for real freedom. His warm emotional nature was being starved in surroundings where he was a stranger. None of the amenities of his life in the Middle West attended the young traveler among journeymen. Many lines in his letters indicate that he was seeking for an excuse to return home. He

[20] *The Writings of Thomas Paine* (ed. M. D. Conway), I, 170. In this connection, I have found only one hint of a Paine influence on Mark Twain—in Carl Van Doren's *The American Novel*, p. 181. In the next chapter some more definite evidence of such influence will be offered.

[21] *The Writings of Thomas Paine*, II, 278.

[22] *Letters*, I, 24.

dreaded the cold winter. Their letters from Hannibal were not satisfactory. "You can write me nothing that will not interest me," he declared.[23] The only reason he desired to return, he assured them, as he imagined them nodding their heads with an I-told-you-so, was that night work was injuring his eyes. He inquired of Orion how much his Muscatine paper was paying. His letters for it would not be satisfactory, he feared, because night work was dulling his ideas. He couldn't understand why it was that he could not set type as fast as he could at home. "I would like amazingly to see a good old-fashioned negro!"[24] the last of his Philadelphia letters concluded.

§3

SAM CLEMENS's first excursion into the world was undertaken before he was quite ready to leave his family, or his native section; but he had proved to himself that he could be wholly self-supporting and that he could amuse himself traveling. No hint of an expanding genius is noticeable in his letters of this time. He was merely a normal youth away from home for the first time, perhaps a little more resourceful than the ordinary eighteen-year-old at finding interests outside himself. He remembered life in Hannibal for its charm, he said in after years. His introduction to great cities did not admit of his knowing the people who could have given his life there the same zest. It was not until he went to San Francisco that he became wholly independent of his family and his Mid-West connections. In the late summer of 1854, after something over a year's absence, he returned to his mother and Orion, then living in Muscatine, Iowa. Arriving in Mus-

[23] *Ibid.*, I, 28.                    [24] *Ibid.*, I, 29.

catine in the middle of the night, he utilized the hours at the hotel, till daybreak, learning the chief facts in the reigns of English kings, from a history he found on the table.

He went back, before winter, to his old place on the *Evening News* in St. Louis. There he was near his sister, Mrs. Moffett. During the winter of 1854 Orion was married and gave up his Muscatine paper to start a job-printing office in Keokuk, Iowa, where his wife's people lived. He employed both Sam and Henry to help him, Sam returning from St. Louis and remaining in Keokuk almost two years. His biographer's account of his life there is not unattractive. He made his first speech at a printers' banquet celebrating Benjamin Franklin's birthday, with such success that he was at once invited to join a debating society. He had a pleasant circle of friends and kinspeople, among whom he was the joker. With one of these, a pretty girl by the name of Annie Taylor, he seems to have had more than a casual acquaintance. Their romance is a slight chapter in Sam Clemens's life not referred to in his biography. She afterwards became a teacher of English at Lindenwood College, in St. Charles, Missouri, just outside of St. Louis. The following letter seems to have been written at Keokuk in 1855 when she was either visiting or studying in Mount Pleasant, Iowa. It shows why, in spite of his dissatisfaction at working under Orion's haphazard direction, he was better satisfied in Keokuk than he had been in the East. His social contacts there enabled him to lead a better balanced life. The letter shows, also, that he had not given up his ambition to write. His discourse on bugs, a forerunner of Jim Baker's blue-jay yarn, is more nearly in the Mark Twain vein than any piece of his writing preserved, before his San Francisco days.

Sunday, May 25.

Well, Annie, I was not permitted to finish my letter Wednesday evening. I believe Henry, who commenced his a day later, has beaten me. However, if my friends will let me alone I will go through today. Bugs! Yes, B-U-G-S! What of the bugs? Why, perdition take the bugs! That is all. Night before last I stood at the little press until nearly 2 o'clock, and the flaring gas light over my head attracted all the varieties of bugs which are to be found in natural history, and they all had the same praiseworthy recklessness about flying into the fire. They at first came in little social crowds of a dozen or so, but soon increased in numbers, until a religious meeting of several millions was assembled on the board before me, presided over by a venerable beetle, who occupied the most prominent lock of my hair as his chair of state, while innumerable lesser dignitaries of the same tribe were clustered around him, keeping order, and at the same time endeavoring to attract the attention of the vast assemblage to their own importance by industriously grating their teeth. It must have been an interesting occasion—perhaps a great bug jubilee commemorating the triumph of the locusts over Pharaoh's crops in Egypt many centuries ago. At least, good seats, commanding an unobstructed view of the scene, were in great demand; and I have no doubt small fortunes were made by certain delegates from Yankee land by disposing of comfortable places on my shoulders at round premiums. In fact, the advantages which my altitude afforded were so well appreciated that I soon began to look like one of those big cards in the museum covered with insects impaled on pins.

The big "president" beetle (who, when he frowned, closely resembled Isbell when the pupils are out of time) rose and ducked his head and, crossing his arms over his shoulders, stroked them down to the tip of his nose several times, and after thus disposing of the perspiration, stuck his hands under his wings, propped his back against a lock of hair, and then, bobbing his head at the congregation, remarked, "B-u-z-z!" To which the congregation devoutly responded, "B-u-z-z!" Satisfied with this promptness on the part of his flock, he took a more imposing perpendicular against another lock of hair and, lifting his hands to command silence, gave another melodious "b-u-z-z!" on a louder key (which I suppose to have been the key-note) and after a moment's silence the whole congregation burst into a grand anthem, three dignified daddy longlegs, perched near the gas burner, beating quadruple time during the performance. Soon two of the parts in the great chorus maintained silence, while a treble and alto duet, sung by forty-seven thousand mosquitoes and twenty-three thousand house flies, came in, and then, after another chorus, a tenor and bass duet by thirty-two thousand locusts and ninety-seven thousand pinch bugs was sung—then another grand chorus, "Let Every Bug Rejoice and Sing" (we used to sing "heart" instead of "bug") terminated the performance, during which eleven treble singers split their throats from head to heels, and the patriotic "daddies" who beat time hadn't a stump of a leg left.

It would take a ream of paper to give all the ceremonies of this great mass meeting. Suffice it to say that the little press "chawed up" half a bushel of the devotees, and I combed 976 beetles out of my hair the next morning, every one of whose throats was stretched wide open, for their gentle spirits had passed away while yet they sung—and who shall say they will not receive their reward? I buried their motionless forms with musical honors in John's hat.

Now, Annie, don't say anything about how long *my* letter was in going, for I didn't receive *yours* until Wednesday—and don't forget that I *tried* to answer it the same day, though I was doomed to fail. I wonder if you will do as much?

Yes, the loss of that bridge almost finished my earthly career. There is still a slight nausea about my stomach (for certain malicious persons say that my heart lies in that vicinity) whenever I think of it, and I believe I should have evaporated and vanished away like a blue cloud if John—indefatigable, unconquerable John—had not recovered from his illness to relieve me of a portion of my troubles. I think I can survive it now. John says "der chills kill a white boy, but sie (pronounced see) can't kill a *Detch*-man."

I have not now the slightest doubt, Annie, that your beautiful sketch is *perfect*. It looks more and more like what I suppose "Mt. Unpleasant" to be every time I look at it. It is really a pity that you could not get the shrubbery in, for your dog fennel is such a tasteful ornament to any yard. Still, I am entirely satisfied to get the principal beauties of the place, and will not grieve over the loss. I have delighted Henry's little heart by delivering your message. Give the respected councilman the Latin letter by all means. If I understood the lingo well enough I would write you a Dutch one for him. Tell Marie I don't know what Henry thinks of the verb "amo," but for some time past I have discovered various fragments of paper scattered about bearing the single word "amite," and since the receipt of her letter the fragments have greatly multiplied and the word has suddenly warmed into "amour"—all written in the same hand, and that, if I mistake not, Henry's, for the latter is the only French word he has any particular affection for. Ah, Annie, I have a slight horror of writing essays myself; and if I were inclined to write one I should be afraid to do it, knowing you could do it so much better if you would only get industrious once and try. Don't you be frightened—I guess Marie is afraid to write anything bad about you, or else her heart softens before she succeeds in doing it. Don't fail to remember me to her—for I perceive she is aware that my funeral has not yet been preached. Ete paid us a visit yesterday, and we are going to return the kindness this afternoon. Good-by.

Your friend,                                                    SAM.[25]

[25] The two letters to Annie Taylor included in this chapter were first published in the Kansas City *Star Magazine*, Sunday, March 21, 1926, in a story entitled

The comment on essay-writing, apparently a disclaimer, if Annie suspected him of sending her a practice-exercise, indicates, nevertheless, that there was a literary foundation to their friendship.

Other hints out of the scant records of his two years in St. Louis on the *Evening News* and in Keokuk, are of significance to the student attempting to trace Sam Clemens's development as a litterateur.   In St. Louis he roomed with a journeyman chair-maker, Frank E. Burrough, a young man who had a taste for "Dickens, Thackeray, Scott, and Disraeli."   The two were "comrades and close friends."[26]   There is no note of what books the youngsters discussed, but a Mark Twain letter to Burrough, written years afterward, in 1876, contains the first suggestion discoverable that the young printer's system of philosophy was in process of formation at this time.   The hint is notable as a follow-up after his quotation of Tom Paine in the Philadelphia letter.   Burrough had evidently, in a letter to which Mark Twain's was an answer, described the Sam Clemens of 1855, as he remembered him.   The humorist's comment, with his own self-accusing analysis, was, "You have described a callow fool, a self-sufficient ass . . . imagining that he is re-modeling the world and entirely capable of doing it right.   Ignorance, intolerance, egotism, self-assertion, opaque perception, dense and pitiful chuckle-headedness—and an almost pathetic unconsciousness of it all."[27]   "Imagining that he is remodeling the

---

"Letters Young Mark Twain wrote in 1857" (pp. 3-5).   The author of the story quotes the owner of the letters as saying that Annie Taylor was "very talented and brilliant.   She and 'Sam' Clemens had similar tastes and were always very congenial friends.   The letters and other things she used to write were strikingly original and humorous.   She always saw the humorous side of life."   *Cf.* Lorch, *op. cit.*, pp. 422-425.

[26] A. B. P., I, 103.                    [27] *Letters*, I, 289.

world" would be a description of a youth who had come to conviction about where all the trouble lay, possibly through reading Tom Paine.

His letters show that he worked hard in Keokuk and received little pay, but he had congenial friends there and a normal social life. There is a little evidence all along that he spent his leisure time reading. His Keokuk companions remembered afterwards that he often "carried a book under his arm—a history or a volume of Dickens or the tales of Edgar Allan Poe."[28] The earliest hint of any ambition to exploit his humor comes from a reminiscence of his friend Ed Brownell, of Keokuk. When Brownell asked him, on one occasion, what he was reading, the young printer replied, "Oh, nothing much—a so-called funny book—one of these days I'll write a funnier book than that, myself."[29]

It was because of the vision of a fortune awaiting him in South America, suggested by a book that he happened upon at this time, that the *wanderlust* seized him and rescued him a second time from the worrisome position of assistant to Orion. The late autobiographic sketch entitled "The Turning Point of My Life" describes the way in which Fate aided him by blowing a $50 bill in his path. This, he said, was the point that turned him toward a literary career. But, like Ibsen's Great Boyg, circumstance of one sort or another kept him away from his appointed goal for a good many years.

Another premature attempt to get something published, however, was the immediate outcome of this intervention of Fate. It has been noted that before he left Hannibal he suggested, in joking vein, that he might

[28] A. B. P., I, 106.          [29] *Ibid.*, I, 107.

some day write travel letters; and that in Keokuk he had announced his intention to write a funny book some day. Buoyed up with the thought of the fortune he was to make in cocoa in Brazil, he went to St. Louis to say good-bye to his mother, who was making her home with Mrs. Moffett. There the happy thought came to him that he might try his hand as a real newspaper correspondent. He returned to Iowa, consequently, and arranged with the editors of the Keokuk *Post* to send back travel letters to help defray the expenses of his South American trip. He was offered five dollars a letter, and went on his way again "jubilant in the prospect of receiving money for literature."[30]  He went to New Orleans by way of Chicago, Indianapolis, and Cincinnati. At the last named place he worked as printer from November until April. His first letter to the *Post*, according to his biographer's record, was sent from Cincinnati in November, 1856, and was signed with the pen name, Thomas Jefferson Snodgrass. He had had practice during his Hannibal days in inventing pen-names for himself.

Albert Bigelow Paine believed that there were only two Snodgrass letters published in the Keokuk *Post;* the second also dates from Cincinnati, four months later than the first, March 14, 1857. But Charles Honce of Chicago, by diligent search, discovered in files of the 1856 Keokuk *Post* an earlier letter with the same signature, written from St. Louis, October 18, 1856. This may explain a clause from a letter of Sam Clemens to his brother Henry in the summer of 1856. He speaks of the necessity of going to South America against Orion's wish. His mother favors the plan, he says: "I could not depend upon

[30] A. B. P., I, 112.

him [Orion] for ten dollars, so I have 'feelers' out in several directions."[31] The discovery of the St. Louis letter indicates that Sam probably had a well developed plan for the Snodgrass correspondence and that he sent the St. Louis letter to the *Post* as what he later called "a specimen letter."

Charles Honce published the three early letters in a small volume entitled *The Adventures of Thomas Jefferson Snodgrass* and noted in his introduction, as Albert Bigelow Paine does in the biography, that even then the young humorist had a book of travel letters in mind.[32] In the first Cincinnati letter the author says:

You know arter going down there to St. Louis, and seein so many wonderful things, I wanted to see more—so I took a notion to go a travelin, so as to see the world, and then write a book about it—a kind o' daily journal like—and have all in gold on the back of it, "Snodgrass' Dierrea," or somethin' of that kind, like other authors that visits forren parts.

Evidently the *Snodgrass Letters* anticipated *Innocents Abroad*.[33] The first of the earlier pair is a sort of burlesque travel diary of his trip to Cincinnati. A theme that became a favorite of the humorist later is touched upon: "a guide to heaven," which "ain't much use to a feller in Chicago."

These early letters were attempts at the kind of humor coming into vogue at this time in the Middle West—humor conveyed by a representation, in both spelling and grammar, of the speech peculiarities of the region—that

[31] *Letters*, I, 34.
[32] C. Honce, ed., *The Adventures of Thomas Jefferson Snodgrass*, p. xiii.
[33] *Ibid.*, p. 19.  Cf. A. B. P., I, 113.

is, of dialect.[33a]  The first is an account of the disturbance created by Snodgrass, an innocent from the country town of Keokuk, when he attended the play *Julius Caesar* in St. Louis. The police finally ejected him from the theatre. The second, that is, the first Cincinnati letter, is Snodgrass's account of his railway journey to Chicago. He has difficulties about his ticket and about his luggage:

. . . bimeby my vallis made its appearance, with shirts and cravats hangin out at one end, and socks and collars at t'other—lookin considerable like an Irishman that's jest got out of a New Orleans 'lection riot—and dern my cats if I'd a knowed it was a vallis at all, . . .[34]

The second Cincinnati letter is dated March 14, 1857.[35]  The correspondent apologizes for his silence:

It mought be that some people think your umble sarvent has "shuffled off this mortal quile" and bid an eternal adoo to this subloonary atmosphere—nary time. He ain't dead, but sleepeth. That expreshun are figerative, and go to signerfy that he's pooty much quit scribblin.

There is a touch of the kind of satire at the methods of public officials which Mark Twain gave vent to ten or fifteen years later:

An indigent Irish woman—a widow with nineteen children and several at the breast, according to custom, went to the Mayor to get some of that public coal. The Mayor he gin her an order on the Marshall; the Marshall gin her an order on the Recorder; Recorder sent her to the Constable; Constable sent her to the

---

[33a] Artemus Ward was in Cincinnati in 1856, using the city as a center from which he went about the country. In 1857, he was made city editor of the *Cleveland Plain Dealer* and was already well known in the Middle West.

[34] C. Honce, ed., *The Adventures of Thomas Jefferson Snodgrass*, p. 31.

[35] It appeared in the *Keokuk Daily Post*, April 10, 1857, under the heading "Correspondence—written for the Keokuk Post. Snodgrass in an Adventure."

Postmaster; Postmaster sent her to the County Clerk, . . . the unfortunit daughter of Eve. (I say "daughter of Eve" meanin it as kinder figerative or poetastical like, for I forgit, now, whether the Irish come from our Eve, or not.)

Then follows the story of Snodgrass the bachelor's discomfiture when a foundling baby is left on his hands. There can be no doubt that Sam planned that the "Snodgrass Dierrea" should be the "funnier book" he had promised Ed Brownell he would some day write. Like many of his later experiments, however, it miscarried. His biographer says:

From the fewness of the letters we may assume that Snodgrass found them hard work, and it is said that he raised on the price. . . . They are mainly important in that they are the first of his contributions that have been preserved; also the first for which he received a cash return.[36]

Mark Twain did not think well enough of these early experiments in the field of humor to have them reprinted, except for the one-third column "exhibit" in the Paine biography.[37] Cincinnati was the chief literary center west of the Alleghenies in the fifties, but the only hint of the young printer's interests there is in his account of his friendship with a Scotchman named Macfarlane. In that reminiscence is the second suggestion of the trend his thinking was taking. Macfarlane had "histories, philosophies, and scientific works" and was a "direct and diligent talker." The young printer was first introduced to the doctrine of evolution at this time. There in Cincinnati, three years before Darwin published his *Origin of Species*, Macfarlane was discussing a similar theory. But the scheme of evolution stopped with man, according to his

[36] A. B. P., I, 113.          [37] A. B. P., I, 113.

doctrine. Man "had retrograded; . . . man's heart was the only bad one in the animal kingdom."[38] The Scotchman's teaching found such lodgment in the mind of Sam Clemens that it became one of his own cardinal doctrines.[39] The Scotchman's theory that "man's intellect was a brutal addition to him" suggests also a Hobbes influence.

## §4

THE FIRST record so far discovered of Sam Clemens's impressions of New Orleans is contained in another letter to his Keokuk friend, Annie Taylor. It was written, apparently, at the time when he was beginning his apprenticeship on the river. He describes in some detail the French market and the cemeteries, but he is homesick for Keokuk. It would have done his very boots good, he says, "to have met half a dozen Keokuk girls . . . [as he] used to meet them at market in the Gate City." He incloses an orange leaf in his letter.

New Orleans,
June 1, 1857.

My Dear Friend Annie: I am not certain what day of the month it is (the weather being so warm), but I expect I have made a pretty close guess.

Well, you wouldn't answer the last letter I wrote from Cincinnati? I just thought I would write again, anyhow, taking for an excuse the fact that you might have written and the letter miscarried. I have been very unfortunate with my correspondence; for during my stay of nearly four months in Cincinnati I did not get more than three or four letters beside those coming from members of our own family. You did write once, though, Annie, and that rather "set me up," for I imagined that as you

---

[38] *Ibid.*, 115; *Autobiography*, I, 144.  [39] *Autobiography*, II, 7.

had got started once more you would continue to write with your ancient punctuality. From some cause or other, however, I was disappointed—though it could hardly have been any fault of mine, for I sat down and answered your letter as soon as I received it, I think, although I was sick at the time. Orion wrote to me at St. Louis, saying that Marie told him she would correspond with me if I would ask her. I lost no time in writing to her—got no reply—and thus ended another brief *correspondence*. I wish you would tell Marie that the Lord won't love her if she does so.

However, I reckon one page of this is sufficient.

I visited the French market yesterday (Sunday) morning. I think it would have done my very boots good to have met half a dozen Keokuk girls there, as I used to meet them at market in the Gate City. But it could not be. However, I did find several acquaintances—two pretty girls, with their two beaux—sipping coffee at one of the stalls. I thought I had seen all kinds of markets before—but that was a great mistake—this being a place such as I had never dreamed of before. Everything was arranged in such beautiful order, and had such an air of cleanliness and neatness that it was a pleasure to wander among the stalls. The pretty pyramids of fresh fruit looked so delicious. Oranges, lemons, pineapples, bananas, figs, plantains, watermelons, blackberries, raspberries, plums, and various other fruits were to be seen on one table, while the next one bore a load of radishes, onions, squashes, peas, beans, sweet potatoes—well, everything imaginable in the vegetable line—and still further on were lobsters, oysters, clams— then milk, cheese, cakes, coffee, tea, nuts, apples, hot rolls, butter, etc.—then the various kinds of meats and poultry. Of course, the place was crowded (as most places in New Orleans are) with men, women and children of every age, color and nation. Out on the pavement were groups of Italians, French, Dutch, Irish, Spaniards, Indians, Chinese, Americans, English, and the Lord knows how many more different kinds of people, selling all kinds of articles—even clothing of every description, from a handkerchief down to a pair of boots, umbrellas, pins, combs, matches—in fact, anything you could possibly want—and keeping up a terrible din with their various cries.

Today I visited one of the cemeteries—a veritable little city, for they *bury* everybody *above* ground here. All round the sides of the inclosure, which is in the heart of the city, there extends a large vault about twelve feet high, containing three or four tiers of holes or tombs (they put the coffins into these holes endways, and then close up the opening with brick), one above another, and looking like a long 3- or 4-story house. The graveyard is laid off in regular, straight streets, strewed with white shells, and the fine, tall marble tombs (numbers of them containing but one corpse) fronting them and looking like so many miniature dwelling houses. You can find wreaths of flowers and crosses, cups of water, mottoes, small statuettes, etc., hanging in front of nearly every tomb. I noticed one beautiful white marble tomb, with a white lace curtain in front of it, under which, on a little shelf, were vases of fresh flowers, several little statuettes, and cups of water, while on the ground under the shelf were little orange and magnolia trees. It looked so pretty. The inscription was in French—said the occupant was a girl of 17, and finished by a wish from the mother that the stranger would drop a tear there, and thus aid her whose sorrow was more than one could bear. They say that the flowers upon many of these tombs are replaced every day by fresh ones. These were fresh, and the poor girl had been dead *five years*. There's depth of affection! On another was the inscription, "To My Dear Mother," with fresh flowers. The lady was 62 years old when she died, and she had been dead *seven years*. I spent half an hour watching the chameleons—strange animals, to change their clothes so often! I found a dingy looking one, drove him on a black rag, and he turned black as ink—drove him under a fresh leaf and he turned the brightest green color you ever saw. I wish you would write to me at St. Louis (I'll be there next week), for I don't believe you have forgotten how yet. Tell Marie and Ete "howdy" for me. Your old friend,

Sam L. Clemens.

P.S.—I have just returned from another cemetery—brought away an orange leaf as a memorial—I inclose it.

It has been commonly believed that Sam Clemens's pilot years were the period when he most nearly gave up all literary ambition. Orion seems to have made some kind of suggestion about newspaper correspondence while he was still learning the river—possibly about continuing the Snodgrass letters for the Keokuk *Post*. In a letter to Orion and Mollie Clemens, written from St. Louis in 1858, Sam wrote, "I cannot correspond with a paper, because when one is learning the river, he is not allowed to do or think about anything else."[40]

But the memories recorded in *Life on the Mississippi* show that he must have looked upon all the objects of his experience during those years as literary material. The river was "a wonderful book . . . it had a new story to tell every day." He had grown up loving the river. All that he had read and seen and done before had been preparing him for the reading of that book. It was "a dead language to the uneducated passenger." To him there was "never a page . . . that you would want to skip, thinking you could find higher enjoyment in some other thing."[41] And by this time he was fully awakened to an interest in men. River passengers then offered the same varieties for study that railway travelers do today, and Macfarlane's indictment of the human race had given edge to Sam Clemens's observation:

[40] *Letters*, I, 38.     [41] *Life on the Mississippi*, p. 69.

I got personally and familiarly acquainted with about all the different types of human nature that are to be found in fiction, biography, or history. . . . the feature of it which I value most is the zest which that early experience has given to my later reading. When I find a well-drawn character in fiction or biography I generally take a warm personal interest in him, for the reason that I have met him before—met him on the river.[42]

It is not surprising, in view of these interests that paralleled his acquiring skill as a pilot, therefore, to discover that after he had got his bearings on the river Sam Clemens made a third attempt at newspaper correspondence—an attempt which, like the *Hannibal Journal* adventures and the *Snodgrass Letters*, proved premature. He did not choose to preserve any of these writings[43] except his satire at the expense of Isaiah Sellers, the original Mark Twain, which is reprinted as Appendix B in the third volume of *Mark Twain*, from the New Orleans *True Delta* of May, 1859.[44] Albert Bigelow Paine refers casually to "squibs and skits which he sometimes contributed to the New Orleans papers";[45] and in an 1862 letter to Orion—after the two had gone to Nevada—Sam asked his brother to get him a place on the *Sacramento Union*. After some suggestions about the letter Orion should write he said, "Tell them I have corresponded with the N. Orleans *Crescent*, and other papers."[46] A search through the files of the *Crescent* in the New Orleans city archives in January, 1929, led to the discovery of a series of letters that appear to the present writer to be the ex-

[42] *Ibid.*, p. 163.
[43] A. B. P., I, 149, "If he published any work in those river-days he did not acknowledge it later—with one exception."
[44] *Ibid.*, III, 1593-96; I, 150.
[45] *Letters*, I, 51.        [46] *Ibid.*, I, 82.

periments referred to by his biographer and by Mark
Twain himself. While they are much more than "skits
and squibs," they justify Albert Bigelow Paine's judgment that Mark Twain's genius needed time for growth.[47]

There are four letters in the series. In the issue of the
*Crescent* for January 21, 1861, appeared a communication
which purported to enclose a letter written by one Quintus
Curtius Snodgrass to his "fidae Achates" [*sic*], Charles
Augustus Brown, of Algiers.[48] The name Snodgrass, of
course, suggested to the searcher the Keokuk *Post* series of
1856. The transformation of the *nom de plume* from its
American connotation, Thomas Jefferson Snodgrass, to the
more classical name of Quintus Curtius Snodgrass, as suggesting a more whimsical contrast, had a precedent in Sam
Clemens's *Hannibal Journal* device of abandoning the
name Perkins in his "cognomen" in favor of Blab. W.
Epaminondas Adrastus Blab suited him because it "made
a good jingle."[49] Apparently Sam Clemens was still at
work upon his "funnier book" in New Orleans. The
*Crescent* correspondence would appear to be the final con-
summation of his plan of four years before, were it not
that its matter and tone are entirely different from those
of the earlier experiments. Instead of the innocent from
up-country giving himself away, Quintus Curtius Snodgrass is a city man who is quite consciously literary, a
satirist and an experimenter with words.

The first of the series is printed with the title, "The
Expedition to Baton Rouge." It appeared ten days before

[47] *Ibid.*, I, 51. His note about the letters is that they were pleasing to Mark
Twain's pilot associates, but they were without literary value. Mark Twain was
twenty-five years old. "More than one author has achieved reputation at that age.
Mark Twain was of slower growth."

[48] That portion of New Orleans which lies on the west of the river.

[49] *Hannibal Journal*, Sept. 16, 1852, p. 2, col. 5.

Louisiana joined the Confederacy. Newspapers of the time contain accounts of the drilling of squads of citizens and even of children at play, that foreshadowed the event. The letter contains a highly absurd account of how Snodgrass "hastened to join the Louisiana Guard," sailed with them up the Mississippi to Baton Rouge on the steamer "National," and planted the flag of the Confederacy in front of the State House.

## THE EXPEDITION TO BATON ROUGE[50]

We present to our readers, by the kind permission of our friend Brown, a letter which he received on Tuesday last from his intimate acquaintance Snodgrass, who is a prominent member of one of our newly organized military corps. Mr. Snodgrass naturally unbosoms himself to his *fidae achates* Brown, so that our readers may depend upon his plain unvarnished statement, as being true in every particular:

———

New Orleans, Jan. 14, 1861.

*Dear Brown*—I have this instant returned from the campaign, and am at present occupied in recruiting,—not more men for another trip, but my exhausted energies, that I may be enabled to give you a slight idea of the excitement and *pleasures* of a soldier's life. You may remember, my dear friend, that from my earliest childhood I have panted to "seek the bubble reputation, even in the cannon's mouth," as somebody or other in the literary line beautifully remarks; in fact I date my infatuation from the day when a besotted uncle, in a moment of temporary imbecility, gave me a wooden sword, with which I succeeded in inflicting severe flesh wounds on all the very small children of the neighborhood, which gallant deed resulted in my being ignominiously spanked with my own weapon, which was then with

[50] New Orleans *Daily Crescent*, Monday morning, Jan. 21, 1861. Vol. XIII, No. 275, p. 2, cols. 1 & 2.

much formality consigned to the flames. This little episode would have cooled the ardor of many, but the Spirit of Quintus Curtius Snodgrass may be conquered but never subdued! No, never!

When, therefore, a short time since, the opportunity presented itself of my covering myself with glory and a blue uniform with buttons all over it, you must remember, my dear friend, how, to use a military phrase, "I took time by the firelock," how I hastened to become a member of the Louisiana Guard, and hurried to the tailor to be measured for clothes that were destined to make me a worthy son of Mars. All this you know, and it is therefore useless for me to dwell upon it longer. I will therefore proceed at once to tell you of what occurred subsequent to our embarkation on the good steamer National, bound for Baton Rouge, where we were to defy the powers that be, and perform certain feats calculated to cause considerable mental discomfort to the O. P. F. We pushed into the stream at the cheerful hour of 3 A. M. amid the cheers of about 34 individuals, all of whom exhibited unmistakable signs of intoxication. We were then ordered to go to bed, an order which, viewed theoretically, was a most desirable one; but as going to bed consisted in sitting upon a chair or lying on the bare floor with a spittoon for a pillow, it was, practically speaking, not as luxurious as an unreflecting mind might deem it.

Just as we were endeavoring under these slightly disadvantageous circumstances to woo the dreamy goddess, we were startled by a severe concussion followed by a series of jerks, while above the din rose the stentorian voice of our noble Colonel, who, in a pathetic but commanding tone, implored us in the never-to-be-forgotten words of Ed'ard Cuttle, Mariner, to "Stand-by." Several of our gallant men were on the point of jumping overboard, doubtless with the noble intention of saving some unknown party who was supposed to have fallen over previously; but they were fortunately dissuaded from their philanthropic purpose by some of their friends, who collared them and dragged them kicking into the cabin. We had run down a flatboat, but for the disregard of human life which particularly characterizes military men, I neglected to inquire whether the proprietors of said flatboat survived this fearful catastrophe or not. If they, like the immortal Webster, "still live," I trust they will, through the medium of the public press, inform our anxious public of the fact. When we arose from what was jocularly supposed to have been our night's sleep, I noticed almost all our men busily engaged with flasks which contained, I am told, tooth-wash, and which, I presume, must have been that necessary article of toilette, as I did not notice that any of them cleaned their teeth in any other way during the campaign. We then feasted like sybarites on hominy, beans and other esculents of a most nutritious and invigorating description, immediately after which we were requested, in the most blandishing terms of endearment, to fall in by our orderly sergeant. Oh, Brown what a jewel of an orderly we have in our corps! He tells us to fall in so often that we are constantly on the point of falling out; the interest he takes in our being dressed is really affecting, while the solicitude he manifests as to whether our eyes are right or left, must create feelings of ardent love for him in the breast of every true soldier. Then the playful way in which he would inquire whether we were all asleep, when it was a fact potent to all that the "balmy" had not been indulged in by any one for 48 hours, was calculated to create a smile and disseminate cheerfulness even in that dark hour that tried men's souls.

Brown, never make a bosom friend of an orderly sergeant! I am willing to concede the fact that in private life he may be all that is estimable—a loving husband, an affectionate father and an obedient son; but as a public character he has a duty to perform, and to that duty he will sacrifice his dearest friend should said dearest friend happen to turn his toes in or his chin out. To get back to our muttons, as the Mounseers say, we were drilled all that day till any one could have knocked us down with a feather, by which time we were considered fit to meet the enemy. That night we arrived at our destination, and on the receipt of the news that the arsenal was to be defended to the last, the quiet determination of both officers and men to win or die was, to say the least, unpleasantly startling, particularly to "Yours, Truly," who felt that he had very little chance, individually, for the win, and every prospect in the world for the die. (Just his luck). Revolvers were loaded and bowie knives sharpened, but having been informed that the attack would not be made till the next morning (which I looked upon very much in the light of a reprieve) we lay down again and tried to fancy we were going to sleep. Three or four succeeded, but as they all turned out to be violent snorers, they most effectually prevented anyone following their example. And now while these merciless snorers are keeping everyone awake, let me speak to you, my dear friend, of our officers; by our officers I mean those of our immediate corps, for of those in command of the battalion you will hear praise everywhere. While the amiable regard for our personal comfort; the kind feeling of good fellowship and general, jolly, *brickish* sort of conduct of the lieutenants of the Louisiana Guards to the members of that corps, are only known and appreciated by the men who experienced it at their hands. In fact, if I had not purchased so many coffee beans on board the boat, and kept backing my opinion with said coffee beans, that a pair of threes was a pretty good hand to go in on, I should have published a card of these gentlemen generally for their kindness, and the first Lieutenant in particular, for two of three pulls at the bottle where he kept his toothwash, and which he told me, in his impressive way, to "use with discretion." But the fact is, as many hands come out better than mine, that I have been compelled to give up my intention, owing to an intense stringency in the money market.

Fancy had been busy during the dark hours picturing the blaze of enthusiasm with which we should be received in the morning by the high-minded and patriotic Baton Rougians, nor were we deceived: The sun was high in the heavens, and there, upon the shore of the Father of Waters, it darted down its ardent rays upon one old donkey ladened with a basket of apples, and some half dozen urchins, the latter more attracted by love of said apples, I fear, than by love of country or of martial glory. Rather discouraged, we were compelled to fall back on our trump card to-wit: the band, the members of which played until they exhibited alarming symptoms of exhaustion, by which time the crowd had been increased by the arrival of four more boys, two white men, a rival apple vendor, and a white cow.

The fact is, my dear boy, that during our whole stay, no one bade us God speed, no one said smoke, no one said imbibe, in short no one said "turkey" once. But stay! I have one exception to make. Brown, if you ever meet Tom Morgan, make the most of him, for many like him you are not likely to meet in life's weary pilgrimage.

I should like to see the man who would think of speaking of him as Thomas Morgan. No, indeed! plain, honest, warm-hearted *Tom;* how kindly he greeted old friends or new acquaintances; and when all others had forgotten the common courtesy due, at least to strangers, if not to men who had come to risk their lives for our common mother State, can any one forget how he, and he alone, marched his company of Fencibles down and gave us those brotherly cheers of God Speed, as we were about to turn our faces homeward. His cheerful face and kindly words are not forgotten.

On Friday morning at 11 o'clock we marched into the town, and after remaining under arms in the principal street for about an hour and a half, under a broiling sun, at what is facetiously termed a parade *rest,* (which, for your information, I would state consists in standing straight as a ramrod, staring immediately in front of you like a Dutch doll, with your hands meekly folded over your musket, with a view of inducing any credulous bystanders to believe that you are comfortable,) we repaired to the arsenal. Speaking of repairing, reminds me of the Baton Rouge mud. Do you know, Brown, I firmly believe that Spalding's glue, that is creating such a sensation now-a-days, must be manufactured largely from that same article. The Japanese may possess some composition more obstinately adhesive, but I've never heard of it.

When the battalion formed before the arsenal, the Louisiana Guard was permitted the honor of first entering the grounds and placing guards at the gates. I have reasons for believing that this honor was accorded us in consequence of the individual good humor of your friend, the writer; but do not let this go farther, as Q. C. Snodgrass would be the last to speak his own praise or to create jealousy among his comrades. After detailing some unhappy beings to stand on guard all night in the rain, and others to act as hewers of wood and drawers of water, we were dismissed to amuse ourselves as best we might. Some of the more fortunate, among whom was Q. C. S., were in the officer's room in a decided case of dishabillé, where we supped beautifully of crackers and cheese, and were indulging in a feast of reason and a flow of Soul in the shape of the Darby Ram and other intellectual and musical *morceaux*, when a couple of shots were fired, whereby the Darby Ram came to an untimely end, and the Louisiana Guard were hurried into their pantaloons, which latter feat our worthy Second Lieutenant performed most systematically in one time and two motions.

This alarm having been ascertained to have resulted from a white-faced heifer looking over the fence at a nervous sentry, we adjourned to our blankets. In the morning (Saturday) we prepared to hand over the post to the Baton Rouge battalion, after which we marched down to the boat, our baggage (such of it as was left) following us in drays.

The rest of this day was occupied in brushing uniforms and wondering when we should start for New O. The next morning at parade all the men appeared with uniforms spotlessly clean, when we received the satisfactory intelligence that we were to march up to the arsenal again to raise the flag of the Southern Confederacy, and we should be, "as we were," i. e., exceedingly muddy. Off we started again to the appropriate air of the "serious Family Polka." The Stars and Stripes, (with but 15 stars) was raised in the barracks yard to the air of "Hail Columbia," and a salute of 15 guns was fired by a detachment of the Washington Artillery, all of which detachment returned to their ranks with the usual allotment of arms and fingers, which astonished as much as it delighted me.

After this impressive ceremony we started again for the boat, where large quantities of "six bits" were again disbursed to have boots and uniforms cleaned, and it did seem to me that the mud in Baton Rouge was the only thing in the place that manifested any attachment for us, and it certainly did stick to us through thick and thin.

At 3 P. M. we backed out (and it was the only time we did "back-out" during the whole trip) and started on our homeward course.

At Plaquemine we were saluted with cheers, cannon and every demonstration of enthusiasm.

Night coming on, I succeeded by my intriguing and cajolery, in securing that part of a mattress which was not occupied by the other five who had laid hands upon it, and dreamed that I was attacking a military post, which contained my hair brush, comb, and all the luxuries of the toilette which I had brought with me. Just as I reached the summit of the breach, and had seized with determined grasp a stick of cosmetic that I recognized as my personal property, a ball struck me and felled me to the ground— when I awoke and found myself vigorously clinging to the nose of one of my comrades, while the foot of another was across the place where my cravat would have been had I been wearing such an article. Shortly after, we arrived at New O., and for the appearance we made then, I refer you to the papers. I can only

say, in conclusion, my dear friend, that I forgive the Baton Rougians for selling me terpentinery whiskey and tobacco largely sprin-
kled with fine shavings; that I am at peace with my fellow-man,
although I have not recovered my lost baggage; and that I have
tied up a fresh supply in a clean towel, ready to start any where
that the South may call me, at a moment's notice.

> Yours, with a military salute,
> Quintus Curtius Snodgrass,
>          One of the Veterans of 1861.
> To Chas. Augustus Brown, Esq., Algiers.

As this new Snodgrass series was written four years
later than the first, the style and mood would, naturally,
be different.   Instead of the vernacular of the traveler
from the country, the language of Snodgrass, metamor-
phosed with a classical given name, is ambitiously literary.
He quotes from Shakespeare, Dickens, and Tom Paine.
All three, according to evidence cited below, Sam Clemens
knew.

The "uncle" mentioned in the first paragraph suggests
Mark Twain's device already mentioned in "My First
Literary Venture."

The opening sentences of the fourth paragraph have
a Mark Twain ring, and the adaptation of the French expression in "to get back to our muttons" is of some significance, inasmuch as the heading of Chapter XXII of
*Life on the Mississippi* is "I Return to My Muttons."

In the seventh paragraph is a defense of Mark Twain's
favorite "given" name for sons of his brain.   Tom Sawyer
and Tom Canty bear evidence of his preference; it was the
name of the boy he remembered most vividly from his
truant days in Hannibal, Tom Blankenship.

Some details here—the spittoon serving for a pillow and the irony directed at tooth-wash—are of the cruder type of fun-making of the earlier Snodgrass letters—of the sort that Mark Twain later trusted his wife and William Dean Howells to censor out of his writings.

The satire directed at the dehumanizing, mechanical-doll effect of military manners would have been characteristic of Mark Twain at any time. It is like the satire at the expense of the important technique of detectives in "The Stolen White Elephant." And, furthermore, the broad satire upon the pride, pomp, and circumstance of glorious war suggests the autobiographic sketch, "A Campaign that Failed," although the mood and style of the two are wholly different. That story was based upon Sam Clemens's two weeks' service in the Confederate Militia, which enlistment came, in fact, only a few months after his contributions to the New Orleans papers.

Brown, the trusted friend, may be an ironical allusion to his partner pilot, Brown, whom he chastised effectively for mistreating his brother Henry.

The second Quintus Curtius Snodgrass communication appeared in the *Crescent* February 25, 1861, somewhat more than a month after the first. The young pilot may have prepared it on his intervening trip up the Mississippi. He seems to have developed out of his thrust at military tactics an ambition to write a more extended satire at the expense of the military profession and its efficiency in making automatons out of men. Quintus Curtius Snodgrass, Esq., High Old Private of the Louisiana Guards, writes *Hints to Young Campaigners: with the Manual of Arms.*—"Dedicated to Charles Augustus Brown, Esq." "Men desiring to become soldiers" are instructed to "do everything briskly and in a series of jerks," and details follow.

The third letter of the second Snodgrass series was printed in the *Crescent* Monday morning, March 11, 1861. After a foreword in which he apologizes because the "dissipated Snodgrass" has not continued his *Hints to Young Campaigners*, the author reverts to his original device of making the letters intimate stories written to his friend Brown. The letter contains the account of a night's epicurean adventures in which Snodgrass, his friend Larryndor Kydd, and a few other happy companions participated. In a letter sent to his brother Orion, Sam Clemens had written:

Yesterday, I had many things to do, but Bixby and I got with the pilots of two other boats and went off dissipating on a ten dollar dinner at a French restaurant—breathe it not to Ma!—where we ate sheep-head, fish with mushrooms, shrimps and oysters—birds—coffee with brandy burnt in it, &c &c,—ate, drank and smoked from one P.M. until five o'clock. . . .[51]

The Larryndor Kydd adventure reported by Snodgrass appears to be the literary residium from Sam Clemens's experience six months before.

The fourth letter of the series is different in vein. Snodgrass has become "special correspondent of the New Orleans *Crescent*" and reports a dinner at which he was a guest at the president's mansion in Washington. The letter reflects the common southern ridicule of "Old Abe" and his family at the beginning of the Civil War.

None of the *Crescent* letters suggests the later Mark Twain as satisfactorily as one wishes they did. The peculiar type of exaggeration, anti-climax, and irony which

[51] *Letters*, I, 48; A. B. P., I, 155.

give flavor to his sentences is discoverable in the earlier
Snodgrass letters, but not here—though the satire at the
expense of the military profession was often a theme during the earlier period of American humor. And yet, if it
can be proved that they are authentic, they are immensely
significant as a link in Mark Twain's development as a
humorist. Can they be admitted to the Sam Clemens
canon? If so, why should Sam Clemens have abandoned
his own middle western vein temporarily in favor of a
more sophisticated manner?

Two answers seem to lie in a letter to Orion Clemens
dated from St. Louis in March, a year before the publication of these. Sam had gone with Pamela to an exhibition
in St. Louis of Church's picture, "The Heart of the
Andes." In a consciously careful way he described the
picture to Orion. They had taken the opera glasses so as
to "examine its beauties minutely." All the youngster's
impressionable nature had been given over to discovering
the secret of its charm: "You will never get tired of looking at the picture, but your reflections—your efforts to
grasp an intelligible Something—you hardly know what
—will grow so painful that you will have to go away from
the thing, in order to obtain relief."[52] This from a
twenty-year-old Middle Westerner, who was to devote
his life to the search for dependable fact. "So much for
the Heart of the Andes," he said as he finished his attempt
at art criticism. It is apparent that his efforts to acquire
conventional culture were bearing fruit. There has been a
question that naturally interests the searcher for elements
that went into the making of Mark Twain's mind and art.
What did his contacts in the cultural centers of New Or-

[52] *Letters*, I, 46.

leans and St. Louis do for Sam Clemens during those impressionable four years while he was spending his hours off duty seeking amusement? Here seems to be the answer—in part, at least—and it is the answer to the question why he was deflected temporarily from his own middle western vein of humor. In New York he had devoted himself to the "4,000 books" in the Printers' library. As a printer in Philadelphia, days or evenings when there was no vacant place for him to fill "he visited historic sites, the art-galleries, and the libraries."[53] He had been drawn into the interests of his sister, who was a music teacher. There were art magazines for sale in the bookstores in Hannibal. Both he and Pamela must have received their first notion of art appreciation there. And it is to be remembered, as evidence that this was not merely a matter of satisfying his curiosity about something that he had on his conscience, that Mark Twain was a musician, of an elementary type, and all his life loved music. He anticipated the twentieth-century vogue of negro spirituals.[54] As pilot he had met cultured people on the Mississippi River boats. His letters show that he was exultingly prosperous at this time.[55] Contemporary pictures of him indicate that he was more conventionally handsome than he was at any other time of his life. As he became master of his situation on the river, the itch to write came back upon him. A letter to Orion contains an attempt to analyse types of humor.[56] He had become convinced that the style of the earlier Snodgrass series was in poor taste; so he turned to what then seemed to him a more elegant style for satire.

[53] A. B. P., I, 98.

[54] Cf. "When Mark Twain Sang Spirituals." Etude, XLIII, 845.

[55] Letters, I, 43.        [56] Ibid., I, 45. Discussed below in chap. VI.

§5

MARK TWAIN'S first *Wanderjähre*, from 1853 to 1861, include three stages in his literary development. First, in 1853 in New York, he was enlarging his horizon chiefly through books. His Philadelphia letters, a little later in the same year, show that he was gaining in command of himself and that he had not lost his literary ambition. That he was not able to make a satisfactory life for himself is indicated by his returning, homesick, to the Middle West, after a little over a year. Second, records of the next two years (1854-1856) in Iowa and Missouri, culminating in the publication of the *Thomas Jefferson Snodgrass Letters*, bear evidence of persisting literary habits and ambitions. And third, once he had got his bearings on the river, the young man returned to his early ambition to write and submitted to the New Orleans *Crescent*, toward the end of the period, in 1861, letters which were more conventionally literary—bore greater evidences of a cultural background—than anything he had attempted before that time. The change of tone is to be accounted for from the fact that throughout the period he had been devoting himself, incidentally but steadily, to the things which would contribute to his personal culture.

But this study of the first twenty-five years of Mark Twain's life justifies the conclusion that the emphasis placed by some of his biographers and critics upon his four pilot years has been out of proportion, that while, during those years, he first attained to a fuller and more nearly satisfactory life for himself than he had found up to that time, they were, after all, *Wanderjähre*—a period of taking stock of the world and of himself. In contrast, the fourteen Hannibal years deserve greater consideration. They are the time when most of the trends which were to determine the direction of his life were formed: his glowing interest in a pioneer situation, where there were problems in development fit for the best energies of the competent, and at the same time a family disability which thwarted the necessity he felt to master the situation; preoccupation with the simpler, more elemental aspects of life, on the one hand, and curiosity about the world of men and books, aroused by his *Journal* tasks, on the other; his dissatisfaction with the conventional and artificial teachings of school and church which thwarted his passion for freedom, and which drove him to find recourse in humor; and the miscarriage of his efforts to find self-expression in the only avenue open to him—writing for his brother's paper. These things determined what his interests would be when he departed from his Hannibal world. His return to his family indicates that, with all the limitations of that Hannibal life, it had been so full of healthy interests that his nature rebelled against breaking away from it. Ultimately, it was the life he knew in Hannibal that gave his genius its character.

# VI

## SAM CLEMENS'S READING

### §1

WITH THE GENERAL trend of the first twenty-five years of Sam Clemens's career in view, we can now take stock more definitely of his literary provenience. Mark Twain's own emphasis upon the original elements in his culture has obscured the facts even more than has the misconception of his critics. In the fragment of a letter written when he was fifty-five years old to some unknown correspondent— British, from internal evidence—he speaks of his assets as a novelist: "I surely have the equipment, a wide culture, and all of it real, none of it artificial, for I don't know anything about books."[1]

The implication is that he considers his own culture to be as nearly original as a man's can be, and that he discredits the kind of culture to be derived from reading. It brings to mind the judgment of Henry James, in which he placed Mark Twain in a class with those Americans whom he has gone to Europe to escape; and it seems to confirm the judgment of Howells that Mark Twain was the most unliterary of literary men. The disclaimer, "I don't know anything about books," is like the pleasure the author had in telling of his wife's "torture" when she had to admit to a foreign guest that her husband had not read Balzac and Thackeray. Both are to be taken as half-

[1] *Letters*, II, 543.

humorous acknowledgments of his sense of contrast between his equipment as a writer and that of Hawthorne,
for instance, or his friend Brander Matthews.  Possibly
he did not know "enough to hurt" about books, "Only a
few languages and a little history."[2]  This comparative
little, however, he continually minimized.  It was a part
of the legend he deliberately created about himself, either
because it pleased his vanity to believe that what he had
read had been of small value in his development, or because he knew that he was more interesting to his American
public in the rôle of an original, than as a man who had
from boyhood extended his powers and his horizon by
diligent reading.  He was unacademic but not unliterary.

The use he made of books to help out his own narrative is surprising to those who have been impressed with
Mark Twain's apparent freedom from bookishness.  *Innocents Abroad* has over nine thousand words borrowed
from books, letters, and notices of various sorts.  *Roughing It* and *Life on the Mississippi* both have almost eleven
thousand, exclusive of the appendices; while *Following
the Equator* has over twenty-five thousand words, or one
twenty-fifth of borrowed material.  However, it was because he ordinarily wrote spontaneously in spite of his
reading that he was restive when he did allow himself to
depend upon information of this sort.  "How it wears a
man out to have to read up a hundred pages of history
every two or three miles!" he exclaimed.[3]

Accepting Mark Twain's account of himself, western
critics as well as eastern have recently used his case as an
example to justify their repudiation of the frontier.  Its
tendency, these critics believe, was to crush down the rarer

---

[2] A. B. P., III, 1350.          [3] *Letters*, II, 614.

spirits that failed to secure the approval of its low level of intelligence. One of the most effective pleaders for the broader view of American literature describes the Hannibal of 1839-1853 as "a kindly, ignorant, slave-holding, Calvinistic village."[4] But ignorance is a relative thing, a thing of many facets, as any group of intelligentsia will exemplify. Previous chapters have shown that the region of which Hannibal was the center had developed an authentic culture by the middle of the nineteenth century and that the Clemens family had had a part in the forming of that culture.

Leaving out of account all other aspects of his training except the literary aspect, the present chapter will trace the steps by which Sam Clemens became a reader and critic of the best in literature by the time he was twenty-five years old.

Albert Bigelow Paine's story of Sam Clemens's conversion to the reading habit is that the youthful Sam found a scrap out of an old life of Joan of Arc floating about on a street in Hannibal, which depicted the "maid" tormented by ribald soldiers. His adolescent rage, aroused by the pity of her situation, took him to the library to learn more of her story. "The first result was that Sam began to read. He hunted up everything he could find on the subject of Joan, and from that went into French history in general—indeed, into history of every kind. Samuel Clemens had suddenly become a reader—almost a

---

[4] The late Vernon Parrington, *Main Currents in American Thought*, III, 87. Parrington's school seems merely to have followed the Van Wyck Brooks view on this point. Mrs. Hazard says that Mark Twain's childhood was passed "in squalid, straggling towns on the southwest frontier."—*Frontier in American Literature*, p. 221. Professor Blankenship cannot see the real significance of Mark Twain's life and work for regret that the Gilded Age caused his gift as a satirist to miscarry.—*American Literature as an Expression of the National Mind*, p. 469.

student."[5]   The mere fact that his village furnished him
with the clue and with the resources to satisfy his newly
aroused curiosity is significant.

It is fairly clear that he came from a family of
readers. "Orion was fond of books, and Pamela, . . . and
Henry had read everything obtainable."[6]  When Sam
wanted facts, he was in the habit of "asking Henry." He
had "cared little for reading himself, beyond a few exciting tales, though the putting into type of a good deal of
miscellaneous matter had beyond doubt developed in him
a taste for general knowledge."[7]   These "exciting tales"
were apparently his first course in reading—a supplement,
that is, to the classics in his McGuffey's readers.  It was
from such barn-loft thrillers, doubtless, that the "histrionic poison entered his bones" and won him supremacy
with his Hannibal gang.[8]

Reading of this kind would have been frowned upon
by Sam's family, of course. His brother Orion tried to
persuade him to read Dickens in their early days. "I was
ashamed," said Mark Twain years later, "but I couldn't
do it."[9]  The statement has a double significance.  Orion
Clemens was evidently of the sort that read those things
without which no gentleman's library is complete, while
Sam had to be independent. As an old man, however,
Mark Twain remembered that he had felt guilty because
he could not read what he ought to read, and this helps to
explain his feeling that his knowledge of books could not
pass muster with any competent judge. Since his knowledge of books was unorthodox, he felt, it counted for
nothing. He would have to abide by his limitations and

[5] *The Boys' Life of Mark Twain*, p. 45.
[6] *Ibid.*, p. 65.          [8] *Ibid.*, p. 60.
[7] A. B. P., I, 80.          [9] A. B. P., III, 1350.

defend them as best he could. "There is much to be learned . . . without going to books . . . books do not cover the whole domain of esthetic human culture," he declared late in life—with his cap and bells on.[10]

There is no evidence that Jane Clemens cared for any book but the Bible. John Marshall Clemens sometimes bought books, and, as has been said, was instrumental in founding the first Hannibal library. Following the example of St. Charles, Hannibal formed a chartered company, which in 1844 founded the Hannibal Library Institute, the second town library in the state. John Clemens was a stockholder in the company and, the year before he died, its president. It was a kind of chamber-of-commerce enterprise to attract a desirable class of settlers to the community. The St. Louis Mercantile Library, now a valuable repository of early American travel books and a good general library, was founded in 1846, two years later than the Hannibal library and under the same plan. These institutions provided lecture courses as well as library facilities. Orion Clemens, who succeeded his father as a stockholder in the library company, published in the *Journal* three months before Sam left Hannibal a statement of a committee of stockholders which reported that the library contained 425 books.[11] If the titles of these books could be discovered, they would be the best indication of what Sam Clemens's reading was at that time.

Besides the Library Institute, the book stalls in Hannibal would have attracted Sam Clemens, with their array

---

[10] "The Bee," *What is Man? and Other Essays*, p. 284.

[11] *Hannibal Journal*, March 31, 1853. *"Report of the Committee of Stockholders of the Hannibal Library Institute:* The library was organized under a regular charter in the year 1844 . . . stockholders 70 . . . number of books, 425 . . . attempting to procure lectures. . . . Signed: Z. G. Draper, O. Clemens, H. Meredith."

of magazines.   We know that he sometimes took magazines to Laura Hawkins—"exchanges from the printing-office—Godey's and others."[12]   There were advertisements of four different bookstores in Hannibal in the early papers.[13]   In the *Tri-weekly Messenger* for August 11, 1853, D. K. Garman advertised, at the New Book Store, *Putnam's, Harper's, Peterson's, Godey's, Graham's, Knickerbocker, Illustrated Magazine of Art.*   The *Western Union* for May 15, 1851, contains this notice:

### MORE NEW BOOKS

Just received from New York, Philadelphia, Baltimore, Louisville, and St. Louis, an extensive assortment of books and stationery, embracing histories, biography, poems, miscellanies, Latin, French, and Greek books, scientific works—a great variety of moral and religious books—in short, every article usually kept in the best book stores, all of which will be sold very cheap for cash, wholesale or retail. . . .

Sign of the Big Book<br>F. B. McElroy[14]

But of course the great source of the boy's reading at this time, as his mother had anticipated, was the printing-office itself, and there he was not reading idly, but with a purpose.   As sub-editor he was watching for what could be used to advantage in the *Journal.*   He was forming standards: "One isn't a printer ten years without setting

[12] A. B. P., I, 80.

[13] It is to be remembered in this connection, that Hannibal spoke of itself as the "Second city in the State" in the early fifties and that it was in direct daily communication with St. Louis, whose papers were advertising Emerson as a lecturer (*St. Louis Intelligencer,* Dec. 30, 1852)—an advertisement that Orion and Sam may be assumed to have had an interest in.

[14] Two other bookstores are advertised in the *Courier.*   On May 23, 1850, J. H. Triplett advertised "Shakespeare, Shelley, Sheridan, Moore, Milton, and all the eminent poets"; J. L. Matthews (March 20, 1851) advertised text books and general literature.

up acres of good and bad literature, and learning—unconsciously at first, consciously later—to discriminate between the two, within his mental limitations. . . ."[15] The chances are that as printer's devil the boy knew not only what was in his brother's paper, but what was in the other four town papers and those of the district, including St. Louis, from all of which they drew "select. material" to fill out their pages. When Orion Clemens bought the *Hannibal Weekly Dollar Journal*, he announced that his paper would be "Devoted to Politics, Literature, Poetry, Miscellany, Arts, Sciences, Amusements, Commercial Affairs, News of the Day, Local Matters, &c."[16] Orion and Sam Clemens proposed to keep their readers informed about literature and poetry. Before sporting news and matters of scientific interest required much space in newspapers, literary notes were welcome in the body of the paper—material which the literary supplement now takes care of. As has already been shown, incomplete columns in any part of the paper were filled out with anecdotes about Samuel Johnson, Gray, Pope, Cowper, Middleton, Macaulay, Byron, Franklin, Hawthorne, Poe—often with quotations from their works. In the April 7, 1853, issue of the *Daily Journal* is an anecdote about Charles Lamb:

Charles Lamb, once called upon for a toast at a dinner party, during which some unruly and ill-bred children had been causing him much personal annoyance, got up and stammered out with a serious-comic air, "Here's to the m-m-memory of the m-m-much calumniated g-g-good King Herod!"[17]

---

[15] "The Turning Point of My Life," *What is Man? and Other Essays*, p. 136.
[16] *Cf.* p. 103 above.
[17] What appears to be an echo of this anecdote is an exclamation in one of Mark Twain's letters to Mr. Howells. He fears that his eldest child may have thrown his third section of *Life on the Mississippi* into the fire and that the stack of MS. may have to be written over again. "If so, O for a return of the lamented Herod!" he says.—*Letters*, I, 241.

§2

T HERE REMAINS something to be said about the reading of
the region of which Hannibal was the center, for the effect
it may have had on Sam Clemens's interests.  As was
pointed out earlier, it was like the rest of early America:
it had it on its conscience to know what was in books.
When Martin Chuzzlewit, on the railway train going to
St. Louis, asked General Choke whether he had been in
England, he replied, "In print I have, sir . . . not otherwise.  We air a reading people here, sir.  You will meet
with much information among us that will surprise you,
sir."[18]

Either at the town library or in Hannibal bookstores
would be found, no doubt, the Harper *Family Library,*
which was a sort of five-foot shelf of the fabulous forties.[19]
There Sam Clemens might have had a chance to read
Michelet's *Modern History* (No. 40), Fraser's *History of
Persia* (No. 70), two volumes of *Lives of Distinguished
Men* (Nos. 123 and 124), including Burke possibly, the
history of the *Lewis and Clark Expedition* (No. 154).
This and the *School District Library* contained early nineteenth-century writings for the most part, but the *Evangelical Family Library* and Wesley's *Christian Library,*
published by the American Tract Society, contained, more
numerously, such eighteenth-century writings as were

[18] *Martin Chuzzlewit,* chap. XXI.

[19] The *Family Library* proposed to make it possible for every family to buy
books of "history, biography, travels, voyages, natural history, natural philosophy,
astronomy, natural theology, physiology, intellectual and moral philosophy, institutions, manners and customs of nations, *belles lettres,* etc." The authors advertised are "Dr. Franklin, Sir Walter Scott, Paley, Abercrombie, Dick, Brewster,
Paulding, James Montgomery, Tytler, Combe, Southey, Gleig, Thatcher, Mudie,
James Turner, Russell, Milner, Leslie, Cunningham, Bush, Griscom, etc."—Vol.
100—Publishers' Foreword.

answers to the atheistical doctrines of Hume, Paine, and Gibbon. The latter, as a consequence, the boy might well have read surreptitiously, with some feeling of heroism; he was defying a Providence that would send a special judgment upon him for his wickedness.

In his *Life on the Mississippi,* Mark Twain says that in the residence of the principal citizen of almost any Mississippi Valley town, among the books to be found on the parlor center-table were

Tupper,[20] much penciled; also, *Friendship's Offering,* and *Affection's Wreath,*[21] with their sappy inanities illustrated in die-away mezzotints; also, Ossian; *Alonzo and Melissa;*[22] maybe *Ivanhoe;* also "Album," full of original "poetry" of the Thou-hast-wounded-the-spirit-that-loved-thee breed; two or three goody-goody works—*Shepherd of Salisbury Plain,*[23] etc.; current number of the chaste and innocuous *Godey's Lady's Book;* . . .[24]

Two things are to be said about taking this list as showing the level of Sam Clemens's reading at the time. First, it represents the Main Street standard, while any town of the Middle West, then as now, had a saving remnant of people not of Main Street complacent sentimentality. In the second place, the parlor center-table represented the woman of the household in the early day. If the husband was a professional man, he usually had a domain of his own on a corner of the lot. In this "office" were the books that represented his tastes—for often he was an advanced thinker—religious and political controversial books, and

---

[20] Martin Farquhar Tupper, *Proverbial Philosophy.*

[21] *Cf.* CHAL, II, 516-17.

[22] By Daniel Jackson (or I. Mitchell). *Cf.* Loshe, *The Early American Novel,* p. 53.

[23] By Hannah More, a writer most popular in Sam Clemens's youth. Harper published a seven-volume edition of her works in 1847.

[24] *Life on the Mississippi,* 317-18.

good substantial classics. The library of Dr. Lenoir, who lived at Old Providence on the Missouri River half way between St. Louis and Kansas City in the early forties may be taken as representing the sort of thing professional men read in river towns (that is, in places on the main avenues of travel) in the section.[25] Besides his own medical books and school texts, his library contained more books on religion than on any other one subject, among them:

Thomas Fuller's *Maxims* (1787)
Alexander and Archibald, *Christian Evidences* (pub. 1842)
George Combe, *Vestiges of the Natural History of Creation* (1846)
E. W. Hooker, *Memoir* of Sarah L. H. Smith, Late of the American Mission in Syria (1845)
Philip Doddridge, *Rise and Progress of Religion* (n. d.— Bought 1847)
Matthew Hale Smith, *Universalism not of God* (1847)
John W. Nevin, *A Summary of Bible Antiquities* (n. d.)
Francis Wayland, *Elements of Moral Science* (1847)
Rev. Thomas Chalmers, *A Call to the Unconverted* (n. d.)
Thomas Dick, *Complete Works* (n. d.)

Dr. Lenoir had a taste also for history and biography. There are many such books as

Philips's *Life and Times of John Bunyan* (n. d.)
Plutarch's *Lives* (1850)
J. H. Merle, *Germany, England, and Scotland* (1848)
S. S. Goodrich, *Modern History from the Fall of Rome* (1848)
Smedley's *Sketches of Venetian Life* (1840)

[25] The library was accumulated during the forties and fifties, part of it after Dr. Lenoir moved to Jefferson City. His son, who lives five miles south of Columbia, Missouri, kindly permitted me to have a list of the books left him by his father. There are 165 titles in all. I am indebted to Mrs. Bernard Matson and Mrs. Sara Saper Gauldin for listing the titles, etc.

Russell's *View of Ancient and Modern Egypt* (1841)
James Fletcher's *History of Poland* (1840)
Sparks's *Life of Washington* (1850)
Knightly's *History of Greece* (1848)
Wm. Paley, *Theology* (1842)
Tooke's *Pantheon of Heathen Gods and Illustrious Heroes* (1838)

Of *belles lettres* the library had the following:

Two editions of the *Spectator* (1819 and 1851)
Young's *Night Thoughts* (1848)
Franklin's *Autobiography* (1848)
Burton's *Anatomy of Melancholy* (1837)
Shakespeare's *Works* (1850)
The *Decameron* (n. d.)
Goldsmith's *Roman History* (1818)
A one-volume *Works of Laurence Sterne* (1850)
Hervey's *Book of Essays and Reflections* (1746)
Byron's *Verse, Prose, Letters, Journals,* etc.

With three exceptions the books are American publications —most of them published in Philadelphia, a few in Cincinnati. Many of the titles and authors are identical with those in the *Family Library* already described. It is not unreasonable to suppose that Sam Clemens, in Hannibal, a larger town, had access to many books of the same sort. Such occasional reminiscences as that in *Following the Equator* suggest that his early interest in books was more extensive than any record he left of it shows: "Fifty years ago, when I was a boy . . . vague tales and rumors of a mysterious body of professional murderers [a sect called thugs] came wandering in from . . . India; . . . The matter died down and a lull followed. Then Eugène Sue's *Wandering Jew* appeared, and made great talk for awhile."[26]   It must be repeated that the educational ideals of the section in which Hannibal was situated were above the average of the time.   As has been shown, Marion had been a college county, and Hannibal itself had three academies in 1852.   The percentage of illiteracy among the whites was lower than it is today.

British and Eastern American magazines were advertised much more extensively in the Hannibal papers of the period than they would now be in middle western papers.[27]   Often the table of contents was printed, and a "Grand Literary and Artistic Combination" was offered— three magazines at special rates.   The *Daily Journal* for March 22, 1853, printed the notice of a special rate for the *London, Edinburgh, Westminster, North British Quarterly,* and *Blackwood's* to a single subscriber!

An important influence resulting from the reading of his region is seen in Mark Twain's obvious familiarity with the Bible.   This familiarity makes us take him at his word when he speaks of having read the Bible through "before I was 15 years old."[28]   In his numerous biblical allusions, in the ease with which he falls into biblical phraseology, and in many of the titles of his minor pieces, he shows a knowledge of the Bible that could have come only from early and prolonged exposure to the Sacred Book.[29]

[26] *Following the Equator,* II, 111.

[27] *Scott's Weekly Paper, Peterson's Prospectus of DeBow's Review, Southern Literary Messenger, Blackwood's, Graham's, Harper's New Monthly Magazine, Godey's Lady's Book, Arthur's Home Gazette, Knickerbocker Magazine, Dodge's Literary Museum,* and the New York *Tribune* are advertised.

[28] A. B. P., III, 1281.

[29] Henry Pochmann discovers 124 allusions to the Bible in Mark Twain's writings—more, by far, than to any individual author.   Twain falls into Bible phrases in such expressions as "you have clothed her in garments meet for her high degree" (*Letters,* II, 722); "There was weeping and wailing and gnashing

No one, moreover, has used Bible stories as mythology to the extent that Mark Twain has. What he called "its picturesque and amazing customs and superstitions"[30] had taken such hold on his imagination that he turned to them again and again for themes. One of the earliest uses (and almost the latest) was his burlesque of the Christian heaven as seen by Captain Stormfield (1868-1907). In 1870 he began *Shem's Diary*, the action of which is laid in Noah's Ark. He returned to the manuscript at various periods of his life, but never finished it.[31] In 1905 he revised *Adam's Diary* as a companion piece to *Eve's Diary*.[32] Besides these there is "A Monument to Adam," "Adam's Soliloquy," "Eve Speaks," and "That Day in Eden [passage from Satan's Diary]." Satan was, without doubt, the Biblical character that appealed most strongly to his imagination, as to Milton's. Besides numerous allusions to him, there is "Sold to Satan," "A Humane Word from Satan," the Satan analogy in "Is Shakespeare Dead?," besides *The Mysterious Stranger*, with Satan's nephew as its hero.

What may be called Mark Twain's second period of Bible study came in connection with his reports of the "Quaker City" excursion into Palestine. Chapters XV and XXI of *Innocents Abroad* show unmistakably with

of teeth" (*Life on the Mississippi*, p. 137); often it is a matter of his taking advantage of familiar biblical ideas for their imagery: "Like Satan's own kitchen" (*ibid.*, p. 93); "be content and praise God"; "a sort of Middle-Age night and slavery which would last till Christ comes again" (*Letters*, II, 693); ". . . Such is the human race. Often it does seem such a pity that Noah and his party did not miss the boat" (*Christian Science* [1907], p. 200). His titles show the same interest: "Was It Heaven or Hell?", "What is Man?", "To a Person Sitting in Darkness," "The Second Advent."

[30] *Letters*, II, 440.          [31] *Ibid.*, II, 486, 488.

[32] *Ibid.*, II, 962. It was written in 1893 and "degraded as an advertisement of the Buffalo Fair."

what care he supported these reports with Bible reading. But it was, after all, because of what his region had done for him that he was so competent a traveler in Palestine. "He who takes with him the wealth of the Indies, brings back the wealth of the Indies." It was by means of tentacles developed in Hannibal that he found his largest interests in a new situation.

It is to be concluded that Sam Clemens, when he left Hannibal, had what would even now be considered a very fair comprehension of what the world of books contained, and had made a good many excursions into it. This was possible because he had access to a town library and to up-to-date bookstores, besides such exchanges as came to his brother's printing office; and because the taste of his family and of his Hannibal world fostered an interest in books.

## §3

IN NEW YORK Sam Clemens was free to turn to what interested him most. Notes in two of the first letters he wrote back to the family after he went East bear evidence of a well developed reading habit. It will be remembered that in the second letter he wrote to his mother from New York he expressed satisfaction that the printers had two libraries in town. "If books are not good company," he asked, "where can I find it?" And in a letter to his sister he said, "You ask me where I spend my evenings. Where would you suppose, with a free printers' library containing more than 4,000 volumes within a quarter of a mile of me, and nobody at home to talk to?"[33] A boy's desire to reassure his family concerning his habits in his new situation is ap-

---

[33] *Letters*, I, 22.

parent; yet the fact remains that the statement is of a piece with the story of his life-long interests that Sam Clemens had already in 1853 literary curiosity sufficient to tide him over the time when he first felt strange in a large city.

We know what sort of thing he chose to read in those libraries. "I like history, biography, travels, curious facts and strange happenings, and science. And I detest novels, poetry, and theology," he wrote twenty years later.[34]    In general, this represented his actual choice of books throughout his life.

In Philadelphia also, as we have seen, the youngster supplemented his sight-seeing expeditions with excursions into history and checked up on what interested him by referring back to his Hannibal reading.    The interest in Benjamin Franklin that his Philadelphia letters show must also have had its origin in Hannibal.    The *Journal* contains frequent allusions to the Philadelphia wise man,[35] and Sam Clemens may have had to know him only too well.    The fact that Orion Clemens called his Keokuk job-printing office the Ben Franklin Book and Job Office indicates that he admired the author of "Poor Richard." With all his own impecuniousness, he would have been merely human if he had reminded his young assistant, boarding at the best hotel in Keokuk, that "a groat a day's a penny a year."    It sounds like a mood of rebellious reminiscence—of satisfaction at least that he is finally getting even—when Mark Twain writes in 1870, "His

---

[34] A. B. P., I, 512.

[35] In the *Hannibal Journal,* Dec. 27, 1849, Dr. Franklin is reported to have quoted Cotton Mather as saying, when he saw a man strike his head against a beam: "Stoop a little as you go through this world, and you will avoid many hard thumps."    In another issue he is quoted as saying, "Always select your wife from a bunch."

maxims were full of animosity toward boys. Nowadays a boy can't follow out a single natural instinct without tumbling over some of those everlasting aphorisms and hearing from Franklin on the spot."[36]

If history and biography were what he was most interested in during his days in the East, his reading during the fifteen months he was in Keokuk, was, in some respects, different. There he was "a popular young man," "thoroughly happy," Fred W. Lorch says. "He had never in his life been under less restraint."[37] A letter of the time, quoted in the preceding chapter, shows that he was interested in writing. It is not surprising, therefore, to find that he sometimes read novels, and "so-called funny books." His biographer, as has been mentioned, notes his reading of Dickens and Poe in Keokuk. Stuart P. Sherman has spoken of the "Dickens flavor" in Mark Twain's writings.[37a] In view of the latter's disclaimer of a knowledge of Dickens, the case of Dickens in Mark Twain's early reading is of special interest. There are many references to Dickens and Thackeray in the *Hannibal Journal*. Though Dickens was never approved of as Thackeray was, his *Household Words* was advertised and quoted, and references to *Pickwick Papers* in all the newspapers of the region show that it was much read in the Middle West. Moreover, the "funny book" Ed Brownell found Sam Clemens reading was probably *Pickwick Papers*. When he began his own "funnier book" he adopted the name Snodgrass. The "poetic Snodgrass" would be the member of the Pickwick Club that would amuse Sam Clemens most; *Pickwick Papers* consists of re-

---

[36] "The Late Benjamin Franklin," *Sketches New and Old.*
[37] *Op. cit.*, p. 419.          [37a] CHAL, III, 6.

ports on travel adventures for which "Innocents Abroad" would be a good title; and the satire in "The Thomas Jefferson Snodgrass Letters," though cruder, is of a kind with that in Dickens's book.  A tempting theory would be that *Innocents Abroad* was written in long-pent-up retaliation upon the English for Dickens's strictures upon American civilization, had there not been so many other strictures.  There is no doubt about Mark Twain's later reading of Dickens,[38] and his disclaimer of early knowledge may have come from any one of several causes—one of those lapses of memory to which his literary habit made him prone, or boredom at the critics' insistence upon a Dickens influence and his own belief that his knowledge of Dickens was too slight to justify any such critical assumption.

The case of Poe supports still further the theory that Mark Twain read more than he left any record of.  As in the case of Dickens, there is no doubt concerning his reading of Poe at some later time,[39] but his early curiosity may

[38] According to Henry Pochmann's findings, there are only eight references to Dickens in Mark Twain's biography and writings.  Three of these are to the *Tale of Two Cities*, which he told Mr. Fisher he read "at least every two years." —H. W. Fisher, *Abroad with Mark Twain and Eugene Field* (1922), pp. 59-60. He and his family "all read" it in Paris.—A. B. P., I, 106; II, 644.  In *Life on the Mississippi* is a reference to the social theory of *Martin Chuzzlewit* (Chap. XXXVIII), and in his London speech, "The Ladies," Sairey Gamp is humorously mentioned among the "sublime women" of history.—*Speeches* (1910), p. 97. The others are vague general references.—A. B. P., I, 106; II, 644.  It cannot be denied that there are a good many things in Dickens's *Martin Chuzzlewit* to which Mark Twain might have owed an unconscious debt, but it is also true that the resemblance so often pointed out between *The Gilded Age* and *Martin Chuzzlewit* may result from the fact that both writers had as common material the careers of William Muldrow and other western promoters.

[39] *Letters*, II, 830: "Your [Howells's] Poe article delighted me; . . . I am in agreement with substantially all you say about his literature.  To me his prose is unreadable . . . you grant that God and circumstance sinned against Poe, but you also grant that he sinned against himself—a thing he couldn't do and didn't do."

The most apparent indebtedness is in the story of dual personality entitled "Concerning the Recent Carnival of Crime in Connecticut" (1876).  The perwell have been aroused by anecdotes and quotations from Poe which, as compositor, he set up for the *Hannibal Journal*. The *Journal* for May 23, 1853, contains a one-column story entitled "A Great Man Self-Wrecked," in which the facts of Poe's death are told as temperance propaganda. It is clear, too, that Poe was much read in the Middle West from the fifties on.[40]

In all his early reading, Sam Clemens perhaps was merely amusing himself, but his remark in Keokuk about the sort of book he would write some day shows what latent purpose persisted in his mind and makes it clear how materials were storing themselves in his unconscious memory which he would someday draw upon. The most notable thing about his earliest *Wanderjähre* is that in his first taking stock of the world, he went habitually to books, partly because his nature craved a larger experience than his trade put him in the way of getting, but partly also because of his desire to correct and broaden his own impressions.

## §4

The habit of resorting to books for pleasure and profit was invaluable to him when he went on the river—when he proceeded to his "university" career.[41] There his "minor" in reading consisted of Milton, Shakespeare,

sonification of the writer's accusing conscience in this story—the small visitor that perches on top of the book-case in his study to taunt him—must be a burlesque of Poe's raven. Furthermore, as a study of dual personality, the story contains fantastic suggestions of "William Wilson." The writer obtains his freedom by killing his other self. (The resemblance of both "The Recent Carnival" and "William Wilson" to Dickens's *The Haunted Man* gives chance for further conjecture.)

[40] M. M. Brashear, "Missouri Verse and Verse-Writers," *Missouri Historical Review*, XVIII, 335. According to R. L. Rusk, Poe was not known up to the 40's.—*The Literature of the Midwestern Frontier*, II, 32.

[41] J. W. Rankin, Introduction to *Life on the Mississippi* (Harper's Modern Classics), p. xii. *Cf.* Melville's *Moby Dick*, chap. XXIV, last lines.

Goldsmith, Tom Hood, and Cervantes, with, probably, supplementary reading in the eighteenth-century novelists, Tom Paine, and, possibly, Voltaire. His biographer says: "The pilots regarded him as a great reader—a student of history, travels, literature, and the sciences—a young man whom it was an education as well as an entertainment to know. When not at the wheel, he was likely to be reading. . . ."[42]

He was studying Milton and Shakespeare with definite things to look for, while he was on the river. In a letter to his brother written toward the end of 1858, he says, "What is the grandest thing in 'Paradise Lost'—the Arch-Fiend's terrible energy!"[43] Apparently it was their common interest in Satan that made him value the Puritan poet.[44] It was after the ironies of life had got possession of his spirit that he used *Paradise Lost* to illustrate his definition of a classic as "something that everybody wants to have read and nobody wants to read."[45]

With his habit of iconoclastic humor he would have put Shakespeare among the same boresome classics, and yet there is good evidence that he knew his Shakespeare well at the time when it was worth most to his personal development to know him. The earliest proof of his study is the first of the Snodgrass letters, written apparently after he saw a production of *Julius Caesar* in St. Louis. The writer represents himself as an illiterate fellow from up-country in trouble at the play. The piece bears

[42] A. B. P., I, 151.
[43] *Ibid.*, I, 146.
[44] *Innocents Abroad*, I, 276; *Roughing It*, I, 119; A. B. P., I, 469; *Speeches*, pp. 134, 278.
[45] "I don't believe any of you have ever read *Paradise Lost*, and you don't want to. That's something that you just want to take on trust."—"Disappearance of Literature," *Speeches*, p. 194.

evidence of having been suggested by Addison's "Sir Roger at the Play." Mark Twain did not choose to preserve his earliest humorous letters, but when he began writing for California papers, with Bret Harte's coaching, he returned to Shakespeare and published in the *Californian* (1864 or 1865), "The Killing of Julius Caesar Localized," preserved in *Sketches New and Old*. In it he anticipated John Erskine's method in *The Private Life of Helen of Troy*, except that this novel is "localized" in the approved, best-seller style of the first after-the-world-war decades, while Mark Twain's sketch uses the best editorial phrases of the period following the Civil War. On the surface it is an effort to get the facts of the murder case stated, as gleaned from all reportorial accounts. The sketch shows a closer knowledge of Shakespeare's lines than would hold over in the writer's memory from merely seeing the play acted. As an exercise in verisimilitude, the editorial dignity of style is delightful.[46] One could forget that one is reading pure burlesque if it were not for those grave words, "Papilius Lena . . . closed his left eye temporarily" when Cassius asked, "What enterprise?" One begins to suspect, at any rate, that the humorist really knew Shakespeare better than did the ordinary man.[47]

If one of Mark Twain's first exercises in literary criticism was an interpretation of Shakespeare, in his final

[46] That both pieces referred to here (the first Snodgrass letter and "The Killing of Julius Caesar Localized"), belong with American types of humor described by Franklin J. Meine (*Tall Tales of the Southwest*, pp. i-xxxii), helps to confirm the impression that the methods of the eighteenth-century writers formed a large contributing element in the American vein.

[47] Henry Pochmann lists twenty allusions to Shakespeare in Mark Twain's writings, leaving out the monograph, "Is Shakespeare Dead?"—almost twice as many as to any other writer.

discussion of the Shakespeare-Bacon controversy, one of the last experiments of his pen, he expressed incidentally his doubt about literary interpretation as an aid to historicity. Written two years after he published *Christian Science*, with its analysis of Mary Baker Eddy's literary style, it continues the method used there.

The piece was originally intended as a part of his autobiography. Its first two sections are the story of his experience with a "Shakespeare-adoring Mississippi pilot" named George Ealer, who resented Delia Bacon's claims. He is returning to the controversy after the lapse of half a century:

A friend has sent me a new book, from England—*The Shakespeare Problem Restated*—well restated and closely reasoned; and my fifty years' interest in that matter—asleep for the last three years—is excited once more. It is an interest which was born of Delia Bacon's book—away back in that ancient day— 1857, or maybe 1856. About a year later my pilot-master, Bixby, transferred me from his own steamboat to the *Pennsylvania*, and placed me under the orders and instructions of George Ealer—dead now, these many, many years. I steered for him a good many months—as was the humble duty of the pilot-apprentice: stood a daylight watch and spun the wheel under the severe superintendence and correction of the master. He was a prime chess-player and an idolater of Shakespeare. He would play chess with anybody; even with me, and it cost his official dignity something to do that. Also—quite uninvited—he would read Shakespeare to me; not just casually, but by the hour, when it was his watch and I was steering.[47a]

This account indicates that Sam Clemens's college course in debate, taken while he was pilot-apprentice under

[47a] "Is Shakespeare Dead?", in *What is Man? and Other Essays*, pp. 298-99.

George Ealer, was based upon Shakespeare.[48] At first he helped Ealer out in his defense of Shakespeare's claims, but gradually he discovered that the politic plan was to take the opposite position in order to give his chief a chance to vent his spleen.

Then the thing happened which has happened to more persons than to me when principle and personal interest found themselves in opposition to each other and a choice had to be made: I let principle go, and went over to the other side. . . . Study, practice, experience in handling my end of the matter presently enabled me to take my new position almost seriously; a little bit later, utterly seriously; a little later still, lovingly, gratefully, devotedly; finally: fiercely, rabidly, uncompromisingly.[49]

One of the first hoaxes he ever perpetrated was a paraphrase of Macbeth's "What man dare, I dare" speech to the ghost, with "steamboatful interlardings." He wrote it to impose upon Ealer with the argument that Shakespeare could not have written his plays, for the reason that "a man can't handle glibly and easily and comfortably and successfully the argot of a trade at which he has not personally served."[50] He was learning Shakespeare at that time for a definite purpose.[51] And later, phrases from the

[48] Mark Twain's knowledge of Cervantes and Goldsmith, and even Tom Hood, may have dated from his acquaintance with Ealer, for he says: "When a man has a passion for Shakespeare, it goes without saying that he keeps company with other standard authors. Ealer always had other high-class books in the pilot-house, and he read the same ones over and over again. . . ." *Ibid.*, p. 305.

[49] *Ibid.*, p. 302.      [50] *Ibid.*, p. 304.

[51] Mark Twain returned to the controversy two years before he died, after he had written *The Mysterious Stranger*, with its dream philosophy; and he had a glorious time with the research. He had all his life been obsessed with the importance of facts. Now he fairly juggled with them—set up the five known facts of Satan's career by the side of those "verified facts, established facts, undisputed facts" of Shakespeare's history. Unfortunately the piece was expanded into a book by Harper's "by means of large type and thick paper," and the critics were very severe. All but the *Independent* took the discussion as a serious attempt of the humorist to contribute something to the controversy. Read now, in the light of

Shakespeare learned during his "college years" made their way unobtrusively into his vocabulary.[52]

More important, however, than his reading of Milton and Shakespeare was his study of Goldsmith and Cervantes. Considered in connection with his dissatisfaction with the humor in *Pickwick Papers*—if that was the book he criticized in Keokuk—the sentence quoted by O. H. Moore from an 1860 letter to Orion takes on new significance:

Your last has just come to hand. It reminds me strongly of Tom Hood's letters to his family, (which I have been reading lately). But yours only *remind* me of his, for although there is a striking likeness, your humor is much finer than his, and far better expressed. Tom Hood's *wit*, (in his letters), has a savor of *labor* about it which is very disagreeable. Your letter . . . resembles Goldsmith's "Citizen of the World," and "Don Quixote,"— which are my *beau ideals* of fine writing.[53]

There are important points here as regards Sam Clemens's way of reading, as regards his training as a humorist, and as regards the literary models that were eventually to make him dissatisfied with the "buffoonery" which delighted his American public. Somehow or other he had discovered what joy and stimulus there is in active, "crea-

the reconsideration of Mark Twain's work since the publication of his life and letters, the book appears to be what the *Independent* ventured to surmise that it might be, a "skit" to "hoist the Baconians with their own petard—an exquisite parody."—*Independent*, LXVII, 90. The best evidence that Mark Twain intended the piece as an "exquisite parody" is his conclusion to the Satan analogy: ". . . he thought that I would make fun of Satan and deride him, laugh at him, scoff at him; whereas I had . . . only a warm desire to make fun of those others and laugh at them." Helen Keller, in her chapter, "Our Mark Twain," *Midstream*, p. 58, speaks of telling the humorist that a friend of hers had found proof that Bacon wrote plays. "He was at first skeptical," she says, "and inclined to be facetious at our expense, yet less than a month elapsed before he brought out . . . 'Is Shakespeare Dead?' "

[52] *Ibid.*, p. 355.          [53] *Letters*, I, 45.

tive" reading. And he had apparently become an intelligent critic of wit and humor. The artificiality of Tom Hood's *wit*—he italicised the word—was distasteful to him. He must, by this time, have read such American humorous books as Longstreet's *Georgia Scenes* (1835) and Baldwin's *Flush Times of Alabama and Mississippi* (1853), but in his strenuous youthful mood[54] he was finding nineteenth-century models, English or American, forced and superficial. He was bent upon finding out for himself what models of art and what manner of life the past could furnish. Only what was clearly first-rate was agreeable to him. What satisfied him when he was twenty-five years old was the "finer," "quiet" style, without *"labor."* Tom Hood's vein was not to be compared with the deeper vein he had discovered in Goldsmith and Cervantes. We have here in embryo the conception of humor which was to come to mature expression in his essay "William Dean Howells":

I do not think that anyone else can play with humorous fancies so gracefully and delicately and deliciously as he does, nor has so many fancies to play with, . . . they are unobtrusive and quiet in their ways. . . . His is a humor which flows softly all around about and over and through the mesh of the page, pervasive, refreshing, health-giving, and makes no more noise than does the circulation of the blood.[55]

An inquiry into the nature of the Tom Hood letters which he criticized in the passage quoted above leads into further "conjecturabilities." The only letters included in the Putnam six volumes of Hood's *Complete Works* (1865) are in the volume entitled *Up the Rhine*, a story

[54] A. B. P., I, 146, 154.
[55] *Harper's Magazine*, CXIII (July, 1906), 223-24.

of a family travel party which contains definite suggestions, even before the reader glances at the Preface, of
Smollett's *Humphrey Clinker*,[56] while in the Preface to
the first edition (1839), reprinted in the 1865 edition, he
discovers this sentence: "To forestall such critics . . . the
following work was constructed, partly on the ground
plan of *Humphrey Clinker*, but with very inferior materials and on a much humbler scale.  I admire the old
mansion too much, to think that any workmanship of mine
could erect a house fit to stand in the same row." As Sam
Clemens was an avid reader by this time, according to the
testimony of his fellow pilots, he would more than likely
have searched out the "old mansion," particularly if he
already had a half-formed plan in his mind, as there is
some evidence that he had, to publish travel letters of the
humorous sort himself some day.  Such a title as *Up the
Rhine* would have attracted him at a time when he was
taking boats up and down the Mississippi; and what he
found inside the book would have attracted the pilot's
notice.  His interest in types of people traveling on Mississippi river boats would have found an echo in an early
letter of Frank Somerville's in *Up the Rhine:* "To believe our tourists and travellers, our Heads and our Trol-
lopes, it is impossible to take a trip in a hoy, smack, or
steamer, without encountering what are technically called
characters.  My first care, therefore, on getting aboard,
was to look out for originals. . . ." As will be pointed
out in the next chapter, Mark Twain was to make his first
reputation as a writer in a chronicle of a "character."

There is also a little internal evidence in the 1860

---

[56] So far as the author has been able to discover, there were no other letters in
the early editions of Tom Hood.

letter to Orion that it was the *Up the Rhine* volume of letters that Mark Twain referred to. In the first letter of this volume, which purports to be written by Frank Somerville, leader of the party, the young man says that his uncle, the center of the group, is "the *beau ideal* of a fine old country gentleman."[57] In Mark Twain's comment on the Hood letters he borrows the term *beau ideal*.

Furthermore, it is possible that Mark Twain got the sub-title of his first volumes of travel letters from this same volume, as well as some suggestions for their content from the Preface to the second edition. Frank Somerville says in the introductory letter in *Up the Rhine* already referred to, "There seemed plenty of lions in the path of such a Pilgrim's Progress."[58] The humorous analogy to *Pilgrim's Progress* runs through the volume. Richard Orchard, a friend of Frank Somerville's, says, "Our life below is only a tour."[59] Such expressions as "the pilgrimage of life"[60] are common, and on page 86 Frank Somerville refers again to their "Pilgrim's Progress." Such expressions may have stuck in the pilot-reader's memory as apt for the literary description of a journey and caused him, nine years later, to call *The Innocents Abroad* the "New Pilgrim's Progress."

Even if it cannot be said that the American Pilgrim's Progress belongs in the tradition with either *Humphrey Clinker* or *Up the Rhine*, the Preface to the second edition of the Hood book[61] may have furnished a suggestion for the trend the *Quaker City* letters were to take:

[57] *Up the Rhine*, p. 8.          [59] *Ibid.*, p. 67.
[58] *Ibid.*, p. 7.          [60] *Ibid.*, p. 38.
[61] *Up the Rhine* went into a second edition in January, 1840, and subsequent editions printed both prefaces.

A plain manufacturer of Roman cement, in the Greenwich road, was once turned, by a cramped showboard, into a *"Manufacturer of Romancement"*; and a Tour up the Rhine has generally been supposed to convert an author into a dealer in the same commodity. There was some danger, therefore, that readers might be disappointed or dissatisfied at not meeting with the usual allowance of real or affected raptures, sentimental lays, romantic legends, euthusimoosy and the foodle ages.   In fact, one of my critics (it is now the fashion for the reviewed to retaliate on their reviewers, as Roderick Random flogged his schoolmaster) plainly snubs my book, for . . . not treading more exactly like an Indian disguising his trail, in the footprints of his predecessors.   According to this gentleman . . . I engaged in a somewhat heretical enterprise, which no man of ordinary sensibility would have embarked in.   I took my apparatus of caricature up the Rhine, quizzed Cologne Cathedral and the facade of the English National Gallery, and turned the storied scenery, the fine traditions, and the poetic atmosphere of the abounding river into a succession of drolleries. In reply to these serious charges, I can say that heretical enterprises—witness Luther's—are sometimes no bad things.

It is apparent that this might very well be an apologia for *Innocents Abroad*.   Indeed, there seems to be little doubt that the allusion in Sam Clemens's letter was to *Up the Rhine* and that the phrase "to his [Tom Hood's] family" was an inadvertence, in that Mark Twain referred to the author as writing the letters in *Up the Rhine* rather than to the author's fictional character, Frank Somerville, as the writer of the letters.

So far, then, as the history of Sam Clemens's reading up to 1861 can be pieced out, it is based upon half a dozen "undisputed facts."   He had read the "unexpurgated Bible" through by the time he was fifteen years old, had read it so effectively that its influence is noticeable in much of his writings. A page out of an old life of Joan of Arc came his way in Hannibal and fired him with a desire to know history. He read the Horace Walpole Letters through when he was "a boy." In New York and Philadelphia he read history and biography. He was often seen, when he was twenty years old, with a volume of Dickens or Poe, or a history under his arm. During his pilot years, possibly earlier, he read Cervantes, Tom Hood, Goldsmith, Milton, and Shakespeare—read them actively enough to form definite convictions concerning them.

Furthermore, it may be said that Sam Clemens profited by his reading in the various ways that we know Mark Twain did later. As a young journeyman, he sought out books to supplement his impressions, and as an experienced writer Mark Twain was accustomed to draw from his reading to fill out his own narratives. In youthful argument, on the river, he made his reading from Shakespeare serve his purpose to support a theory. In five of his later writings Mark Twain used what he read as documents to help him establish a thesis: in his "Defense of Harriet Shelley," in "Fenimore Cooper's Literary Offenses," in "What Paul Bourget Thinks of Us," in "Is Shakespeare Dead?" and in *The Personal Recollections of Joan of Arc*. Furthermore, the youth's reading brought on either a positive or a negative reaction that took form in writings of his own. The Snodgrass letters were written after he felt the challenge to write "a funnier book" than one he was reading. Mark Twain all his life felt the same kind of challenge. What he read excited him mentally and emotionally, and stimulated him to get his reaction expressed. He wrote *A Fireside Conversation in the Year*

*1601* to out-Rabelais Rabelais.  Elizabeth Stuart Phelps's *Gates Ajar* called forth *Captain Stormfield's Visit to Heaven, A Double-Barreled Detective Story, Tom Sawyer, The Prince and the Pauper, Huckleberry Finn,* and *A Connecticut Yankee at King Arthur's Court,* leaving out of account many minor pieces, had their literary provocations.  It is because this kind of stimulus is constantly apparent and its influence on Mark Twain's later writing well established that the student feels justified in assuming a more extensive debt to books than the records have shown.

# VII

## MARK TWAIN AND THE "SHADOW OF EUROPE"

### §1

MARK TWAIN was so vivid a part of the life of his country and century that his commentators have been interested, for the most part, to note how he was related to men and forces of his own day. Stuart P. Sherman's super-American, William Dean Howells's individual-recording-his-unique-vision, realist-at-heart-romantic, are accounted for from contemporaneous points of view. In their preoccupation with the all-American Mark Twain, in fact, critics have unwittingly neglected the consideration of Mark Twain, heir of Virginian ancestry and Colonial mental temper, the mental temper, immediately, of eighteenth-century England. By failing to take into account this more remote debt, the critics have obscured the fact that it existed. And even more have Mark Twain's own mood and emphasis obscured it. His casual, informal insistence upon himself as a representative American, the apologist, it may be said, for western Americanism, has seemed to place him in a sphere far removed from the Age of Reason—and of devotion to tradition and to elegance of form. But it is not illogical to expect that, beyond the mere fact of his general unconscious heritage in common with other Americans, there can be found in the development of the mind and art of America's greatest humorist some more or less definite indebtedness to books and men of the preceding age.

The prevalence of eighteenth-century ideas on the western frontier, where Mark Twain grew to manhood, has often been noted. "The pioneer was close to those who founded this republic," says the curator of the State Historical Society of Missouri. "He kept many of the good features of the 18th century."[1] No phrase out of the classics is more commonly quoted in the periodicals of the Middle West than that which has to do with the proper study of mankind. "Nowhere else," declares one of the latest foreign critics of America, "could the ideas of the eighteenth century assert themselves in their purity so long."[2] Mark Twain's preference for the robust world of men, his common sense founded on reason, his prepossession with man as the center of the coil in which the world finds itself enclosed, all admit of new emphases when they are considered in answer to the question, What of the eighteenth century is discernible in Mark Twain?

In his preference for the world of men, he was like both his father and his mother. John Clemens had not been a wilderness-loving man like Daniel Boone, but one who, it may be inferred, felt the need of people about him —partly, to be sure, to keep his courage steady; but, in general, it was in terms of social contacts that life was

[1] F. C. Shoemaker, "The Pioneer," *Missouri Historical Review*, XIX (Jan., 1925), 254.

[2] ". . . as far as inner experience goes, there has practically been no nineteenth century in America . . . I found the spirit of John Locke there still . . . and next to him of all the other leaders of eighteenth century thought. The peculiar optimism of America has its roots in the outlook of the eighteenth century. . . . America's disbelief in any sort of distinction, with its corollary, the overrating of the values of good-fellowship . . . also belongs to the eighteenth century. So does its moralism, and to a great extent, its educationalism and institutionalism."— Hermann Keyserling, *America Set Free*, p. 156.

worth living to both Jane Lampton and John Marshall Clemens. Their son was that kind of man. Until life was virtually finished for him, Mark Twain sought the places where men most do congregate. When he was alone, his reading was about men.[3] It was a fact so patent to him that it needed no Pope-like assertion, that the proper study of mankind is man. Nineteenth-century preoccupation with a developing physical economy, while it touched his imagination, took little hold upon his practical thinking. Evangelicalism, and transcendental speculative philosophy detached from man's use and wont, found slight entertainment in his mind or soul. Given the world—his care was about man's position in it as an ethical component of society. If his conclusion was that whatever is, is not right, it was because his concentration upon the human point of view made the general human situation appear to him intolerable. This bias determined both the materials he chose and his treatment of his materials. He was one of the apologists for humanity, "Member at Large for the Human Race," he called himself.[4]

§2

To SAY that Mark Twain's treatment of his materials may have been influenced by suggestions that filtered through to him out of the preceding century appears at first thought absurd. Such seeming lawlessness of manner, the casual reader feels, can have had no spring in the Augustan Age. But certain of Mark Twain's characteristic types, the character, the informal essay, the apologue, the maxim, and the picaresque-like narrative as adapted by Defoe and Smollett—models which had already established them-

[3] A. B. P., III, 1539.          [4] *Letters*, II, 718.

selves in American humorous writing—appear to be more akin to eighteenth-century forms than to those of the nineteenth century.

The character, as adapted by seventeenth-century writers, was an essay-like portrayal of the faults and foibles of a person that represented a type. As adapted by Addison and Steele in the next century, it emphasized the humorous and moralizing intention of the earlier experiments, for the purpose of taking off an "original." In the earliest sketches of Mark Twain, while the moralizing purpose is lost, the device representing the more sophisticated man's amusement at such eccentric characters as the pioneer West produced seems to have been suggested by Mr. Spectator's interest in Will Wimble and Sir Roger. "Odd and uncommon characters are the game I look for and most delight in," said Addison.[5]

It was Jim Smiley who first brought Mark Twain literary renown, and, however uncomfortable Will Honeycomb would have been in the company of the owner of the jumping frog, Jim Smiley was like a *Spectator* rarity whom the fates cast high and dry in Western America. His historian, Simon Wheeler, done only in a thumb-nail portrait, is of the same sort:

He never smiled, he never frowned, he never changed his voice from the gentle-flowing key to which he tuned his initial sentence, he never betrayed the slightest suspicion of enthusiasm; but all through the interminable narrative there ran a vein of impressive

---

[5] Chalmers, ed., *The Spectator*, IV, 225. Mark Twain's experiments are not the best example of the persistence of Addison's influence in the United States, of course. The portrayal of Frank Meriwether and his friends and neighbors in John Pendleton Kennedy's *Swallow Barn* (1851) is more obviously modeled upon Addison than Irving's or Paulding's or Mark Twain's characters. *Swallow Barn*, with its loosely woven plot, in fact, is an intermediary stage between the *De Coverley Papers* and the carefully constructed novel, just as a good deal of Mark Twain's longest fiction is.

earnestness and sincerity, which showed me plainly that, so far
from his imagining that there was anything ridiculous or funny
about his story, he regarded it as a really important matter. . . .[6]

Simon Wheeler, Jim Smiley, and Jim Wolfe were the
studio exercises by means of which the author developed
skill for his full-length portrayal of Colonel Mulberry
Sellers, the most engaging of his eccentrics. This harmless visionary, with a fortune always in sight, accruing
through some clever scheme of his own, is a Clemens
replica, as most of these originals are.[7] Tom Sawyer is
the western play-boy Clemens, Huck Finn the picaresque
Clemens. Pudd'nhead Wilson is the prophet without renown, never admitted among those who "belong"—like
Sam Clemens among western miners, perhaps. Less well
known are Hurricane Jones[8] and Nicodemus Dodge.[9]
None of these is a type in the sense in which Overbury's
"Braggadocio Welshman" is a type. They are incapable
of standardization. Each has his individual humor and
each, except Tom Sawyer, represents the person as he
would appear if no one were looking on. Each is a whim-
sical sidelight on human nature—on western American,
Clemens nature, to be sure, which is nearer to Will
Honeycomb than it is to Wieland or Arthur Dimmesdale.
Natty Bumppo has many points in common with the Mark
Twain character, but its real American forerunner is Rip
Van Winkle,[10] and Rip is more nearly related to Tam

---

[6] "The Jumping Frog," *Sketches New and Old.*

[7] "If Byron—if any man—draws 50 characters, they are all himself—50 shades, 50 moods, of his own character."—Mark Twain, quoted in A. B. P., III, 1540.

[8] "The Captain's Story," *Some Rambling Notes of an Idle Excursion.*

[9] *A Tramp Abroad*, pp. 224-29; also in *Editorial Wild Oats* (1905), pp. 30-40.

[10] "Those intimate with Mr. Clemens will certify that he was one of the charmers. Joe Jefferson is the only man who can be conceded his twin brother in manner and speech, their charm being of the same kind. ["Uncle Remus,"

O'Shanter and Will Wimble than to Natty Bumppo; he belongs in some neglected spot and has to be sought out there.  It was necessary for Mark Twain to be a personage, seen among men, but he too was an eccentric,[11] and each of his characters might find himself reflected in some facet of the many-sided nature of Samuel Langhorne Clemens.  Like Addison, Mark Twain was "much pleased with the novelty of the character."

So far developed and unique did the "character" become in Mark Twain's hands that it forms a class apart, a type that its author, following the terminology of earlier southern humorists, usually called yarns; it cannot be grouped with his essays.  At the same time, the informal essay is a more extensive type, if not so distinguished, in the body of his works.  It is a further hint that his interest was more fundamentally in models developed prior to his own century that the sort of essay Mark Twain worked out for himself—and believed, in truth, to be original—bears a close resemblance to the *Spectator* and *Rambler* papers.

George W. Cable, and Josh Billings had it] . . . In Rip Van Winkle's words: 'All pretty much alike, dem fellers.' "—Andrew Carnegie, *Autobiography*, p. 295.

[11] So accustomed are we to the finished Mark Twain that it is difficult to realize what an odd and uncommon figure he presented when he first went to live in the East.  Mrs. Thomas Bailey Aldrich, in *Crowding Memories* (pp. 128-32) tells of her dismay when her husband first brought him to call upon her, introducing him as Mr. Clemens: ". . . a most unusual guest, clothed in a coat of seal-skin, the fur worn outward; a seal-skin cap well down over his ears; the cap half revealing and half-concealing the mass of reddish hair underneath; the heavy mustache having the same red tint . . . the gentleman showed marked inability to stand perpendicular, but swayed from side to side, and had also difficulty with his speech; he did not stammer exactly, but after each word he placed a period.  His sentences were whimsical, and host and guest laughed loudly with and at each other."  After he had left, without her inviting him to remain to dinner, her husband turned to her for an explanation of her want of cordiality.  She mentioned the apparent cause of the peculiar speech and manner of the guest.  Mr. Aldrich replied, so his wife reports, " '. . . did you not know who he was?  What you thought was wine was his mannerisms and idiosyncrasies, characteristic of himself, and born with Mark Twain.' "

His most distinguished German critic discovers this resemblance and points to the influence of Goldsmith, "Ad-
disons originellster Schüler." But he says that a study of
Addison's influence in the United States would have to
cover the whole literature of the country, from Franklin
through the early essayists and humorists, through Irving
and Hawthorne and Holmes, to the later writers of the
short story.[12] After emphasizing the point further that,
through Goldsmith and Irving, Addison influenced the
whole development of the essay in America, he adds that
while Mark Twain as an essayist has never hitherto been
connected with these, he undoubtedly belongs in the same
line of development.[13] His essay-method, like theirs, is
to beguile the public into swallowing a good deal of useful
information, and, what they considered more important,
many a moral lesson. In defensive mood in one of his letters he said, "I have seldom deliberately tried to instruct
them, but have done my best to entertain them"; but in
almost the same breath he revealed his real motive: "I
had two chances to help to the teacher's one."[14] And he
acknowledged to his biographer that his purpose was to
teach.

Although Mark Twain's essays are, for the most part,
like those of Montaigne, a medium through which he
dramatizes himself before the world—an extension of his
lecture platform and banquet hall tone, the speech quali-

[12] "Ein Buch über Addison in America würde die ganze Literaturbewegung
der Vereinigten Staaten umfassen: von Franklin an, dessen erklärtes Stilideal
Addison war, über die frühen Essayisten und frühen Humoristen, über Washington
Irving zu Hawthorne und Holmes bis zu den 'short story writers.' "—Friedrich
Schönemann, *Mark Twain als Literarische Persönlichkeit*, p. 96.

[13] "Mark Twain ist bisher nie in einem Atem mit diesen Essayisten genannt
worden, abwohl er unbedingt in diese ganze Entwicklung gehört."—*Ibid.*, p. 97.

[14] *Letters*, II, 527. *Cf.* A. B. P., III, 1277.

ties of spontaneity and directness that give to so much that he wrote the convincing quality of human documents, were characteristic of Queen Anne's men. It is a commonplace of criticism that the wit and satire of Addison and Steele and, later, of Johnson and Goldsmith, took much of their character from the coffee-house discussions that preceded them. Critics have commented upon this quality in Mark Twain as an evidence of his originality. In this, again, the German critic sees the effect of the teaching of Goldsmith, who, in the preface to the *Citizen of the World*, uses the term "colloquial ease" in describing a good prose style.[15]

How completely Mark Twain conformed to the recommendation of Goldsmith's preface, whether consciously or unconsciously, may be seen in the volume, *What is Man? and Other Essays*. The title piece is a Socratic dialogue, probably as effective an adaptation of that classical model as the Augustan Age could have produced—exposition dramatised. "The Death of Jean" is an attempt to represent the poignant experience of the death of a member of one's family—lyric exposition: "Would I bring her back to life if I could do it? I would not. In her loss I am almost bankrupt, and my life is a bitterness, but I am content: for she has been enriched with the most precious of all gifts—that gift which makes all other gifts mean and poor—death." The third essay in the volume, "The Turning Point of My Life," is an autobiographical sketch,

---

[15] "In der Vorrede zum 'Citizen of the World' hatte ein Wort von *colloquial ease* gestanden, das des Verfassers Prosastil sehr gut charakterisierte. Es war die verkörperte Leichtigkeit der guten Umgangssprache, frisch, lebendig, ungekünstelt, dabei niemals Umgepflegt und nachlässig, vielmehr anmutig und schön. Er hatte die Unmittelbarkeit des Zweigesprächs, der Diskussion im Klub und zugleich gepflegten literarischen Glanz. Als Vorbild des Stils konnte der junge Clemens nichts Besseres haben."—Schönemann, *op. cit.*, p. 94.

which has an expository purpose: "Now what interests me as regards these details is . . . none of them was planned by me. I was the author of none of them. Circumstance, working in harness with my temperament, created them all and compelled them all."

Another *Spectator* type developed by Mark Twain into a form of his own is the apologue—the narrative with the same kind of ulterior purpose that *The Vision of Mirza, Gulliver's Travels,* and *Rasselas* have. These apologues contain the allegorical element with such varying degrees of explicitness that it is difficult to classify them, but two classes stand out with sufficient clearness to justify special comment—the fable proper and what may be called the "moralized legend."[16]

Mark Twain's experiments with fables were not extensive. The most successful, perhaps, is "The Five Boons of Life" (1902), that grim fairy tale in which man, failing to choose the "dear, sweet and kindly" gift of death, finds himself left with only "the wanton insult of Old Age." No reference to Aesop[17] or La Fontaine is to be found in his writings.

The second type of narrative with a symbolical aim is worthy of more extended consideration. The term "moralized legend" fits well the tale that stands at the head of this group, *The Man That Corrupted Hadleyburg* (1899). It has something of the generalized character and the detachment of the parable, along with the in-

---

[16] Hawthorne's term, the sub-title of his story, "Feathertop."

[17] In an article entitled "From Aesop to Mark Twain," *Sewanee Review,* XIX, 43-49, Killis Campbell traces the various possible sources of the story upon which "A Dog's Tale" is based. His final conjecture is, however, that "Mark Twain was not conscious of any acquaintance whatsoever with the ancient story, that it was with him a case of 'unconscious assimilation.' . . . But that the two stories are ultimately one and the same we may, I think, be reasonably sure."

timacy of the folk tale.   It is the once-upon-a-time and
once-upon-a-place story.   If *Rasselas* were not a story of
aristocratic life rather than of common life, it would be an
eighteenth-century prototype of Mark Twain's story,
which is as idyllic as *Rasselas*.   Here Mark Twain does
not choose the feverish ways of legislatures and markets
to show how greed betrays men.   In his story, greed
worms its insidious way among people leading quiet and
God-fearing lives.   At the same time the story is as re-
lentless in its indictment of mankind as anything in
*Gulliver's Travels*.   It belongs in the eighteenth-century
tradition.

Two other stories from the same general period have
the same stern ethical purpose.   "The $30,000 Bequest"
(1904) has almost the theme of the earlier story.   Developed without supernatural intervention, it perhaps
gains something in immediate human significance; it seems
more nearly what might have happened to people in
reality, but it misses something of the universality of its
predecessor.   The same may be said of the study of the
Puritan New England conscience, "Was It Heaven? or
Hell?" (1902).   In the same class are "A Dog's Tale"
(1903) and "A Horse's Tale" (1906), both the first-
person stories of animals speaking.   The first was used as
a tract by the national anti-vivisection society.   The second
was written at the request of Mrs. Minnie Maddern Fiske
for the cause of prevention of cruelty to animals in Spain.
More successful than these are stories that make their
point in lighter vein.   "A Curious Experience" is a satirical
presentation of the fact that reading dime novels is likely
to stimulate a lad's latent histrionic talents.   "The Stolen
White Elephant" is a humorous warning to the man who

contemplates entrusting his problem to a detective bureau, with its tortuous and important technique. These stories, have a more or less obvious symbolical significance. It is in the close resemblance of many of his shorter stories and sketches to the older models of the moral apologue that Mark Twain's writings approach most nearly the eighteenth-century periodical essay.

Finally, Mark Twain's study of mankind takes the form of an eighteenth-century model in what is perhaps his greatest literary achievement.\ His adaptation of the picaresque romance in *The Adventures of Huckleberry Finn* is more nearly a cross between the *Humphrey Clinker* and the *Robinson Crusoe* patterns than like anything in nineteenth-century literature. As in *Humphrey Clinker* there is a strong Le Sage influence in the story of the "river rat."[18] It is like *Humphrey Clinker* not only as travel literature, but (and here it surpasses *Robinson Crusoe*), in its humor and irony.

It is like *Robinson Crusoe* in its verisimilitude first of all. One stands looking on at Huck and Jim fending for themselves on the island, just as one stands looking on at Robinson Crusoe making shift with what conveniences he salvages from the ship. But both *Huckleberry Finn* and *Robinson Crusoe* are significantly different from the early rogue tale in their more searching representation of

[18] One point is to be noted in the attempt to show that Mark Twain may really have owed a debt to Smollett. The eighteenth-century novelists were much interested in Le Sage and Cervantes. Smollett translated the masterpieces of both writers, and both translations were to be found in American libraries in the fifties. When he finished *Tom Sawyer*, Mark Twain wrote to Howells: "I have finished the story and didn't take the chap beyond boyhood. I believe it would be fatal to do it in any shape but autobiographically—like *Gil Blas*."—*Letters*, I, 258. It is more than likely that Sam Clemens read both *Don Quixote* and *Gil Blas* in Smollett's translations. The two copies of *Gil Blas* in the University of North Carolina library are both Smollett's translations. Sam Clemens might also have read Voltaire in Smollett's translation.

human nature. If man were deprived of the props that civilization has built up around him, if he were stripped of his clothes,[19] both authors seem to have asked themselves, how could he maintain himself? Has he the vigor for animal independence? Could he sustain his part with any grace of spirit? Robinson Crusoe, as if in answer to Hobbes's theory that man is of worth only as a cog in a tyrant state, is "unaccommodated man" with physical and spiritual courage to accommodate himself. Huckleberry Finn would be as nearly "unaccommodated man" were it not that he has his man Friday along from the first to fortify him. But he is resourceful for both of them in the river wilderness, with all the handicap of his youth. Robinson Crusoe is in the prime of manhood. Both heroes are humane in all essentials. Mr. Howells was the first to point to the kinship between the two authors: "His invention is of the good old sort, like De Foe's more than that of any other English writer, and like that of the Spanish picaresque novelists."[20]

## §3

CERTAIN ASPECTS of Mark Twain's humor also point to an eighteenth-century provenience; and hints here and there indicate that he knew such books as *Roderick Random* and *Humphrey Clinker* better than the records of his reading show. In *A Connecticut Yankee*, written in the late eighties, speaking of King Arthur's court, he said:

[19] "Show me a lord and I will show you a man whom you couldn't tell from a journeyman shoemaker if he were stripped, and who, in all that is worth being, is the shoemaker's inferior."—A. B. P., II, 874. *Cf.* "An honest man's aboon his might," a sentiment to which Carlyle and Mark Twain hark back.

[20] *My Mark Twain*, p. 142. See also Howells's comment on picaresque elements in *The Prince and the Pauper*, *Life in Letters*, I, 290.

. . . many of the terms used in the most matter-of-fact way by this great assemblage of the first ladies and gentlemen in the land would have made a Comanche blush. Indelicacy is too mild a term to convey the idea. However, I had read *Tom Jones* and *Roderick Random*, and other books of that kind, and knew that the highest and first ladies and gentlemen in England had remained little or no cleaner in their talk, and in the morals and conduct which such talk implies, clear up to a hundred years ago; in fact, clear into our own nineteenth century. . . . Suppose Sir Walter, instead of putting the conversations into the mouths of his characters, had allowed the characters to speak for themselves? We should have had talk from Rebecca and Ivanhoe and the soft lady Rowena which would embarrass a tramp in our day. However, to the unconsciously indelicate all things are delicate. King Arthur's people were not aware that they were indecent. . . .[21]

Ten years before, under the inspiration of Pepys's *Diary* Mark Twain had experimented with a *Fireside Conversation in the Time of Queen Elizabeth* (1876), which was circulated privately among his friends and has at various times been surreptitiously printed. In a notebook of a later period he said that it had been his purpose in it to out-Rabelais Rabelais. The broadest parts of *Roderick Random* and *Tristram Shandy* are more nearly quotable than the fun-making in this imaginary conversation. It has been taken as an evidence of where Mark Twain's real tastes lay that he, like Lincoln, was a master of the salacious, smoking-room joke. His friend Howells said, "He had the Southwestern, the Lincolnian, the Elizabethan breadth of parlance, which I suppose one ought not to call coarse without calling one's self prudish." How nearly he might have followed in the footsteps of his freer predecessors if his lot had not been cast in the Victorian Age is

[21] *A Connecticut Yankee*, pp. 38-39.

a question which has interested many of his critics; but if a *Fireside Conversation* is the nearest approach to felicity in the Rabelaisian manner that he was capable of, most people will believe that he more nearly found himself as a writer in *Roughing It* and *Huckleberry Finn*. Many of his risqué jokes, however, are rare and delightful—such as might have been struck off before Samuel Johnson's group in a coffee house, like those parts of *Tristram Shandy* in which "the whim and wit of them blow away the scandal." In a letter to Howells about the heroism of a family servant, written about this time he said: "Delicacy—a sad, sad false delicacy—robs literature of the best two things among its belongings: Family-circle narrative and obscene stories. But no matter; in that better world which I trust we are all going to I have the hope and belief that they will not be denied us."[22]  However humorously the remark was made, there can be no doubt that he chafed under anything that limited his freedom of expression; and whether his taste for the "obscene" is to be taken as something vigorous and wholesome or as something reprehensible, it identifies him with the preceding century, in its literary aspect, even if it does not relate him in any accurate way with Smollett and Sterne.

If Mark Twain, the "border Ruffian from Missouri," was more nearly related to the Elizabethans, and to Smollett and Sterne, as an imitator of Rabelais, he was, in his more highly developed manner, a kinsman of Goldsmith and Fielding—of both, as of Swift, in his tendency to make humor the handmaid of ethics; of Goldsmith in his finer, more humane vein; and of Fielding in his deeper study of human frailty.

[22] *Letters*, I, 310.

Friedrich Schönemann has sought to find in Gold-smith the source of many of Mark Twain's themes. While his results are not very conclusive, his discussion serves to deepen the impression that eighteenth-century writings must have had a formative influence upon the American humorist. From both Goldsmith and Cer-vantes, he says, the American learned early the uses of humor as a weapon, "den künstlerischen Erfolg in Ge-brauch dieser Waffe." But he finds it much easier to discover traces of the Spaniard in Mark Twain's develop-ment than of the author of *A Citizen of the World*.[23]

The only evidence that Mark Twain knew Fielding lies in the *Connecticut Yankee* statement, already quoted, that he had read *Tom Jones*, but there are re-markable resemblances in the mental and emotional trends of the two men and in the themes they chose. This resem-blance, of course, lies outside of the realm of provable literary influence, although Sam Clemens's early reading of Horace Walpole's letters and Goldsmith's *Citizen of the World* may have confirmed in him the temperamental traits that made him and the author of *Tom Jones* con-genial spirits with Cervantes. Both turned to *Don Quixote* as the model for their most representative writ-ings; a strong masculine tolerance for human frailty led both to the great Spaniard. Mark Twain's defense of his friend Dan Sloat—"I have got a splendid immoral, to-bacco-smoking, wine-drinking, godless room-mate, who is as good and true and right-minded a man as ever lived," —might be Fielding defending his hero Tom Jones.

The resemblance of Mark Twain to Swift has been remarked upon ever since the time of Bret Harte's Cal-

---

[23] Schönemann, *op. cit.*, p. 89.

ifornia comment.[24]  Friedrich Schönemann has pointed
out the parallels most fully.[25]  Different as the general
slant of the two men is, there are striking similarities;
Gulliver calls men "curious little vermin"; Satan, in *The
Mysterious Stranger*, condemns them as "shabby, poor
worthless vermin."  Both contrast animals with men to
the disparagement of men.  Both are stern moralists.  It
would be difficult to find two writers, in fact, who more
consistently employed their satirical pens to reveal how
far the human race falls short in disinterested social ethics,
and what a sorry failure civilization is, than Swift and
Mark Twain.

To seek Pope influence in writings so apparently casual
as most of Mark Twain's is likely to draw forth some
such dictum as that pronounced by a not unfriendly critic
of his who said, "In the conventional sense, Mark Twain is
no more a literary artist than, in the conventional sense,
Lincoln was a gentleman."[26]  This is an expression of the
handed-down opinion embraced especially by persons
who like to look upon Mark Twain as a self-made American.  Even his friend Howells thought of him somewhat
as an adventurer among literary men.  Since the appearance of O. H. Moore's proofs of his indebtedness to
Cervantes, however, such opinions have been looked upon
as untrustworthy.  There is no proof that the author of
*Pudd'nhead Wilson's Calendar* was indebted to Pope, but
the literary tastes and habits of his time and region, together with a certain elegance in his wit, make such an in-

[24] *Overland Monthly*, I, 101: "Mr. Swift has made one or two neat long shots
with a rifled Parrat, and Mr. Mark Twain has used brickbats on stained glass
windows with damaging effect."

[25] *Op. cit.*, pp. 42-43.

[26] C. M. Thompson, "Mark Twain as an Interpreter of American Character,"
*The Atlantic Monthly*, LXXIX (April, 1897), 443.

fluence probable.  His early introduction to Franklin indicates an American influence as well, but most of his witty
sentences have an elegance of form different in quality
from Poor Richard's homely aphorisms:

There is no character, howsoever good and fine, but it can be
destroyed by ridicule, howsoever poor and witless.

If a man is a pessimist before forty-eight, he knows too much; if
he is an optimist after that age, he knows too little.

The task of discovering how great a debt American
southwestern and western humor owed to the eighteenth
century will become easier as both recede into better per-
spective.  The vein of Mark Twain, the most representative of American humorists, makes it clear that it was no
small debt: his writings hark back to the coarse fun-making of Smollett and Sterne, to the more understanding and
democratic humor of Goldsmith and Fielding, to the wit
of Pope and Swift.  And traces of his reading show unmistakably that as a young man he drew inspiration from
certain eighteenth-century sources.  "One does that unconsciously," he said, "with things one likes."[26a]

## §4

THERE SEEMS to be no doubt that along with his literary
activities Sam Clemens's philosophy was also forming
itself while he was on the river—that any doubts which
may have insinuated themselves into his mind before this,
about the religion he had inherited, came to a head about
the time he was first attaining real personal independence.
His doubt about the efficacy of revealed religion, he expressed in the same letter (1860) in which he declared his

[26a] *Speeches*, p. 215.

devotion to Goldsmith and Cervantes—the same also in
which he showed his determination to master the secrets of
Church's effects in his picture, the "Heart of the Andes."
Every object in the picture, he found, had its own *personality* [his italics]. The year before he had exclaimed,
"What a vast respect Prosperity commands!" Now he
dared think for himself about religion. Apparently he
had arrived at the stage of the Harvard youth who has
discovered that there is no God.

Mark Twain's philosophy of life, one is forced to conclude, must have had its foundation in the more rigid
eighteenth-century trends of thinking. If he could have
realized the scope of nineteenth-century speculation, his
conclusions concerning man's place in the cosmos would
have been a larger and more valuable contribution to
human thought. He would have been drawn into some
theory concerning the whence and whither of man in the
universe of mind and matter. Instead, he was almost
wholly preoccupied with the narrow, bitter problem of
why men are not supermen.[27] The question of the im-
mortality of the soul found, after all, a rather slight place
in his thinking, as well as the implications of the theory of
evolution as they concern man's destiny.

This restriction can best be accounted for by comparing
his philosophical system with trends of thought that seem
to have gone into its forming—for Mark Twain had a
system, which he believed to be his unique contribution to
the cause of truth.

Something of his beliefs undoubtedly came from his

---

[27] The value a trained philosopher would place upon Mark Twain's system
may be inferred from William James's phrase in a letter to Henry James, in
which he speaks of the humorist as "that dear little genius."—William James,
*Letters*, II, 264.

father and mother, though the vague but potent suggestions that he received from them have to be guessed at.
Both were mentally alert—aristocrats, if they are compared with the poor whites that seeped through to Missouri from the South. That Judge Clemens, whose large
ambition was fated to small accomplishment, was a shut-
in man[28] may have been partly because, feeling the southern gentleman's prerogative to entertain advanced ideas,
he found himself out of touch with his Presbyterian
household and community. He came out of an age of
controversialists; and as a lawyer, a contemporary of Lincoln, living in Lincoln's region, he must have been drawn
into the interests of the keener intelligences of his time.
It was noted in an earlier chapter, besides, that John
Quarles, a childhood hero of Sam Clemens's, was the same
type of free-thinker. Jane Lampton Clemens had the
intelligence and wit of a Kentucky belle, sharpened in a
continuous battle with frontier conditions. To her Calvinistic teaching must have been due the ineradicable feeling in Sam Clemens that life is controlled by an im-
movable power; and the losing struggle of his father, a
conscientious man and a gentleman, may have confirmed
in him the feeling later in life that the power was inimical.

But while these influences may have prepared the
ground for his reception of the rationalists' doctrines, they
do not account for the direction the young man's thinking
took. His early interest in the cool, cynical, and witty
letters of Horace Walpole would have made him familiar
with the general mental temper of Walpole's age. And
it would account to some extent for his interest in Lecky's
*History of European Morals.* Traces of the influence of

[28] A. B. P., I, 74.

this book in *Tom Sawyer* show that he must have known
it as early as 1874.[29]   During the summer of 1874 at
Quarry Farm, in fact, when he was beginning the boy's
book, he and his brother-in-law, Theodore Crane, read the
book on European morals avidly and discussed it in original and unorthodox ways.   "Mark Twain," Mr. Paine
continues, "found an echo of his own philosophies in
Lecky."[30]   The last clause seems to justify the inference
that his beliefs were already formulated by the early seventies.   From the *History of European Morals* he would
have made the acquaintance of the main lines of eighteenth-century thinking.   Its Chapter I, "The Natural
History of Morals," contains extensive references to the
doctrines of Hobbes, Locke, and Hume.   Later he knew
the author himself in England.[31]   In his library was an
1887 edition of the English writer's *History of England
in the Eighteenth Century*.

The real source of Mark Twain's philosophy, however, must be discovered much earlier than in his reading
of Lecky at Quarry Farm.   A theory concerning it was
offered in the chapter on his years as journeyman printer
—a theory which answers the question how, out in the
Middle West, his thinking, forsaking the freer trends of
his own generation, was turned back into eighteenth-century channels.   It was found that in his late teens he became interested in Tom Paine.   It is wholly possible that,
imposed upon the foundation Calvinistic belief, received
from his mother, that what is to be will be, his life-view
took on an unchangeable shape from his interest in the

[29] O. H. Moore, "Mark Twain and Don Quixote," *PMLA*, XXXVII (June,
1922), p. 329.                                     [30] A. B. P., I, 511.
[31] "Once with Mrs. Clemens he dined with the author of his old favorite,
*European Morals*, William E. H. Lecky."—*Ibid.*, II, 1104.

writings of the apologist for American freedom; and that it was due to this shaping that his philosophy remained a cramped thing—tragic, indeed, from his own point of view. It is impossible to discover how early he made the acquaintance of Tom Paine, but he said to his biographer in 1907, in reply to a remark that it "took a brave man before the Civil War to confess that he had read *The Age of Reason*," "So it did, and yet that seems a mild book now. *I read it first when I was a cub pilot, read it with fear and hesitation, but marveling at its fearlessness and wonderful power.*[32] I read it again a year or two ago, for some reason, and was amazed to see how tame it had become. It seemed that Paine was apologizing everywhere for hurting the feelings of the reader."[33] The significant points in this remark are at once apparent. He read *The Age of Reason* as "cub-pilot,"—two or three years, it may be, before writing the letter to his brother. The arguments he found there had been taking possession of his mind, until, in 1860, when he had attained to prosperity and independence, he couldn't see what a man wanted with religion at all—the first expression we find of his "free-thinking." It made a stupendous impression upon his mind, an impression so great that when he returned to the book late in life he was surprised to discover that its tone seemed mild and apologetic. Furthermore, he had originally read it as a thing banned and forbidden, and hence, it may be assumed, with some youthful feeling of heroism. There was no quality that Mark Twain admired more than "fearlessness," and none which, at that time, would have been a greater matter for emulation than the "wonderful power" he found in the book.

[32] My italics.                    [33] A. B. P., III, 1445.

While this reading, as will be shown, would account for the main points in the philosophy of Mark Twain, another possible source from this period of his life may be mentioned here by way of parenthesis. It is suggested in an earlier notation by his biographer, who, writing of his river days, says: "He began the study of French. . . . He must have studied pretty faithfully when he was off watch and in port, for his river note-book contains a French exercise . . . and it is from the *Dialogues of Voltaire.*"[34] This evidence of a Voltaire influence at the *Sturm und Drang* period of his life cannot be neglected. At first view it brings the inference that necessarily, during the years while he was in and out of the most French city in the United States every month, he would have picked up an interest in Voltaire. The note becomes more significant in the light of a passage from Woodbridge Riley's *American Thought:*

Within two decades [after 1794, when *The Age of Reason* was published] the pamphlet was to be found on the banks of the Tennessee and Ohio; within two more decades it was circulated among the readers of Volney and Voltaire and in those places in Tennessee and Kentucky whose names still attest the French sympathies of the first settlers . . . a friend of Abraham Lincoln reported that in Indiana *The Age of Reason* passed from hand to hand, furnishing food for discussion in tavern and village store.[35]

Two suggestions may be taken from this extract: first, that Mark Twain's father, sojourning in Kentucky or coming down the Ohio in the thirties, may have acquired an interest in both Voltaire and Tom Paine, and that his son may have caught from him hints of such an interest that aroused his curiosity and motivated his later reading; sec-

[34] *Ibid.*, I, 151.     [35] P. 99.

ond, that Sam Clemens, himself, if not in Philadelphia or New York, certainly from Macfarlane in Cincinnati, and on the Ohio in 1856, heard discussions of both authors that started him reading them—if he had not been initiated earlier.[36] By Tom Paine, of course, he might have been incited to read Voltaire, and by Goldsmith, if the young man read him extensively enough to discover his interest in the French philosopher. Undoubtedly, ideas from the French "Enlightenment" found their way into Mark Twain's thinking. His denial of free will, his indictment of the Christian civilization, his belief in property as an enhancement to personality,[37] and his view of history as "nothing more than a picture of crimes and misfortunes," might have been confirmed, if not first suggested, by Voltaire. The reference to his reading of *The Age of Reason*, therefore, takes on greater significance. The remark quoted from the letter of 1860 shows that his religious revolt had gone beyond that of his teacher. *The Age of Reason* defends the God of the deists, though it advocates that each man shall follow "the religion and worship he prefers. . . . My own mind is my own church," Paine declared.

From the first part of *The Age of Reason* Mark Twain as a young man might have got his initial glimpse of the mechanical theory of human life, which he finally formulated into a philosophical system. Part I explains the principles of Newtonian deism as based on the phenomena of planetary motion. It contains coarse ridicule

---

[36] In Mark Twain's library was a 1784 edition of Voltaire's *Memoires pour servir à la Vie*, and an 1881 edition of a *Life* by J. Parton, with "numerous marked paragraphs and marginal notes."—Anderson Galleries Catalogue.

[37] *Cf.* "The Curious Republic of Gondour," *The Atlantic Monthly*, XXXVI (Oct., 1875), 461-63.

of what Paine considered superstition, along with many eloquent passages in favor of a pure morality founded upon natural religion. Its moral idealism must have constituted a large part of its appeal to Sam Clemens. And the place that orthodox Christianity had occupied in the thinking of the Clemens family, even if he had acquired no other point of contact with Paine up to that time, would have insured that the deistic arguments against Christian proofs, reviewed in the passionate spirit of a rough and ready controversialist, would arouse him either to accept or refute Paine's position.

It is difficult to understand why there is no mention of Tom Paine in Mark Twain's writings. In London he knew Moncure D. Conway,[38] the chief authority on the sceptic's life. In 1908 Mark Twain received an incomplete list of the world's "One Hundred Greatest Men," men who had "exerted the greatest visible influence on the life and activities of the race," with the request that he suggest names that should be added to it. To the list of statesmen he added the name of Thomas Paine.[39]

As has been said, Mark Twain's thought was not much touched by nineteenth-century speculative philosophy. It remained within the limits of the narrower experiences of the preceding age. In its main lines it seems to follow the doctrines of Hobbes (1588-1679), one of the precursors of English deism, and of Locke, Hume, and Newton. His theory of the will is like that of Hobbes, who says, "For as much as the *will to do* is *appetite,* and the *will to omit, fear,* the cause of *appetite* and *fear* is the cause also of our will."[40]

---

[38] A. B. P., II, 570; 547; III, 1540.
[39] *Letters,* II, 817.     [40] *Discourse on Human Nature,* p. 9.

The central problems of Mark Twain's system are two, the first involving the answer to the question, How far is man a free agent? and the second, whether he is influenced from within or without. The answers to these questions are given by the Old Man to the Young Man in the dialogue, "What is Man?" The answer to the first is that man has no more responsibility than a machine has; to the second, that the influences which determine a man's conduct come from the outside. The Old Man says, "Whatsoever a man is, is due to his *make,* and to the *influences* brought to bear upon it by his heredities, his habitat, his associations. He is moved, directed, COM-MANDED by *exterior* influences—*solely.* He *originates* nothing, not even a thought."[41] In a copy of Lecky's *History of European Morals,* opposite a passage in which the author refers to those who believe that a desire to obtain happiness and avoid pain is the only possible motive to action, Mark Twain's marginal note was, "Sound and true."[42]

Mark Twain's conception of the human understanding was much like that of Locke. Innate, speculative ideas he shied away from, just as he did from poetry and romance. What his eyes could see, what his ears could hear—fact—was the rock that he set his faith upon, both for his art and his philosophy.

Closely related to his ideas that might have been derived from Hobbes and Locke is the point in which Mark Twain's philosophy resembles that of Hume. Like Hume, ruling out everything but empirical knowledge, he could not admit the idea of God into his universe, nor

[41] Mark Twain, *What is Man? and Other Essays,* p. 5.
[42] A. B. P., I, 511.

hope for any interposition on man's behalf. The Mysterious Stranger that controls the destinies of his puppets is a nephew of Satan. Hume, however, could no more admit the idea of a destroying power than of an all-ruling Providence. "It seems to me," he says, "that this theory of the universal energy and operation of the Supreme Being is too bold ever to carry conviction with it to man."[43] He saw mere chance reaction; conscious experience was merely the succession of isolated impressions. If a pattern is ever discernible, according to Hume's belief, it is such a passing pattern as a kaleidoscope produces. Both Hume and Mark Twain were thoroughgoing sceptics, but whereas the eighteenth-century man found stimulation and satisfaction in scepticism, the nineteenth-century man found in it sorrow and, finally, despair. A maleficent power set the machine going, he believed, whose victim man is. Unlike Hume, he found that all chance is direction, but it is the direction of a malign power. He believed that whatever is, is not right.

It was in this last finding that Mark Twain's account differed from Newton's. Newton saw in the perfect mechanism of the cosmos the design of Providence. Except for this difference, it almost appears as if Mark Twain adopted the Newtonian universe ready made. Of all the trends that went into eighteenth-century thought, in fact, Newton's was the system, in its broader, more obvious lines, at any rate, that must have appealed most strongly to Mark Twain's imagination. The evidences of mechanism in the whole scheme of things—the idea of the

---

[43] *Inquiries* (ed. Selby-Bigge), p. 63. Henry Pochmann does not find any references to Hume's philosophy in Mark Twain's writings, but he notes that in *The Prince and the Pauper* are five passages quoted from Hume's *History of England*.—"The Mind of Mark Twain," p. 171.

world as "a vast perpetual motion machine, every event of which is deducible from universal mechanical principles" would have been just as convincing to the humorist as to the philosopher. Mark Twain's humorous representation of the heavens, with Halley's comet, in his "Captain Stormfield's Visit to Heaven," might have been a clown's play through the heavens of Newton.

His firmly fixed conception of a materialistic universe was the source both of his strength and of his limitation. To refuse to recognize fact and its implications would, to him, have been to depart from his own honesty. His need of solid fact to plant his universe upon, and his trust in the human intellect—though the Mysterious Stranger, the embodiment of pure intellect, betrays man, according to his final representation—made it impossible for him to be reconciled to uncertainty. His mood seems almost an atheist's revolt against the attitude that in agnosticism may be found satisfaction. It was not that of the man who could feel that "no conclusion can be more agreeable to scepticism than such as make discoveries concerning the weakness and narrow limits of human reason and capacity.[44] He could not "embrace the doubt." His convictions brought sorrow and bitterness to him. He wanted passionately to be assured of the validity of man's faith in the unseen, but his principle of following his intellect fearlessly whither it led him was his undoing. There is no overseeing Providence directing the world, he was forced to conclude; man is a selfish animal incapable of choosing a noble rôle for himself, though Mark Twain desired passionately to discover that he and his fellows could hold themselves to a noble rôle. Every man has his price, as

[44] Hume, *op. cit.*, p. 76.

surely to his way of thinking as to Robert Walpole's, as *The Man that Corrupted Hadleyburg* shows. There is nothing real about religion. It is pretty much a part, he suspected, of the world of poetry and romance.

That his ethical and social teaching is a larger and more trustworthy thing than his religious and philosophical system, is due to the fact that his sympathy for man and his fretful fever was vigorous enough to modify and impose balance upon his rational faculty. He gave his chivalrous heart authority when it came to the practical conduct of life. All that was broadest and best in his father's and mother's ethical teaching, all the faith in humanity that he discovered in Goldsmith, intensified his passion for honesty and justice, and his belief that whether or not the masses are capable of developing toward a more nearly ideal life, certain evils can be removed.[45]    But his nature impelled him to submit himself to the stream of life in its stormy places, and there he had to flounder with his fellows. When he discovered that his ideals of honesty and justice could not hold in the current, he railed at himself and others, but his great sympathy, the passion of pity that swept him into defense of the helpless in various parts of the world, preserved him from the more blighting phases of cynicism and misanthropy.

He was born with a hungry heart. In his own personal life he half remolded the sorry scheme of things— only to have it broken by fate. His tragedy was that, by the time he left the river, he had anchored himself so firmly to external reality that he could not find assurance in anything but reason and concrete fact; and the facts about life he found to be negative. During the years while

[45] *Letters*, II, 527.

his spirit was robust, he did not become unbalanced by this finding; but when old age and disappointment came upon him, all the intellectual and emotional forces of his nature were surrendered to a great melancholy, brought on in part by a noble sense of the tragedy of the human situation, in part by a sense of his own limitation. As he grew older, his creative powers expanded, but the lines of his thinking, instead of taking the advancing directions of his own century, assumed increasingly more fixed limitations from that which had preceded it.

# VIII

## AT THE CROSS-ROADS OF THE NATION

THESE CHAPTERS have been, first of all, an essay at presenting some neglected aspects of the region out of which Mark Twain came—a small region, a backwater, if you will, of the fabulous forties; and that is not to say that it is to be discredited. "All that goes to make the *me* in me was in a Missourian village, on the other side of the globe," Mark Twain wrote in India, looking back through the vista of three-score years. Sam Clemens's region had too vivid and too highly idealized a life of its own to be drawn authentically by a satirical pen, by any historian who cannot catch the spirit of what it tried for. More nearly approached today in some parts of Texas, perhaps, than elsewhere in America, the Missouri of Mark Twain's boyhood is not accounted for by any of the attempts so far made to describe the American frontier—partly in that it developed a culture that was favorable for the nurture of a literary ambition.

In religion Sam Clemens's habitat was, by and large, puritanical, whether of the Church of England, brought from Virginia, as in early Pike County country communities, or, more commonly, of the evangelical churches, especially the Presbyterian. Because the church had been trusted from the first to lift border society out of ruffianism, its interests were enthusiastically supported, though professional men in the district were likely, in a silent kind of way, to be free-thinkers of the Jefferson type. If their beliefs came from Tom Paine, they did not much acknowledge it.

On its worse side, the obvious paradoxes of the social structure, as well as the futility of being committed to un-attainable ideals, made for hypocrisy and errors of the flesh. The aristocratic, Church-of-England woman knew that her husband's western, hail-fellow-well-met man-ners and easy conscience furthered his political ambitions. Free-thinking political leaders knew that the religious sanction made for the success of their enterprises—for the founding of colleges as well as the securing of votes for congressmen. Senator Dillworthy in *The Gilded Age* made his religion pay. The appraising glance could always detect the equivocation, which, when the prosper-ous days after the Civil War came, made so rich a harvest for satire. But the life of the country before the Civil War was lived on such a generous scale and tried so gen-uinely for the noble way of life necessary for the success of the American social experiment, that its insincerities were not the most real thing about it. The big thing about it as a culture, in contrast to the industrial society that has grown out of it, was that, because every man in that broad expanse might have his own domain, however small, whereon his individuality could express itself, it did not lend itself readily to standardization. And this fostering of individual gifts was due as much to the influence of early evangelical churches as to an agrarian economy.

The region was western—western in its belief in "honest toil" for all men, in its undivided adherence to the progressive doctrines of agrarian democracy, with a belief in its own perfectibility, and a trust in the Manifest

Destiny of the West. To its citizens as to their contemporary, Emerson, whom they may have heard lecture in St. Louis, there was "virtue yet in the hoe and spade." "The dignity and necessity of labor to every citizen," if less transcendentally interpreted, was a more fully developed principle with them than with him. The year before Orion Clemens took over the *Hannibal Journal*, that newspaper voiced this spirit for the West: "The cultivation of the soil, in a free country, is the highest and noblest profession in which man can be engaged—as it is the foundation of all true wealth." The *Western Journal and Civilian*, published in St. Louis (1848-1855), found a deeper significance in this favorite doctrine of the region: No pursuit of man, it declared, is "so free from vicious contamination"; none "requires closer observation of natural facts, more rigid analysis of cause and effects . . .; none better calculated to impress on man the duties of this life and lift him to the habitual contemplation of another." The development of an early culture in Missouri was possible because the rich new lands brought in quick returns for all labor bestowed upon them. Waterways offered a means of reaching St. Louis markets. In less than a generation people had money for securing the merchandise of civilization which makes for better living and better thinking. This quick turn-over, with the hope that went with it, gave a hearty trust to life there that was western more than it was southern.

To say that the region was agrarian, however, is not to say that it was of peasant quality—as a recent foreign visitor to the Valley characterized its descendants of the present generation. The poorest of its citizens had often a spirit and social grace that lifted them out of the com-

mon-place.  The truly homespun among them were objects of amusement.  Society did not exclude them, though
where it was southern rather than western it was likely
to give them a rope to hang themselves with.  Mark
Twain's story of Nicodemus Dodge in *A Tramp Abroad*
concerns a Hannibal rustic of this sort.

The region was both southern and western in that it
was a man's world.  The men spurred forth to California
to seek a fortune, Joe Bowers fashion, to lay at the feet of
the women they left behind.  They rode off to the Seminole and the Mexican wars, rationalizing their thirst for
adventure as the call of honor.  In general, they were
sporting men, whose ideals of integrity and ethical standards came from giving authority to their passions: at its
best, it was the disciplined and trusted impulses of the
southern gentleman that actuated its men, with something
of the solid substance of the British squire riding to the
hounds.  Men engaged in hot debates over political issues.
They might be aided and abetted by the wit of their wives,
but the women themselves had no aspiration to such public
preëminence as Mrs. Emily Newell Blair's "Courageous
Woman" attained to.  They would have disapproved of
her aspiration heartily.

But this was not because either the women themselves
or their men doubted their importance in the general social economy.  The chief glory of the region, in fact, in
both its southern and its western aspects, was its women.
Mariolatry, one of Mark Twain's American critics dubs
the regard for women represented in his life and writings.
It was as queens of earth rather than of heaven, however,
that he viewed them; Sam Clemens touched off their
harmless vanities and peccadilloes in his Assistant's Col-

umn.  But the place assigned to women in his region was an element in the epic of the West.  The wives and daughters of the men who built up the economic substructure of its society were of charming purity, at the same time that they were gay, and often witty.  Their social functions had something of formality and unusual charm.  The principle on which society was maintained was of the simplest kind.  Men trusted women to keep society on the ideal plane to which they desired the new community to attain. Theoretically social intrigue did not exist, and the "fallen woman" was not in the picture.  Her existence was ignored.  In the newspapers of the time France is often referred to acidulously as the country of social irregularities—an attitude which finds an unfortunate echo in "What Paul Bourget Thinks of Us."  Becky Thatcher is typical of the small daughters of the region.  Mark Twain's lifelong delight in the society of young girls is a trail-over from the attitude he naturally felt to be ideal. His own three daughters were considered, by highly bred strangers who met them, to be lovely in a flower-like way, an impression confirmed in his poem "In Memoriam," written after the death of Susie Clemens, and in "The Death of Jean."  Laura Hawkins of *The Gilded Age,* who stepped outside the pale, was an adopted daughter.  She did not properly "belong," was not typical of the women whom the men there delighted to honor.  Mark Twain's description of an acquaintance out of the "beautiful past, the dear and lamented past," whom he happened upon in Calcutta, is typical of his memory of the women of his home town: "Mary Wilson," as he recalls her, "was dainty and sweet, peachblooming and exquisite, gracious and lovely in character."  His attitude found its supreme

expression in his knightly story of Joan of Arc, dedicated
to his wife. Of no small significance in the present study
is the fact that it was in Hannibal that the story of "the
maid" first touched his imagination.

Above all else, the region was proudly southern—but
southern with a difference. Instead of large plantations
with swarms of slaves to support its social fabric, it had a
simpler—at best, an idyllic—type of farm life, where
slaves lived for the most part happily, their only fear being that a turn of fortune might make it necessary for
them to be "sold down the river." These farms supported country towns as centers of the social life of the
region. Their social traditions came down mainly from
Virginia by way of Kentucky. The robust taste for life, as
well as its pride and vanity and curiosity, was indirectly
out of Renaissance England, from which Virginia got her
name. These are seen in the newspapers of the section,
in the tall language of the political speech, in the large
enterprises proposed to the state legislature, and in comments, often satirical, on the social, political, and literary
affairs of the world. A Renaissance taste for life at high
pitch is seen in the hold-over of the duel for settling the
private quarrel, satirized by Mark Twain in *Pudd'nhead
Wilson,* and in the gusto with which wives and sweet-
hearts, with patriotic suppers, sent their men forth to the
wars. The region was southern in that the amenities of
social life and the call of honor took precedence over business interests—an attitude made possible by slave labor.
While their capacity for a vivid leisure saved them from
becoming bound down to business, their taste for good living made them intensely practical. The small thrift of
the Yankee they had no ability for. This transplanted,

new South avoided many of the tyrannies of the old. Its
newspapers reveal an undercurrent of distrust of the institution of slavery—a distrust felt in Jefferson's Virginia,
out of which it came.

Finally, although its citizens were intelligent rather
than intellectual, the region was "literary"—literary, that
is, in an amateur, southern way; it consistently encouraged an interest in the safe and reliable classics. And the
young women of the Hannibal Female Seminary were
just as eager to get their verses into print in the early
fifties as college sophomores are to-day. The newspapers
printed at county-seats and larger towns contained much
quotation from classics and anecdotes and squibs about
their authors. Even though in its practical ambitions the
region looked forward to after-the-war baroque achieve-
ments, in its most approved sentiments it looked backward
to eighteenth-century writers. The speeches of professional men were impressively ornamented with flowers of
rhetoric from the classics—if Greek and Latin, so much
the better. Champ Clark, of the later period, was its
favorite son.

Sam Clemens started on his career as writer with this
kind of oratory ringing in his ears, but from his genuinely
high-minded father and his keen-witted mother he had
somehow inherited a reaching spirit that could not be con-
tented with commonplace performance. All his life he
tried for something that eluded him. His tremendous
curiosity about life kept him turning to new situations. As
printer's apprentice, as sub-editor, as journeyman-printer,
as river-pilot in the Middle West, he paralleled his excursions into life with experiments at writing down the materials of life. The necessity that Joseph Conrad saw for

the artist to render justice to his materials themselves, and to his own temperamental angle of vision, was Mark Twain's necessity. Writing late in life of the need of each man to have his own pattern of patriotism, he phrased what would have been his creed. The artist must *labor it out* in his own "head and heart, and in the privacy and independence" of his own temperament. What he writes must be "fire-assayed and tested and proved in his own conscience."

The culture that produced Mark Twain gave the trend to both his earlier and his later work. *Roughing It* is a realization of travels into Nevada and California which he had already experienced vicariously through many stories of earlier argonauts, set up in print in the Hannibal papers. ⌐His own is of larger proportions than any that preceded it. The epic character of *Huckleberry Finn* and *Life on the Mississippi* is attributable to the glowing, vigorous life of the Mid-West setting which Mark Twain knew. ⌐ His submerged consciousness of the dangers that lurked under the fine ideals of his Missouri world was more real to a young newspaper man than to most men, because it was his part "to castigate the times." It got the better of the artist in him only gradually, however, as life failed to fulfil his vision of what it might be. Then he went about with a lantern in his hand peering into men's faces, scanning his own face in the mirror, to discover whether man could ever show himself trustworthy to act an uncalculating and noble part. His passionate hatred of meanness and cruelty and sham was the hatred felt by a community where life was young and was trusted to perfect itself. To say that he remained a youth till his death is to say that something from that early time lingered in his spirit till the last. He devoted his life to its hope. In his rôle as ideal husband, ideal father, ideal friend, he made his own little world a glorious dwelling-place. But the dreams that his youth had cherished, in the brave new frontier world, miscarried. The transition in America to an industrial economy left him hopeless about man's future. He was one of the first writers to realize whither America was drifting, and because he could see nothing but inescapable doom in the vista ahead, his heart broke. He had had such a glorious vision of the ideals by which America had formed itself that he was glad his own passing would be with their passing. Stimulating as the social and ethical teaching of his later period was, the real significance of his last years lies not primarily in anything that he said or wrote, but in the fight that he fought to the last. His defiance of the powers that ruled the cosmos, as he conceived them, is of heroic proportions. At the end he was an American Prometheus, but the American masses he wrote for were a highly idealized, mythical citizenry, not a congeries of humanity turning daily to the leaders that could promise the largest rewards—"scrambling at the shearer's feast." And because to him the hope of the world lay in America, his despair was for all mankind.

And this is not to say that he betrayed his region in *The Gilded Age*. Looking back from the vantage ground of after-the-war abuses, he saw what had grown logically out of the inconsistencies of the early time. Some unconscious feeling however, that he had failed to get the whole truth about his home country written down, must have caused him to turn to his boys' books. As a boy's world the region had been full of charm. And thus it was by doing the smaller thing that he did the larger thing. Because he was so authentically of Marion and Monroe and Pike counties, he was authentically of Missouri, and authentically of America—for Missouri lies at the cross-roads of the nation.

In whatever Mark Twain was, in his vanity, his curiosity, his ambition to secure what was first-rate, along with his need to keep his spirit clear from the taint of self-interest; in whatever he did: on the lecture platform, in the drawing-room, by the banquet table, at his desk, "beguiling all of the people all of the time," his hope for social justice, for the *raison d'être* of America, was a passion larger than that of ordinary men. In that passion he called to account the very gods of the universe. In his rôle as the supreme apologist for the American experiment he defies final analysis; he will ever be a figure of legend.

# SELECTED BIBLIOGRAPHY

NEWSPAPERS

*Hannibal Commercial Advertiser*, Jan. 4, 1838 (Vol. 1, No. 11); June 22, 1838; Sept. 18, 1838; Sept. 25, 1838; Feb. 27, 1839.

——— *Daily Journal.* March 15–Sept. 21, 1853. Fairly complete file, bound volume, Missouri State Historical Library, Columbia, Mo.

——— *Journal.* Sept. 7, 1848–Sept. 15, 1853. Imperfect file, bound volume, Missouri State Historical Library, Columbia, Mo.

——— *Missouri Courier.* Oct. 12, 1848–June 8, 1854. Imperfect file, bound volume, Missouri State Historical Library, Columbia, Mo. (Known in the state as the *Missouri Courier.*)

——— *Tri-Weekly Messenger.* Oct. 16, 1852–Oct. 13, 1853. Imperfect file, bound volume, Missouri State Historical Library, Columbia, Mo.

——— *Western Union.* Oct. 10, 1850–Aug. 28, 1851.

——— *Whig Messenger.* Sept. 10, 1853–Aug. 31, 1854. Imperfect file, bound volume, Missouri State Historical Library, Columbia, Mo.

*Jeffersonian Republican.* Jefferson City, 1833-1844.

*Kansas City Star Magazine*, "Letters Young Mark Twain Wrote in 1857," March 21, 1926.

*Missouri Gazette.* St. Louis, 1819-1821.

*Missouri Intelligencer.* Columbia, 1831-1835.

*Missouri Republican.* St. Louis, 1823-1828.

*Missouri Statesman.* Columbia, 1848-1853.

*Monroe City News*, Historical Edition, Commemorating the One Hundredth Anniversary of the Organization of Monroe County, Missouri, 1831-1931 Vol. LVII (Aug. 13, 1931), No. 33.

*New Orleans Crescent,* 1857-1861.
———— *Daily Picayune,* 1857-1861.
*Saint Louis Enquirer,* 1819-1823.
*Salt River Journal.* Bowling Green, Mo., 1835.
*Western Emigrant.* Boonville, Jan. 10-Dec. 31, 1839; Jan.-
March 19, 1840.
*Western Journal and Civilian Magazine.* St. Louis, 1848-1855.

BOOKS AND MAGAZINES

Adams, J. T. *The Epic of America.* New York, 1931.
Aikman, Duncan. *The Taming of the Frontier.* New York,
1925.
Alden, Henry M. "Mark Twain—An Appreciation," *Bookman,*
XXXI (June, 1910), 366-69.
Aldrich, P. Emory. "John Locke and the Influence of His
Works in America," *Publications of the American Antiquarian
Society,* April, 1879.
Aldrich, Mrs. T. B. *Crowding Memories.* Boston and New
York, 1920.
Anderson Auction Company. *Catalogue of the Library and
Manuscripts of Samuel L. Clemens (Mark Twain).* Part I.
. . . to be sold Feb. 7 and 8, 1911. No. 892. New York,
12 East 46th Street.
Anon., "Mark Twain's Message of Mirth," in "Musings Without
Method," *Blackwood's Magazine,* CLXXXII (August,
1907), 279-86.
Archbold, Miss Anne. *A Book for the Married and Single, the
Grave and the Gay: and Especially Designed for Steamboat
Passengers.* East Plainfield, Ohio, 1850.
Armstrong, C. J. "Mark Twain's Early Writings Discovered,"
*Missouri Historical Review,* XXIV (July, 1930), 485-501.
Atkeson, Mary Meek. *A Study of the Local Literature of the
Upper Ohio Valley.* Ohio State University Bulletin XXVI,
No. 3. Contributions in English, 2. Columbus, Ohio, 1921.

[Baird, Robert]. *View of the Valley of the Mississippi, or the Emigrant's and Traveller's Guide to the West.* Philadelphia, 1832.

Baldwin, Joseph Glover. *The Flush Times of Alabama and Mississippi: A Series of Sketches.* New York, 1853.

Ball, Isaac. "An Inquiry into Humor," *Sewanee Review.* XIX (January, 1911), 50-60.

Bay, J. Christian. "Tom Sawyer, Detective: The Origin of the Plot," *Anniversary Volume to Herbert Putnam,* pp. 80-88. New Haven, 1929.

Beecher, Lyman. *A Plea for the West.* Cincinnati, 1835.

Bek, William G. "The Followers of Duden," *Missouri Historical Review,* Vols. XIV and XV (Oct., 1919—July, 1921).

Bentzon, Th. "Les humoristes Américains: Mark Twain," *Revue des Deux Mondes,* C, 2 période (July 15, 1872), 313-35.

Birkbeck, Morris. *Notes on a Journey in America, from the Coast of Virginia to the Territory of Illinois.* London, 1817.

Blair, Walter A. *A Raft Pilot's Log: A History of the Great Rafting Industry on the Upper Mississippi, 1840-1915.* Cleveland, 1930.

Blankenship, Russell. *American Literature as an Expression of the National Mind.* New York, 1931.

Bodine, T. V. "A Journey to the Home of Mark Twain," *Kansas City Star Magazine,* May 19, 1912.

Bolton, S. K. *Mark Twain* (Famous American Authors Series). New York, 1887.

Boynton, Percy H. "The West and Mark Twain," *A History of American Literature.* New York, 1919.

Brackenridge, H. H. *Modern Chivalry (containing the Adventures of a Captain, and Teague O'Regan his Servant).* 4 vols. Richmond, Va., 1815. (Philadelphia, 1792-97.)

Brackenridge, Henry Marie. *Recollections of Persons and Places in the West.* Philadelphia, 1868.

———— *Views of Louisiana together with a Journal of a Voyage up the Missouri River in 1811.* Pittsburg, 1814.

Bradford, Gamaliel. "Mark Twain," *American Portraits.* Boston, 1922.

Brashear, M. M. "Missouri Verse and Verse-Writers," *Missouri Historical Review,* XVIII (April, 1924), 315-44; XIX (October, 1924), 36-93.

Britannicus. "England and Mark Twain," *North American Review,* CXCI (June, 1910), 822-26.

Broadhead, G. C. "Early Missouri Roads," *Missouri Historical Review,* VIII (January, 1914), 90-92.

Brooks, Noah. "Mark Twain in California," *Century,* XXXV n.s. (November, 1898), 97-99.

Brooks, Van Wyck. *America's Coming of Age.* New York, 1915.

———— "The Genesis of Huck Finn," *The Freeman,* I (March 31, 1920).

———— *The Ordeal of Mark Twain.* New York, 1920. [New edition, 1933]

Brown, Robert. "Life on the Mississippi" (reviewed), *Academy,* XXIV (July 28, 1883), 58.

Burton, Richard. "Mark Twain," *Little Essays in Literature and Life.* New York, 1914.

Cairns, William B. *A History of American Literature.* New York, 1912.

Campbell, Killis. "From Aesop to Mark Twain," *Sewanee Review,* XIX (January, 1911), 43-49.

Canby, H. S. "Mark Twain," *Literary Review,* IV (November 3, 1923), 201-2.

Canfield, Channey. *The Diary of a Forty-Niner.* Boston, 1920.

Carey, W. A. "Memories of Mark Twain," *Overland Monthly,* LXVI (1916), 203.

Carnegie, Andrew. *Autobiography.* Boston, 1920.

Carr, Lucien. *Missouri* (American Commonwealth Series). Boston and New York, 1888.

Carter, John Henton [Col. Rolling Pin]. "Mark Twain," *The Man at the Wheel,* pp. 11-15. St. Louis, 1898.

Carus, P. "Mark Twain's Philosophy," *Monist,* XXIII (April, 1913), 181-223.

Chambers, H. H. *Mississippi Valley Beginnings.* New York, 1922.

Cheiro [Louis Hamon]. *Memoirs. Story of the Origin of Pudd'nhead Wilson.* 1912.

Chittenden, H. M. *Early Steamboat Navigation on the Missouri River.* 2 vols. New York, 1903.

Clapp, Louisa A. [Dame Shirley]. *The Shirley Letters from California Mines in 1851-52,* Originally printed in *Pioneer Magazine* of 1854-55. San Francisco, 1922.

Clark, C. H. *Mark Twain* (Authors at Home Series, J. L. and J. B. Gilder, eds.). New York, 1888.

Clemens, Clara. *My Father, Mark Twain.* New York and London, 1931.

Clemens, Cyril. *Mark Twain, The Letter Writer.* Boston, 1932.

Clemens, Will M. "Bret Harte's Country," *Bookman,* XIII (May, 1901), 223-37.

——— *Mark Twain: His Life and Work.* A Biographical Sketch. San Francisco, 1892.

Cobbett, William. *A Year's Residence in America* (The Abbey Classics). Boston, n. d.

Coman, Katharine. *Economic Beginnings in the Far West.* New York, 1912.

Conard, Howard F. (ed.). *Encyclopedia of the History of Missouri.* New York, Louisville, St. Louis, 1901.

Conway, Moncure D. *Autobiography.* Boston, 1904.

Corey, W. A. "Memories of Mark Twain," *Overland,* LXVI (September, 1915), 263-65.

Crews, E. K. "Illinois in Modern Literature," Illinois State Historical Society *Journal,* III, 26.

Crockett, David. *Autobiography* [First ed., 1834]. New York, 1923.

Dayton, F. E. *Steamboat Days*. New York, 1925.

Delano, A. *Life on the Plains and among the Diggings*. New York, 1857.

De Menil, Alexandre Nicolas. *The Literature of the Louisiana Territory*. St. Louis, 1904.

De Quille, Dan. "Reporting with Mark Twain," *California Illustrated Magazine*, July, 1893.

DeVoto, Bernard. *Mark Twain's American*. Boston, 1932.

Dickens, Charles. *Letters, 1833-1870* (ed. by his sister-in-law and his eldest daughter). London, 1909.

—— *Martin Chuzzlewit*. London, 1834.

Dondore, Dorothy Anne. *The Prairie and the Making of Middle America: Four Centuries of Description*. Cedar Rapids, Ia., 1926.

Du Breuil, Alice Jouveau. *The Novel of Democracy in America*. Baltimore, 1923.

Emberson, Frances Guthrie. "The Vocabulary of Samuel L. Clemens from 1852 to 1884." Thesis (Ph.D.), University of Missouri, 1932.

Espenshade, A. H. "Tom Sawyer's Fiftieth Birthday," *St. Nicholas*, LIV (August, 1927), 808-9.

Fielder, E. D. "Familiar Haunts of Mark Twain," *Harper's Weekly*, XLIII (1899), 10.

Fields, Mrs. J. R. "Bret Harte and Mark Twain in the Seventies," *The Atlantic Monthly*, CXXX (September, 1922), 341-48.

Fisher, Henry W. *Abroad with Mark Twain and Eugene Field: Tales They Told to a Fellow-correspondent*. London, 1924.

Fisher, S. J. "Mark Twain," *Spectator*, CXXX (June 2, 1923), 922.

Flint, Timothy. *George Mason, the Young Backwoodsman, or "Don't Give up the Ship." A Story of the Mississippi Valley*. Boston, 1829.

―――― *Recollections of the Last Ten Years, Passed in Occasional Residences and Journeyings in the Valley of the Mississippi.* Boston, 1826.

Foerster, Norman. "New Viewpoints in American Literature," *The Saturday Review of Literature,* II (April 3, 1926), 677-79.

―――― ed. *The Reinterpretation of American Literature.* New York, 1928.

Forgues, Eugène. "Mark Twain: Les Carevanes d'un Humoriste," *Revue des Deux Mondes,* LXXIII, 3 période (Feb. 15, 1886), 879-918.

Fulton, Maurice G., ed. *Southern Life in Southern Literature.* Boston, 1917.

Genthe, Arnold. *Impressions of Old New Orleans.* New York, 1926.

Gilder, Richard Watson. "A Glance at Twain's Spoken and Written Art," *Outlook,* LXXVIII (December 3, 1904), 842-44.

―――― "Mark Twain's *The Prince and the Pauper,*" *Century,* I, n. s. (March, 1882), 783-84.

Gilmore, James R. *The Advance-Guard of Western Civilization.* New York, 1888.

Goodpasture, A. V. "Mark Twain, Southerner," *Tennessee Historical Magazine,* July, 1931.

Gould, E. W. *Fifty Years on the Mississippi.* St. Louis, 1889.

Greenslet, Ferris. *Life of Thomas Bailey Aldrich.* Boston, 1908.

Guitar, Sarah. "The Arrow Rock Tavern," *Missouri Historical Review,* XX (July, 1926), 499-503.

Hall, Ernest Jackson. "The Satirical Element in the American Novel." Thesis (Ph.D.), University of Pennsylvania, 1922.

Hall, James. *The Romance of Western History, or Sketches of History, Life, and Manners in the West.* Cincinnati, 1857.

Hamby, W. H. "The Literature of the Land," *History of Northwest Missouri* (Walter Williams, ed.). Vol. I. New York, 1915.

Hannay, David. *Life of Tobias George Smollett* (Great Writers Series). London, 1887.

Hannay, James. *Satire and Satirists*. London, 1854.

Hannigan, D. F. "Mark Twain as a Critic," *Free Review*, October, 1895.

Harkins, E. F. *Mark Twain* (Little Pilgrimages among the Men Who Have Written Famous Books). Boston, 1902.

Harte, Bret. "Innocents Abroad" (reviewed), *Overland Monthly*, IV o. s. January, 1870.

—————— *The Lectures of Bret Harte* (C. M. Kozlay, ed.). New York, 1909.

Harte, Bret and Twain, Mark. *Sketches of the Sixties*. San Francisco, 1926.

Harvey, Charles M. "The Dime Novel in American Life," *The Atlantic Monthly*, C (July, 1907), 37.

Haskins, C. W. *The Argonauts of California*. New York, 1890.

Hatfield, James Taft. "Goethe and the Ku Klux Klan," *Publications of the Modern Language Association*, XXXVII, 735.

Haweis, H. R. *American Humorists*. London, 1882.

Hazard, Lucy Lockwood. *The Frontier in American Literature*. New York, 1927.

Henderson, Archibald. *The Conquest of the Old Southwest*. New York, 1920.

—————— *Mark Twain*. New York, 1912.

—————— "Mark Twain from a New Angle," *Current Literature*, XLVII (August, 1909), 166-67.

Higginson, T. W. and Boynton, H. W. *A Reader's History of American Literature*. New York, 1903.

Hingston, E. P. *The Genial Showman: Being Reminiscences of the Life of Artemus Ward*. London, 1870.

Holliday, Carl. *A History of Southern Literature*. New York, 1906.

Holmes, O. W. "To Mark Twain on His Fiftieth Birthday," *Critic*, VII (October 18, 1884), 253.

Holmes, Ralph. "Mark Twain and Music," *Century*, CIV (October, 1922), 844-50.

Honce, C., ed. *The Adventures of Thomas Jefferson Snodgrass*. Chicago, 1928.

Hood, Thomas. "Up the Rhine," *Works* (Epes Sargent, ed). Vol. V. New York, 1865.

Hough, Emerson. *The Passing of the Frontier*. New Haven, 1919.

Howe, Will D. "Early Humorists," *Cambridge History of American Literature*, Bk. II, Ch. XIX. New York, 1918.

Howells, William Cooper. *Recollections of Life in Ohio* (1813-1840). Cincinnati, 1895.

Howells, William Dean. *A Boy's Town*. New York, 1890.

———— *Life in Letters* (Mildred Howells, ed.). 2 vols. Garden City, 1928.

———— "Mark Twain: An Inquiry," *North American Review*, CXCI (June, 1910), 836-50.

———— *My Mark Twain: Reminiscences and Criticism*. New York and London, 1910.

Hubbell, Jay B. "Introduction," J. P. Kennedy, *Swallow Barn*. New York, 1929.

Hudson, Manly O. "Missouri," *These United States* (Ernest Gruening, ed.). New York, 1923.

Hulbert, A. B. *Boone's Wilderness Road*. Cleveland, 1903.

*Humorist's Own Book, The*. Philadelphia, 1833.

Huntington, Ellsworth. *Civilization and Climate*. New Haven, 1915.

Imlay, Gilbert. *A Topographical Description of the Western Territory of North America . . . In a Series of Letters to a Friend in England*. London, 1797.

Irving, Pierre M. *Life and Letters of Washington Irving*. 2 vols. London, 1882.

Irving, Washington. "A Tour of the Prairies," *The Crayon Miscellany*. Philadelphia, 1835.

James, William. *The Letters of William James* (H. James, his son, ed.). 2 vols. Boston, 1920.

Jerrold, Walter. "Mark Twain, the Man and the Jester," *Bookman* (London), June, 1910.

Jones, Howard Mumford. *America and French Culture, 1750-1848.* Chapel Hill, 1927.

Keeling, Anna E. "American Humor: Mark Twain," *London Quarterly Review*, XCII (July, 1897), 147.

Keith, Clayton. *Centennial History of Pike County.* Read at the Centennial Celebration Held at Louisiana, Mo., July 4, 1876.

Keller, Helen. *Midstream.* Garden City, 1929.

Kellner, Leon. *American Literature* (Julia Franklin, trans.). New York, 1915.

Kennedy, J. P. *Swallow Barn* (Jay B. Hubbell, ed.). New York, 1929.

Keyserling, Hermann Alexander. *America Set Free.* New York, 1929.

Kipling, Rudyard. "An Interview with Mark Twain," *From Sea to Sea.* New York, 1899.

Kirkpatrick, J. E. *Timothy Flint: Pioneer, Missionary, Author, Editor, 1780-1840; the Story of His Life among the Pioneers and Frontiersmen in the Ohio and Mississippi Valley and in New England and the South.* Cleveland, 1911.

Kitton, F. C. *Charles Dickens: His Life, Writings, and Personality.* New York, 1908.

Lang, Andrew. "The Art of S. L. Clemens," *Critic*, XIX o. s. (July 25, 1891), 45-50.

Laut, Agnes C. *The Blazed Trail of the Old Frontier.* New York, 1926.

Lautrec, Gabriel de. "Introduction," *Contes Choisies de Mark Twain.* Paris, 1900.

Lawton, Mary. *Lifetime with Mark Twain: Memories of Katy Leary, His Faithful Servant and Friend.* New York, 1925.

Leacock, Stephen. *Mark Twain*. New York, 1933.

Lewisohn, Ludwig. *Expression in America*. New York, 1932.

"Life on the Mississippi" (reviewed), *Harper's Magazine*, LXVII (October, 1883), 799.

Locke, David Ross [Petroleum V. Nasby]. *Ekkoes from Kentucky*. Boston, 1868.

Longstreet, Augustus Baldwin. *Georgia Scenes, Characters, Incidents, etc., in the First Half Century of the Republic*. New York, 1840.

Lorch, Fred W. "Lecture Trips and Visits of Mark Twain in Iowa," *Iowa Journal of History and Politics*, XXVII (October, 1929), 507-47.

———— "Mark Twain in Iowa," *Iowa Journal of History and Politics*, XXVII (July, 1929), 408-56.

———— "Orion Clemens Number." "The Tradition," 353-57; "Molly Clemens's Note Book," 357-63; "Literary Apprenticeship," 364-71; "Adrift for Heresy," 372-80; "The Closing Years," 381-86; "Comment," 387-88. *The Palimpsest* (Pub. monthly at Iowa City by the State Historical Society), X (October, 1929).

Loshe, Lillie Deming. *The Early American Novel*. New York, 1907.

Lowell, James Russell. "Humor, Wit, Fun, and Satire," 33-61; "Swift," 173-200, in *The Function of the Poet and Other Essays*. Boston, 1920.

———— "Pope," in *My Study Windows*, 385-433. Boston, 1913.

Ludewig, Hermann Ernst. *The Literature of American Local History*. New York, 1846. First Supplement, 1848.

Lukens, Henry Clay. "American Literary Comedians," *Harper's Magazine*, LXXX (April, 1890), 783-97.

Mabbott, T. O. "Mark Twain's Artillery, A Mark Twain Legend," *Missouri Historical Review*, XXV (October, 1929), 23-30.

McDougal, Henry Clay. *Recollections, 1844-1909*. Kansas City, Mo., 1910.

Macy, John. "Mark Twain," *The Spirit of American Literature,* 248-77. Garden City, 1913.

Mann, Max. "Mark Twain," Biographical Introduction to *A Tramp Abroad.* Leipzig, 1901.

"Marion City, 'Great Metropolis of the West' " (Quincy, Ill. *Herald,* June 14, 1926), *Missouri Historical Review,* October, 1928.

Marryat, Frederick. *A Diary in America, with Remarks on Its Institutions.* 3 vols. London, 1839.

Martin, Alma. *A Vocabulary Study of the Gilded Age* (pub. by the Mark Twain Society). Webster Groves, Mo., 1930.

Martineau, Harriet. *Retrospect of Western Travel.* 3 vols. London, 1838.

———— *Society in America.* 2 vols. New York, 1837.

Matthews, Brander. "Mark Twain," Introduction to Harper Ed., Vol. I. New York, 1899.

———— "Mark Twain and the Art of Writing," *Harper's Magazine,* CXLI (October, 1920), 635-43.

———— "Mark Twain as Speech Maker and Story Teller," *Mentor,* XII (May, 1924), 24-28.

Meine, Franklin J., ed. *Tall Tales of the Southwest: an Anthology of Southern and Southwestern Humor, 1830-1860* (Americana Deserta Series). New York, 1930.

Melville, H. "The Lightning-Rod Man." *Piazza Tales.* 1856.

*Mentor,* Mark Twain Number. XII (May, 1924).

Merwin, Henry Childs. *Life of Bret Harte, with Some Account of California Pioneers.* Boston and New York, 1911.

Mesick, Jane Louise. *The English Traveler in America, 1785-1835.* New York, 1922.

Michaud, Regis. *The American Novel of To-Day.* Boston, 1928.

Mierow, H. E. "Cicero and Mark Twain," *Classical Journal,* XX (Dec., 1924), 167-69.

Milard, Bailey. "Mark Twain in San Francisco," *Bookman*, XXXI (1910), 369-73.

———— "When They Were Twenty-One," *Bookman*, XXXVII (May, 1913), 296-304.

Minnegerode, Meade. *The Fabulous Forties: A Presentation of Private Life*. New York and London, 1924.

*Missouri History of Marion County* (compiled). St. Louis, 1884.

*Missouri History of Monroe and Shelby Counties* (compiled). St. Louis, 1884.

Mitford, Mary Russell. *Lights and Shadows of American Life*. London, 1832.

Moffett, S. E. "Mark Twain as Interpreter of American Character," *McClure's*, XIII (October, 1899), 523-29 (Also in *The $30,000 Bequest*).

Monette, J. W. *History of the Discovery and Settlement of the Mississippi by the Three Great European Powers, Spain, France, and Great Britain*. 2 vols. 1846.

Moore, Olin Harris. "Mark Twain and Don Quixote," *Publications of the Modern Language Association*, XXXVII (June, 1922), 324-46.

Mumford, Lewis. *The Golden Day: A Study in American Experience and Culture*. New York, 1926.

Musick, J. R. *Stories of Missouri*. New York, 1897.

Noble, James Ashcroft. "New Novels," *Academy*, XXXVII (February 22, 1890), 129-30.

Nolen, Mary Norman. "A Century of Life in Monroe County," *The Monroe City News*, LVII (August 13, 1932), 1-9.

Ogg, Frederick A. *Opening of the Mississippi: A Struggle for Supremacy in the American Interior*. New York, 1904.

———— *The Reign of Andrew Jackson: A Chronicle of the Frontier in Politics*. New Haven, 1919.

O'Higgins, Harvey. *The American Mind in Action*. New York and London, 1924.

O'Rell, Max. "Mark Twain and Paul Bourget," *North American Review*, CLX (March, 1895), 302.

Quick, Herbert. *Mississippi Steamboatin': A History of Steamboating on the Mississippi and Its Tributaries.* New York, 1926.

Pain, Barry. "The Humor of Mark Twain," *Bookman* (London), June, 1910.

Paine, Albert Bigelow. *The Boys' Life of Mark Twain.* New York, 1916.

———— *Mark Twain: A Biography. The Personal and Literary Life of Samuel Langhorne Clemens.* 3 vols. New York and London, 1912.

———— ed. *Mark Twain's Autobiography.* 2 vols. New York and London, 1924.

———— ed. *Mark Twain's Letters, Arranged with Comment.* 2 vols. New York and London, 1917.

Parkman, Francis. *LaSalle and the Discovery of the Great West.* Boston, 1897.

———— *The Pioneers of France in the New World.* Boston, 1897.

Parrington, V. L. *Main Currents in American Thought.* 3 vols. New York, 1927-1930.

Pattee, Fred Lewis. *A History of American Literature since 1870.* New York, 1915.

———— "On the Rating of Mark Twain," *American Mercury,* XIV (June, 1928), 183-91.

Paulding, James Kirke. *Letters from the South* (written during an excursion in the summer of 1816). New York, 1817.

———— *Westward Ho.* New York, 1832.

Paxson, F. L. *History of the American Frontier, 1763-1893.* Boston, 1924.

Peck, Harry Thurston. *Twenty Years of the Republic, 1885-1905.* New York, 1913.

———— "Mark Twain, a Century Hence," *Bookman,* XXXI (June, 1910), 382-93.

Peckham, H. Houston. "The Literary Status of Mark Twain,

1877-1890," *South Atlantic Quarterly*, XIX (October, 1920), 332-40.

Pemberton, T. E. *The Life of Bret Harte.* New York, 1903.

Perkins, James Handasyd. *Annals of the West* (from the discovery of the Mississippi Valley to 1845). Cincinnati, 1846.

Perry, Bliss. *The American Spirit in Literature: A Chronicle of Great Interpreters.* New Haven, 1918.

Perry, T. S. "Huckleberry Finn," *Century*, VIII n. s. (May, 1885), 171-72.

Peyton, John Lewis. *Over the Alleghanies and across the Prairies.* London, 1869.

Phelps, W. L. "Notes on Mark Twain," *Essays on Books.* New York, 1914.

Phillips, Ulrich B., ed. *Plantation and Frontier Documents* (Vol. II, Documentary History of the American Industrial Society). Cleveland, 1909.

Pickard, John, ed. *Report of the Capitol Decoration Commission.* [Jefferson City, 1928].

Pike, Zebulon Montgomery. *An Account of a Voyage up the Mississippi River, from St. Louis to Its Source, . . . Compiled from Mr. Pike's Journal* (1805-1806). [Washington, 1807].

*Pike County, Missouri, History of* (compiled, Des Moines, Ia.) 1883.

Pochmann, Henry August. "The Mind of Mark Twain." Thesis (M. A.), University of Texas, August, 1924.

Pond, J. B. "Mark Twain," *Eccentricities of Genius.* London, 1900.

Priestley, J. B. *The English Comic Characters.* London, 1925.

*"Prince and the Pauper, The"* (reviewed), *Critic*, December 31, 1881.

Ramsay, Robert L. *The Short Story in America.* Boston, 1921.

Randall, John Herman. *The Making of the Modern Mind.* Boston and New York, 1926.

Rankin, J. W. "Introduction," *Life on the Mississippi* (Harper's Modern Classics). New York, 1925.

Reynolds, John. *The Pioneer History of Illinois,* containing the discovery in 1673, and the history of the country to the year eighteen hundred and eighteen when the state government was organized. Belleville, Ill., 1852.

Riley, Woodbridge. *American Philosophy: The Early Schools.* New York, 1907.

———— *American Thought: From Puritanism to Pragmatism and Beyond.* New York, 1923.

Robertson, J. A. *Louisiana under the Rule of Spain, France, and the United States,* 1785-1807. Cleveland, 1911.

Rourke, Constance M. *American Humor: A Study of National Character.* New York, 1931.

Rowe, Henry Kelloch. *The History of Religion in the United States.* New York, 1924.

Royce, Josiah. *California* (From the Conquest, 1846, to the Second Vigilance Committee in San Francisco, 1856): A Story of American Character. Boston and New York, 1886.

Rusk, R. L. *Literature of the Middle Western Frontier.* 2 vols. New York, 1925.

Rutter, John P. *Thirty Years' View in Marion County* (Pamphlet, 1861). Quoted in *History Marion County,* 1884.

Sampson, F. A. "Marion College and Its Founders," *Missouri Historical Review,* XX (July, 1926), 485-88.

Schönemann, Friedrich. *Mark Twain als literarische Persönlichkeit.* Jena, 1926.

———— "Mark Twain and Adolf Wilbrandt," *Modern Language Notes,* XXXIV (June, 1919), 372.

———— "Mark Twains Weltanschauung," *Englische Studien,* LV (January, 1921), 53-84.

———— "Mr. Samuel Langhorne Clemens," *Archiv,* CXLIV (1923), 184-213.

Schoolcraft, Henry Rowe. *Journal of a Tour into the Interior of Missouri and Arkansaw* (1818-1819). London, 1821.

Seabright, J. M.  "A Shrine to the Prince of Humorists," *International Book Review*, II (November, 1924).

Sedgwick, H. D.  "Mark Twain," *The New American Type and Other Essays*.  Boston, 1908.

Seitz, Don C.  *Artemus Ward* [Charles Farrar Browne].  Harper, 1919.

———— "Mark Twain's Autobiography," *Bookman*, LX (December, 1924), 446-48.

Shaw, Albert.  "Our Legacy from a Century of Pioneers," *South Atlantic Quarterly*, V (October, 1906), 311-32.

Shea, William G.  *Discovery and Exploration of the Mississippi Valley*.  New York [1852].

Sherman, S. P.  "The Democracy of Mark Twain," *On Contemporary Literature*.  New York, 1917.

———— "Mark Twain," *Cambridge History of American Literature*, III, 1-20.

———— "Mark Twain," *Nation*, XC (May 12, 1910), 477-80.

———— "The Misanthropy of Mark Twain," *Nation*, CIII (December 21, 1916), 588-89.

Shinn, Charles H.  "Mining Camps: A Study in American Frontier Government."  New York, 1885.

Shoemaker, F. C.  "Herculaneum Shot Tower."  *Missouri Historical Review*, XX (January, 1926), 214-216.

———— "The Pioneer," *Missouri Historical Review*, XIX (January, 1925), 241-255.

Shuster, G. N.  "The Tragedy of Mark Twain," *Catholic World*, CIV (March, 1917), 731-37.

Siegfried, André.  *America Comes of Age*.  New York, 1925.

Skinner, Constance L.  *Pioneers of the Old Southwest*.  New Haven, 1919.

Smith, C. Alphonso.  "Mark Twain und der amerikanische Humor," *Die Amerikanische Literatur*.  Ch. XV, 312-337.  Berlin, 1912.

Sosey, Frank H. (editor, Palmyra *Spectator*).  "Palmyra and Its

Historical Environment," *Missouri Historical Review*, XXIII (April, 1929), 361-79.

———— *Robert DeVoy:* A Tale of the Palmyra Massacre. Palmyra (Press of Sosey Brothers), 1903 (4th ed.).

*Spectator*, "Mark Twain," XCVIII (May 25, 1907), 825-26.

Squires, M. N., "Henry Lewis and His Mammoth Panorama of the Mississippi River," *Missouri Historical Review*, XXVII (April, 1933), 244-56.

Stead, W. T. "Mark Twain: A Character Sketch," *Review of Reviews* (London), August, 1897.

Stephen, Leslie. *English Thought in the Eighteenth Century.* 2 vols. London, 1881.

Stewart, W. M. *A Senator of the Sixties.* Richmond, 1908.

Stoddard, C. W. *A Humorist Abroad. Exits and Entrances: A Book of Essays and Sketches.* Boston, [1903].

"Stolen White Elephant, The" (reviewed), *Nation*, XXXV (August 10, 1882), 119.

Street, J. "In Mizzoura," *Collier's*, August 29, 1914.

Tandy, Jennette. *Crackerbox Philosophers in American Humor and Satire.* New York, 1925.

Taylor, Jean K. "Some Phases of Local Color in the Literature of the Lower Middle West." Thesis (Ph.D.), University of Missouri, 1928.

Thaler, C. Von. "Mark Twain in Deutschland," *Die Gegenwart*, IV (1899), 376-8.

Thompson, C. M. "Mark Twain as an Interpreter of American Character," *The Atlantic Monthly*, LXXIX (April, 1897), 443-50.

Thompson, Robert Ellis. *A History of the Presbyterian Churches in the United States* (American Church History Series). New York, 1902.

Thwaites, Reuben Gold. *Early Western Travels, 1748-1846.* 32 vols. Cleveland, 1904.

Ticknor, Caroline. "Mark Twain's Missing Chapter," *Bookman*, XXXIX (May, 1914), 298-309.

"Tramp Abroad, A" (reviewed), *Athenaeum*, April 24, 1880.

Trent, W. P. "Dominant Forces in Southern Life," *The Atlantic Monthly*, LXXIX, 42-54.

———— "Mark Twain as an Historical Novelist," *Bookman*, III (May, 1896), 207-10.

———— "A Retrospect of American Humor," *Century*, XLI (November, 1901), 45-64.

Trollope, Frances. *Domestic Manners of the Americans*. New York and London, 1832.

*Trollopiad; or, Travelling Gentlemen in America, a Satire*. By Nil Admirari. New York, 1837.

Tuckerman, Bayard. *A History of English Prose Fiction*. New York, 1882.

Turner, Frederick J. "The Colonization of the West, 1820-1830," *American Historical Review*, XI (January, 1906), 303-27.

———— *The Rise of the New West, 1819-1829*. New York, 1906.

———— and Merk, F. *List of References on the History of the West*. Rev. ed., Cambridge, 1922.

Twichell, Joseph H. "Mark Twain," *Harper's Magazine*, XCII (May, 1896), 817-27.

Umphraville, Angus. *Missourian Lays, and Other Western Ditties*. St. Louis, 1821.

Underwood, J. C. *Literature and Insurgency: Ten Studies in Racial Evolution*. New York, 1914.

*United States Census*, 1830.

*United States Census*, 1840.

Vail, H. H. *A History of the McGuffey Readers*. Cleveland, 1911.

Van Doren, Carl. *American and British Literature since 1890*. New York, 1925.

———— *The American Novel*. New York, 1921.

———— *Benjamin Franklin and Jonathan Edwards*. New York, 1920.

—————— "Mark Twain and Bernard Shaw," *Century,* LXXXVII n. s. (March, 1925), 705-10.

Van Doren, Mark. "The Repudiation of the Pioneer," *The English Journal,* XVII (October, 1928), 616-23.

Vedder, H. C. "Mark Twain," *American Writers of To-Day.* New York, 1894.

Venable, W. H. *Beginnings of Literary Culture in the Ohio Valley.* Cincinnati, 1891.

Violette, Eugene Morrow. *A History of Missouri.* New York, 1918.

Wade, John Donald. *Augustus Baldwin Longstreet: A Study of the Development of Culture in the South.* New York, 1924.

Wallace, Elizabeth. *Mark Twain and the Happy Island.* Chicago, 1913.

Watson, Aaron. *Artemus Ward and Mark Twain* (The Savage Club). London, 1907.

Watterson, Henry. "Mark Twain: An Intimate Memory," *American Magazine,* July, 1910.

Weber, Paul. *Survey of German Treatments of America in the German Literature of the First Half of the 19th Century.* New York. 1926.

Webster, Doris and Samuel. "Whitewashing Jane Clemens," *Bookman.* LXI (July, 1925), 531-35.

Wegelin, Oscar. *Early American Fiction, 1774-1830.* Stamford, Conn., 1902.

Wendell, Barrett, *A Literary History of America.* New York, 1900.

West, Victor Royce. *Folklore in the Works of Mark Twain* (University of Nebraska Studies). Lincoln, 1930.

Wetmore, Alonzo. *Gazetteer of Missouri.* St. Louis, 1837.

White, E. "Mark Twain's Printer Days," *Overland,* LXX (December, 1917), 573-76.

White, Edgar W. "The Literature of the Land," *The History of Northeast Missouri* (Walter Williams, ed.). New York, 1913.

White, F. M. "Mark Twain as a Newspaper Reporter," *Outlook*, XCVI (December 24, 1910), 961-67.

White, Stuart E. *The Forty-Niners.* New Haven, 1921.

Whitman, Walt. "Mississippi Valley Literature," *Specimen Days.* New York, 1891.

Williams, Walter. *The Missouri Book.* Columbia, Mo., 1904.

Winsor, Justin. *The Mississippi Basin: The Struggle in America between England and France, 1697-1763.* Boston and New York, 1895.

Woodbridge, Homer E. "Mark Twain and the Gesta Romanorum," *Nation,* CVIII (March 22, 1919), 424-25.

——— "Mark Twain's Fatalism," *Nation,* CV (October 11, 1917), 399.

Wyatt, Edith. "An Inspired Critic," *North American Review,* CCV (April, 1917), 603-15.

# INDEX